W9-ALX-170

CONTENTS

Business Ethics: Case Studies and Selected Readings

Third Edition

Marianne Moody Jennings

Director, Lincoln Center for Applied Ethics

Arizona State University

WEST **West Educational Publishing Company**
an International Thomson Publishing company I(T)P®

Cincinnati • Albany • Boston • Detroit • Johannesburg • London • Madrid • Melbourne • Mexico City
New York • Pacific Grove • San Francisco • Scottsdale • Singapore • Tokyo • Toronto

Publisher / Team Director: Jack W. Calhoun
Sr. Acquisitions Editor: Rob Dewey
Acquisitions Editor: Scott D. Person
Developmental Editor: Mignon D. Worman, Esquire
                                Member, Ohio and California Bars
Production Editor: Sharon L. Smith
Team Assistant: Kristen Meere
Marketing Manager: Michael Worls

ISBN: 0-324-00468-0

1 2 3 4 5 6 7 GP 4 3 2 1 0 9 8

Printed in the United States of America

International Thomson Publishing
West Educational Publishing is an ITP Company. The ITP trademark is used under license.

Using the Manual

This instructor's manual consists of four parts. In the first portion you will find key discussion points, observations and additional information for each of the cases in the book. The second portion of the manual contains transparency masters for the cases. These transparencies offer illustrations and diagrams of the often complex interactions of the characters in the cases. The students will be able to visualize this interaction as opposed to mentally keeping track of who did what and when.

The third part of this instructor's manual offers some additional background and reading in ethics. For those instructors who want their students to be more familiar with the traditional philosophical underpinnings of ethics, there is group of reading materials called Advanced Instructional Materials (AIM) that can be used as a supplement for your preparation and lectures or as background reading for your students.

The final segment of this instructor's manual is a test bank. Many instructors asked for help in developing exams for their courses. This test bank offers a variety of question formats and topics along with answers.

Each case is covered in the manual. The title of the case appears at the top of the page. If there is a transparency associated with the case, its number is noted directly beneath the case title. There is then a section called "Answers and Key Discussion Items." The questions from the book are answered along with embellishments and additional questions to ask the students as a follow-up. In those cases where the legal and ethical issues cross, there is a heading, "Legal Issues" in which the law as applied to that particular case is discussed.

The materials were developed with both students and instructors in mind. The instructor is given additional resources as well as notions for the stimulation of discussion. Students enjoy the benefit of instruction that leads to the heart of the difficult dilemmas presented in the text.

Good luck as you proceed with instruction in an area that is critical to your students in their business and personal lives. I hope the materials are helpful to you. If you have questions or suggestions, please feel free to call at (602)965-2710 or write to me at marianne.jennings@asu.edu or Box 874806, Arizona State University, Tempe, AZ 85287.

Marianne M. Jennings
Professor of Legal and Ethical
    Studies in Business
Director, Lincoln Center for
    Applied Ethics
College of Business
Arizona State University

Foundations of Business Ethics

The materials in this unit of the third edition are expanded from what appeared in the introduction in the second edition. Also, the seminal readings in the field of business ethics have been added to these introductory materials. The readings could be assigned as a means of beginning a course, or they could be assigned throughout a semester as you cover various cases that are particularly germane to the ideas in the readings. If you are using the book as a supplement to your discussion of ethics, these introductory materials need not be covered. If you are using the book as a portion of a course that contains an ethics component, you may wish to begin with a discussion of these introductory materials. There are transparency masters for these introductory materials that can be used to enhance your lecture or discussion. You may wish to also draw on the Advanced Instructional Materials (AIM) that appear in this manual to provide you with more traditional depth for your discussion and/or lecture. Transparency masters for those materials are also included with the transparencies in the final portion of this manual.

I. Why Business Ethics?

    A. Poor ethical choices can lead to devastating losses and often business failures

        e.g.: Orange County, Barings Bank, Union Carbide, Beech-Nut, E.F. Hutton, BCCI, Salomon Brothers, Johns-Manville, Phar-Mor, Kidder Peabody, Bausch and Lomb and others covered in the text

    B. Good ethical choices can have positive effect on earnings

        e.g.: Ethical firms are able to pay dividends consistently
             Ethical firms offer investors a better return

    C. Connection between profitability and ethics/values

        Note: Collins and Porras - BUILT TO LAST
        Note: Ethics Resource Center Study on value of shares in ethical firms
        Note: CEOs belief that ethical standards strengthen your competitive edge

    D. 1997 *Academy of Management Review* study showed firms with criminal and regulatory violations still feel financial impact five years later

II. What is business ethics?

    A. The application of moral standards to business dilemmas

    B. Moral standards are canons of behavior that are neither legislated nor changed by legislation

        1.   Conflicts between law and moral issues: child labor

2.   Moral accountability for business conduct

THE SOCIAL RESPONSIBILITY OF BUSINESS IS TO INCREASE ITS PROFITS
Milton Friedman

Answers and Key Discussion Items

1. Mr. Friedman compares the discussions about social responsibility of business to the story of the Frenchman who was surprised to learn he had been speaking "prose" all of his life. Mr. Friedman feels that such discussions are simply socialism for they attempt to hold businesses accountable to more than just their owners. Mr. Friedman is also dismayed at the lack of rigor in the discussions.

2. The corporate executive is selected by the shareholders (or, more accurately, the shareholders elect a board and the board is in charge of the officers) as an agent of the shareholders and as such, the executive is accountable to those shareholders. He is an employee of those shareholders and has direct accountability to them. To the extent he wishes to become involved in social issues and causes, he should do so with his own money and not the money of the corporation. If he involves the corporation's money in such causes, he is using the money without shareholder consent and is, then, in effect, imposing a tax upon the shareholders to accomplish a public project that can otherwise not be done because citizens have decided otherwise.

3. When unions engage in restraining wages in the name of the social good, the likely result is wildcat strikes, revolts and the emergence of a new work force.

4. Yes, Mr. Friedman does support voluntary actions on the part of the corporation if the corporation can show that there will be benefits that workers, shareholders or customers can gain through the voluntary conduct. For example, if a town where a business plant is located has become so contaminated with pollution that the company can't attract and keep long-term employees, then voluntary action in order to clean up is something Mr. Friedman would support despite no legal requirement to do so.

THE ETHICS OF RESPONSIBILITY
Peter Drucker

Answers and Key Discussion Items

1. Ethics are ethics, whether in business or as an individual. The problem is that people don't change simply because they become vice president. They simply continue doing all the things they do personally. If they lie and cheat in their personal lives, they will lie and steal in their business lives. Stiff punishments serve in personal and business lives to deter unwanted behaviors.

2. Leadership groups create a certain anonymity in the decision-making and business presence. No one can really name the CEOs of companies.

Individuals, therefore, do not make decisions. Leadership groups make decisions.

3. The three areas for application of primum non nocere are executive compensation, use of employee benefits to create "golden fetters," and profit rhetoric.

4. The rhetoric of the profit motive is that managers discuss it constantly, not risk, not cost of capital, not costs, but profit maximization.

5. No, Mr. Drucker sees the ethical standards varying in Japan significantly and somewhat in Western Europe.

   III. The Areas of Ethical Challenges

   Use Transparencies 1 and 1A to cover the areas of ethical challenges to be covered in the book which is organized by units according to these groupings of ethical challenges.

   IV. Recognizing Ethical Dilemmas

   A. Recognizing ethical dilemmas - Observe the language of justification used when people face an ethical dilemma (Use transparency 2)

      1. Everybody else does it

IS BUSINESS BLUFFING ETHICAL?
Albert Z. Carr

ANSWERS AND KEY DISCUSSION ITEMS

1. Have the students discuss the implications of lying during business negotiations in order to answer this question and offer their views on Carr's premise that we are all bluffing in business and so lying is acceptable. For example, what if you relied on a seller's representation that his price was the lowest and he guaranteed that price as lowest. To save yourself some time in checking around, you rely on the seller's representation. Soon you discover another seller with the same product at a lower price. What are the implications for your relationship with that seller? What is the level of trust you have with the seller? Would you continue to do business with that seller?

   Also have the students discuss the implications of not knowing what is just a bluff and therefore part of the big business game and what goes too far. How do we know where to draw the line on what is part of the game and what is fraud?

   Have the students note that even Friedman believes fraud must not be part of business in order for the free market to function effectively. Does Carr introduce fraud into the marketplace as an acceptable part of business?

2. Review with the students the difficulties in having individuals decide what is acceptable vs. unacceptable bluffing. What is bluffing and what is misrepresentation? If bluffing is acceptable, what will happen to legal standards misrepresentation and fraud?

3. Carr characterizes the statement as "self-serving calculation in disguise. He explains that the goal is to make more money and the statement just gives a surface explanation for what is really a strong drive for success.

    2.   If we don't do it, someone else will.

    3.   That's the way it has always been done.

    4.   We'll wait until the lawyers tell us it is wrong.

    5.   It doesn't really hurt anyone.

    6.   The system is unfair.

B. Categories of unethical behavior (Use transparency 3)

    1.   Taking things that don't belong to you

    2.   Saying things you know are not true

    3.   Giving or allowing false impressions

    4.   Buying influence or engaging in conflict of interest

    5.   Hiding or divulging information

    6.   Taking unfair advantage

    7.   Committing personal decadence

    8.   Perpetrating interpersonal abuse

    9.   Permitting organizational abuse

    10.   Violate rules

    11.   Condoning unethical actions

    12.   Balancing ethical dilemmas

V. Resolving Ethical Dilemmas

A. Blanchard/Peale model (Use transparency 4)

    1.   Is it legal?

2. Is it balanced?

3. How does it make me feel?

THE PARABLE OF THE SADHU
Bowen H. McCoy

Answers and Key Discussion Items

Mr. McCoy's poignant experience and piece force students to see the parallels between organizational ethics and his experience. No one in the mountain parties saw themselves as being responsible for the sadhu's problems or fate. They all did a little bit to help, but no one assumed accountability. So it is in companies. All the employees do a little bit of the conduct that results in harm, but no one is ultimately, or feels ultimately responsible for what happens. Everyone designed and manufactured the car, but no one is responsible for what happened to those who purchased and drove the defective car.

Mr. McCoy also points out that achievement of the goal (in his story, it was reaching the top) often blinds us and our values during the journey or climb to that goal. He was so determined to make his goal that he was unwilling to be side-tracked by the needs of another human being in desperate straits. The parallels to business are obvious. In the quest for the goal of sales quotas, quarterly profits, etc., business people often fail to pause and retain their personal values. In fact, they may take ethical and legal shortcuts to get to the goal. As Mr. McCoy notes, sometimes stepping back from the linear path to the goal is the best decision a business person can make. He points out that the times when he could not continue his climb, but was forced to sit in the village, he had a wonderful time and a rich cultural experience that he seems to recall far more than the climb to the top. Students should be challenged with questions about the achievement of success and their lives along the way. Do they take time for family? Do they take time to do volunteer work? Do they take time to help others at work?

B. Front Page of the Newspaper Test (Use transparency 5)

C. Laura Nash model (Use transparency 6)

1. Have you defined the problem accurately?

2. How would you define the problem if you stood on the other side of the fence?

3. How did this situation occur in the first place?

4. To whom and to what do you give your loyalty as a person and as a member of the corporation?

5. What is your intention in making this decision?

6. How does this intention compare with the likely results?

7.   Whom could your decision or action injure?

8.   Can you discuss your decision with the affected parties?

9.   Are you confident that your position will be as valid over a long period of time as it seems now?

10. Could you discuss your decision with your CEO, board, friends, boss, family?

11. What is the symbolic potential of your action if understood? if misunderstood?

12. Under what circumstances would you make exceptions to your position?

ETHICS WITHOUT THE SERMON
Laura Nash

<u>ANSWERS AND KEY DISCUSSION ITEMS</u>

1. How would you define this problem if you stood on the other side of the fence? What does the supplier think you are doing? Does the supplier see this as a way to get the upper hand on bids?

   To whom and to what do you give your loyalty? There is a break in loyalty to your company when you accept gifts from others. The Chrysler corporation refers to gifts as "the hook." The gifts get a hook on the employee for future benefits or breaks for the gift giver.

2. An ethics of attitude sets a standard that ensures a certain action. A firm policy of not cheating customers stops employees from lying to customers even by omission.

   An ethics of absolute ends dictates that the reason for an action does not matter — that so long as the right action is taken, the intention for doing so is not an issue whereas the ethics of attitude produces certain behaviors because the result is the driving force, i.e., not cheating customers. An ethics of absolute ends would be that "we'll get caught if we cheat customers, so we shouldn't cheat customers." An attitude standard is that it is wrong to cheat customers and the employee conduct is derived from the expressed philosophy and goal.

3. Taking a free trip from a supplier who has contract proposals pending

   Taking participation in a golf tournament and a weekend at a resort from a customer with a loan application pending

   Accepting an interest-free loan from someone who wishes to be awarded a contract from your company

4. History is important so that the company can look to see what happened and how they got into this particular ethical dilemma. The company can then go

forward to the future with the problems, processes and procedures corrected so that it need not face that ethical dilemma again.

      D. Perspective: Use that of a reporter or a wage earner

VI. Resolution of ethical dilemmas requires practice in applying the various models.

Make assignments of cases according to your class coverage or use the indexes in the text to assign cases by company, business discipline or topic.

1.1   Commodities, Conflicts, and Clintons

Use Transparency 7.

It will help students visualize the parties' roles and interrelationships.

Answers and Key Discussion Items

1.   Mrs. Clinton was then the wife of a top law enforcement official in the
      state of Arkansas. Mr. Blair was legal counsel for the state's largest
      company, a firm that was heavily regulated at both the state and federal
      levels. Mr. Blair's advice on commodities trades introduced a quid pro
      quo element into the Blair/Clinton relationship. Tyson's and Blair's
      interests in regulation were from a business perspective. Mrs. Clinton
      was the spouse of the state's top regulator who was also a candidate for
      governor. The front page of the newspaper test tells us there was a
      conflict here.

2.   Yes, there was a conflict of interest. Whether Mr. and Mrs. Clinton would
      or would not have been influenced by the helpful advice is not the issue.
      Their interests are at odds as regulator and regulated. The most
      skeptical could argue that the advice was a way of making significant
      campaign contributions outside the legal limitations. There is also the
      appearance of impropriety.

3.   The appointment of the Tyson executives subsequent to Mr. Clinton's
      election as governor creates the appearance of quid pro quo. Tyson's
      regulatory treatment post-Blair advice is some evidence that the advice
      was given in exchange for favorable regulatory treatment.

4.   Yes, Mr. Clinton did have a conflict of interest. Direct influence is
      often not used because of prohibitions -- statutory prohibitions because
      of public official standing. Hence, family members are sought out for
      influence. Influence once removed remains influence and Mr. Clinton had
      a conflict through his wife's conduct.

5.   Mr. Espy's actions as Secretary of Agriculture provide some indication of
      the introduction of a quid pro quo. Further, Tyson was perceived and
      treated as a friend of the Clinton governorship and presidency.

6.   Yes, Mr. Espy had a conflict. He was accepting items of value from a firm
      he was responsible for enforcing the law against and regulating. As a
      former member of Congress, Mr. Espy did not realize the distinction
      between lobbying activities when one is a legislator as opposed to
      influence activities when one is the enforcer/regulator. Lobbying is an
      activity protected by the First Amendment. Influencing regulators and
      enforcers is obstruction of justice.

7.   Under the American Bar Association's Model Rules of Professional
      Responsibility, Mrs. Clinton would have a conflict because of her
      husband's position in government. However, partners of Mrs. Clinton in

the Rose law firm could represent Tyson without a violation of the ABA rules. Again, the lack of a violation of the rules is not necessarily the test for ethical conduct. This representation does not survive the newspaper test: it looks bad to have the governor's wife's law firm awarded the legal business of the state's largest company, a heavily regulated one at that.

8.   None of the decisions made in this case from Blair's advice to hiring the Rose firm to Espy's actions to the hiring of Tyson executives can survive the front-page-of-the-newspaper test. Transparency 7 demonstrates how interconnected and interdependent the parties were and the likelihood of expectation of favorable treatment was high.

9.   What is your intention in providing trading advice to Mrs. Clinton?
     What is your intention in taking trading advice from Mr. Blair?
     Are you as confident about your decision over the long term?
     Could you disclose your decision publicly?

     All of these questions could be applied to Mrs. Clinton's decision to accept the trading advice, the Rose law firm account, the Tyson executives being hired and the Mike Espy situation. As we examine these decisions now, they have created image and other problems for all those involved. The Laura Nash questions would have helped at the time.

10. In conflicts of interest, the issue is not whether one has been influenced. The issue is whether a situation has been created in which influence is possible. The introduction of quid pro quo into the relationship is the ethical breach.

Legal Issues

Indirect campaign contributions may be a problem here. The commodities trades and the sufficiency of cash coverage for the trade may present some legal issues. Laws against bribing public officials may apply as the Espy investigation continues.

1.2 The City Council Employee

Answers and Key Discussion Items

1. No matter how much Bimini needed graphic art work and no matter how good a graphic artist Jake Gilbert is, the newspaper accounts of this relationship if Houston hires Gilbert would be unfavorable. The relationship would be depicted as a suggestive pay-off in which Gilbert's position on billboards is supported by a business dependent upon the continuation of billboard advertising for survival.

2. The headline might read:

   Unemployed Council Candidate Now Employed By the City's Largest Billboard Beneficiary

   The Best Kind of Campaign Contribution: A Job

   Council Candidate Working for Billboard Proponent

3. No. There is no difference. Whether working directly for Bimini or working in a position Bimini obtained for Gilbert, the result is the same: the introduction of quid pro quo into their relationship. Gilbert can no longer vote his constituency or conscience, he must consider Bimini's personal help as an expectation of favorable treatment.

4. Gilbert should not be submitting a bid. The potential for public embarrassment and conflict is too high. His being hired simply cannot be adequately explained or justified. The conflict is so great here that the nature of the bid is irrelevant. He should not be bidding, period. If he does bid, Bimini should not hire him. The potential for damage to them is great as well.

5. Gilbert cannot avoid facing the billboard issue if he is running for office. There is no way to take the job and do a credible job of running for and holding office. He simply cannot take the job.

6. Yes. Gilbert has a conflict of interest whether he is a direct employee or under contract.

Other Observations

The long-term impact of a decision to hire Gilbert would be damaging to Gilbert's, Bimini's and Houston's reputations. Independence is perceived, not explained. Both will cost themselves the issue that concerns them the most.

The students will identify with Dewey because he is an employee who has seen the implications of a decision to hire Gilbert either as an employee or a contractor. Dewey is but a manager who possesses little authority and little job security. Challenge the students to think of ways Dewey might approach the problem:

3

1.2 The City Council Employee (cont'd)

a. Preparation; examples of other elections in which similar relationships have destroyed candidates and cost businesses;
b. Appearance of impropriety; the newspaper test
c. Laura Nash; will I feel as good about this over the long-run?

Legal Issues

In many states, the contracts (either for the work or for employment) might be classified as indirect campaign contributions that might have to be disclosed at a minimum and, quite possibly, could be considered contributions in excess of many of the states' maximums established by campaign finance reform laws.

1.3 Conflicts of Interest in Referrals

<u>Answers and Key Discussion Items</u>

1. Tina is in a difficult situation as she tries to manage the outside activities of physicians, a generally independent and private group. However, Tina needs to think of the various stakeholders affected by her work and decisions. She also needs to think of the long term. Today's high medical care costs, cutbacks in insurance coverage and increasing government regulation demand a responsible approach to cost-containment and conflicts of interest. Tina should institute a mandatory disclosure policy. Tina should take a proactive position, citing current regulation, the Blue Cross study and the Department of Health and Human Services' policies. Tina should implement the policy after discussions with physicians and explanations of her concerns.

2. As a patient, I would want to know who owns the facilities. There might be the need for a second opinion. There might be the need to investigate costs at other facilities. I should be told if the person ordering tests is going to make money from those tests.

3. Whether or not the physicians would be self-serving is not the issue. The appearance of all of the physician-owned facilities is that there is a conflict of interest. The physician owners do not make money if patients are not referred to their facilities or services. A newspaper story about the incestuous relationships between physicians and their companies would not be favorable for them or Tina.

4. Possible headlines:

   Physicians Earn From Prescribing Tests at Their Labs
   Prescriptions for Profit: Your Doctor Might Own the Lab
   Doctor-Owned Labs Earn Lavish Profits in a Captive Market

<u>Legal Issues</u>

Many states already mandate disclosure when a physician makes a referral to a self-owned lab. The AMA position is behind the times in terms of legislative coverage of disclosure.

1.4   Barbara Walters and Her Andrew Lloyd Webber Conflicts

Answers and Key Discussion Items

1. Ms. Walters has her personal interest in her financial investment in Mr. Webber's work and production vs. her objective interest as a reporter and news anchor for ABC News. If Webber's play is successful, she does well with her investment. Touting that new play on network television under the guise of an objective news story is not a bad way of promoting the play.

2. and 3. Ms. Walters should have disclosed her investment when the decision was made to do the Andrew Lloyd Webber piece. She should not have even been part of the process for making the decision to do the piece and she should not have been the anchor assigned to conduct the interview. Also, it should have been disclosed on the air before the piece aired that Ms Walters did have such an investment and that she had no part in the story's idea, production or interview. In fact, in spring 1998, when *20/20* aired a story on the possibility that the segments on Jerry Springer were fake, Ms. Walters disclosed before the segment aired that her daytime television show airs opposite Springer in some markets and that she had no part in the decision to do the story or in its production.

Her decision to make the disclosure was critical for the credibility of the news program. It was a fair disclosure to the viewers who might otherwise have questioned the independence of the piece, particularly if her show's competition was revealed after the story had run.

1.5 The Loan Officer and the Debtors

Answers and Key Discussion Items

1. Shelby, a character most students will identify with, is faced with the classic problem of a new culture and old employees who "have always done it this way." Shelby may find herself in the difficult position of having to turn to someone other than her immediate supervisor for "ethical relief." It may be "just the way business is done", but it should be changed. Shelby is absolutely correct. Shelby will need to express her concerns directly to Ben. She should do so with good preparation. She should use the bank's own code of ethics as well as examples from other banks to demonstrate her position. She should pursue other avenues in the bank if she is unable to convince Ben of the need to avoid the appearance of impropriety. Alternatives would include a hotline, the ombudsperson, audit department, legal counsel and Ben's supervisor. She should look to the persons who are committed to changing the bank's ethical culture and enlist their support.

2. The conflict with the potential borrower paying for the collateral evaluation trip is that the pressure to make the loan increases. The payment necessitates more direct contact and the passage of funds from the potential customer to the bank regardless of the loan decision.

3. The payment for the collateral evaluation trip opens all kinds of doors: will the travel arrangements be "excessive?" how much can the potential borrower expend in making the arrangements? how fancy will the facilities for the loan officers be? Many banks include policies in their codes of ethics that specifically preclude loan officers from allowing potential borrowers to pay for their collateral evaluation trips.

4. The solicitation of donations from bank loan officers is a less direct and more subtle type of pressure that says to the debtor, "either I contribute to this or I am going to lose my line of credit." It is a means of applying pressure to customers who want to maintain good relationships with their loan officers. Many banks, again, have specific provisions in their codes of ethics that prohibit loan officers and others responsible for loan approval from soliciting contributions (in-kind or otherwise) from loan customers to avoid the appearance of pressure.

5. The voluntary contribution of a firm would be accepted but bank employees would not solicit such donations from customers.

6. Again, Shelby needs to present her concerns in a well-reasoned manner. Research on other banks' policies would help as she resents her concerns.

1.6 The Secretary of Agriculture, Chicken Processors, and Football Sky-Box Seats

<u>Use Transparency 8</u>.

<u>Answers and Key Discussion Items</u>

1. No, the value is not the issue. Taking these items, regardless of amount, introduced quid pro quos into Mr. Espy's relationships with the companies he was supposed to be regulating. As a cabinet member and member of the executive branch, Mr. Espy has enforcement responsibilities that preclude the acceptance of any form of gift, regardless of value.

2. No, Mr. Espy's reimbursement does not eliminate the questionable values introduced in the relationship by his having taken items in the first place. Mr. Espy cannot accept items and then reimburse. Mr. Espy simply cannot accept them in the first place.

3. Front page of the newspaper test - looks like sale of influence

   Blanchard/Peale: Is it legal?

   No; this type of conduct in the executive branch, particularly by a heavily regulated company could be called bribery. Is it balanced? No, introduces an unfair advantage to those with access to the secretary. How does it make me feel? Although initially Mr. Espy was not troubled by it all, the aftermath demonstrates that the gifts should have been troubling; creating conflicts of interest.

4. Yes, Mr. Espy allowed the introduction of quid pro quo into his relationships; his acceptance of benefits created a sense of obligation.

5. Mr. Blackley's dual paycheck was a problem; possibly illegal; government employee's outside compensation is regulated. Mr. Blackley's orders on inspections give the appearance of impropriety.

   Tyson's furnishing of lodging and flights to a member of the executive (i.e., law enforcement) branch of government was a conflict.

   The Tyson scholarship to Mr. Espy's girlfriend was just shy of an out-and-out cash payment; a definite conflict.

   Sun Diamond's conduct was suspicious -- who paid for it? Appearance of a conflict.

   Dallas Football Game -- gift of tickets and transportation are conflicts.

6. In this case, as well as in the Starr/Clinton investigation, a typical point of contention in the discussion has been that the special investigations cost so much money and take so much time. However, there are issues of public trust involved in these cases. Mr. Smaltz is pointing out that officials

charged with enforcement of the law were accepting gifts from those against whom the law must be enforced. The issue of public confidence, particularly in this area of food safety, is critical and Mr. Smaltz sees his work as a means of preserving public trust.

1.7   The Purchasing Agents' Wonder World Trip

Answers and Key Discussion Items

1. Sheila is in a position no one enjoys and very few know how to handle. She is the killjoy. However, Sheila needs to keep in mind some of the questions from the Nash test: could I discuss this trip with the CEO, with the Board, with my family? will I feel as good about this decision over the long run? If she is unable to convince the others and the supervisor of her concerns about propriety, she needs to use whatever avenue the company has available. She might try someone outside her immediate supervisor's supervisor such as the legal department or the audit department.

2. Foregoing the trip is enough for Sheila personally but when the incident is later discovered, her ability to take a position and advocate it will be questioned. Many people view Sheila as being in a no-win situation. In fact, Sheila's principles afford her an opportunity to demonstrate leadership skills. She might consider offering examples of other similar incidents from other industries and firms and the results to demonstrate the repercussions for the members of her group.

3. No, the CEO sends a stronger message if Sheila is retained. It would help employees to understand that choosing the correct action ensures protection. If she is fired when she had nowhere to turn, all employees will be reluctant to stay.

4. No, firing the agents is not too harsh. The ethical tone of the department is pervasively poor. Cleaning it out is a good idea because these purchasing agents simply could not see the ethical issue. Whether there are bids pending is not the issue. The perks Rydman is offering will cloud the judgment of the purchasing department in future bidding processes. This type of conduct will not survive the front page of the newspaper test. The trip would simply be reported as the purchasing department accepting trips from a supplier and the appropriate conclusions would be drawn by the public. LA East is in a particularly sensitive position because it is a regulated public utility. Life for these types of firms is one in a fish bowl. Public scrutiny is intense and merciless.

Legal Issues

No statutory violations have occurred. However, the purchasing department is compromising its independence and its duty as an agent for the company to secure those contracts that are most beneficial to the principal (the utility).

1.8   The Sale of Sand to the Saudis

Answers and Key Discussion Items

1. If you can't trust Ms. Morris now, how can you trust her as an employee? Ms. Morris is bringing proprietary information to you. Her information looks like a solution in the short-run. In the long-run you will be forced to cope with her tendencies. She could do the same to you. You will also be working with someone who knows that you hired her because of improper information. You are both on the line at all times.

2. Silt, Sand and Such is harmed by your decision to hire Ms. Morris. You and your firm will be harmed over the long-run. Is this the type of information you would want disclosed on the front page of a newspaper?

3. Could you trust her? Would Silt, Sand and Such sue you for Morris breaking a covenant not to compete? Would you come to rely on "easy" fixes for meeting goals?

4. Ms. Morris might be under a covenant not to compete and you could be held liable. If it is proprietary information, it might be theft. Many students will respond that this type of thing is done all the time: employees leave and take information with them. However, "it's always been done," and "if we don't do it someone else will," are not justifications for actions, they are signals of ethical problems. This information is not just operational or technological. It is information unique to one firm and developed solely by that firm.

5. No, there would be no trust in your relationship with Morris. She betrayed her former employer. She could betray you.

Legal Issues

It is possible that your firm could be sued for interference with contractual relations. You really don't know how much negotiation has gone on and what groundwork has been laid for the contract. The use of Ms. Morris's information could throw your company into a costly legal battle.

1.9 The Compliance Officer Who Strayed

Answers and Key Discussion Items

1. The problem with insiders using information in advance of public disclosure of that information is that the market is forced to operate without full disclosure and full information. Further, to allow insiders to make money without disclosure of such information is an investment deterrent. Investors do not wish to place money into a market in which they can't trust the players and they don't have the same shot at a return that some do. The high returns captured by secret information trading are returns that belong to others who could trade if the information were disclosed. The element of trust breaks down when insider trading is permitted.

2. Trust and investor confidence in the market are at risk when insiders are permitted to trade on non-public information.

3. The case was a shock to those on Wall Street. Compliance officers and compliance programs are clearly a key element in the system of policing inside information use and disclosure and here a key element in that system broke down. The case tells companies that they need individuals of absolute integrity in those positions and their programs broke down at that point. Some feel that Ms. Baridis and others who are place in charged of such programs are simply too young to be able to handle such responsibility and temptation.

1.10 Espionage and Job-Hopping

<u>Answers and Key Discussion Items</u>

DAVIS AND GILLETTE CASE

1. Mr. Davis, although he did not work for Gillette, was still in a position of trust and confidence as an independent contractor/agent for Gillette. There was still an understanding and requirement of fiduciary responsibility as a contractor for Gillette.

2. The case is interesting not just in the ethical breach but in the ethical standards of Gillette's competitors. They in essence refused to take advantage of a competitor and reported Davis's attempts. It would be a crime anyway for the competitors to use the information. Inevitably, the use of such information would end up in litigation and would not serve any company well.

3. Mr. Davis, like so many of the ethically challenged, sees those who refused to cheat with him as the ethical problem, not his initial conduct in trying to steal from Gillette.

LOPEZ AND GM

1. An executive who is part of the senior management team will always have access to sensitive information. Executives at this level must know of developments and future plans in order to do their jobs.

2. An executive can go to work for a competitor with restrictions. Those restrictions could include product line limitations which would be the only way to ensure that the executive did not take advantage of information gleaned from work with his previous employer.

3. The covenants are designed to protect the proprietary information of the employer, but they do restrict the work that employees can do if they leave the company.

4. The planning and research that companies do is their competitive advantage. In many cases, employees are being hired with the idea that they will bring that competitive advantage with them. The employee, in the interest of protecting that information, may have to work in a related field for a time, but not for a competitor until a sufficient amount of time has passed to make the proprietary information obsolete.

1.11 The Rigged Election

Answers and Key Discussion Items

1. Mr. Gunty was trying to get an edge on the job market. Contact with speakers through the president's position might give him an opportunity not available to others.

2. Chances are many students did not care about the club officer positions. But many are hurt by Gunty's actions. The process is undermined, the credibility of the organization and institution are hurt. If those tactics are allowed to continue, they eliminate equal opportunities for all students to hold office.

3. Anonymity offers some security. Often it is used when there is insufficient evidence available and an investigation is warranted.

4. Many students make the point that this is "just school" and that the standards are different. Standards of personal honesty are always the same. Further, have the students examine the consequences to Mr. Gunty. He is known to his classmates and readers of the *Wall Street Journal* as someone who cheated on something as insignificant as "just school." Could you count on Mr. Gunty in an honesty sense in any setting? Mr. Gunty's long-term damage to his reputation is significant.

   Further, Mr. Gunty may have encountered life's worst punishment: having to write an extra paper!!!

1.12   Puffing in the Resume

Answers and Key Discussion Items

1. The point should be made that there is nothing wrong with presenting yourself in the best light possible. The line for unethical resumes is crossed when the information is not accurate. For example, you could put "Denny's Restaurant Manager," or you could list your activities, "Coordinated scheduling, handled purchasing, performed payroll, customer satisfaction, etc." and then list Denny's as the place of employment. Saying you performed those management duties when, in fact, you were a fry cook would be unethical. It is wrong to place false information in a resume. You may not have the chance to correct it.

2. Rather than misstate the degree, you should take care of the debts or fines. Either way you handle this one, you are going to have to disclose unethical behavior. You have not defined the problem accurately. Why go through the job process having to explain why you don't have a degree? Get the degree.

3. A thirteen-month lapse is not so unusual these days. Concealment from a prospective employer will only damage your relationship even if you do get the job. And, as the Honeywell case illustrated, deceit is something an employer can use against you at any point in the employment relationship.

4. There is a difference between marketing yourself effectively and lying. You should never claim to have a skill, degree or prior employment experience that you do not have. The lack of candor will ensure that you don't keep the job you do get. It all works out the same. The idea in an employment search is to match skills, experience and personality with the right job. The lack of candor only postpones the ability to find that position.

5. Puffing is acceptable so long as there are no false impressions. Misrepresentation may get you a job, but it may also get you fired. It is a high risk activity and a truly short-term solution.

6. Ms. Green was a capable individual who thought it would look better if she put down a degree that did not exist. While there were many things going on in her life, the additional stress from work should never have happened. Working on the basis of honest credentials is a critical part of the employer/employee relationship. Also, if Ms. Green had come forward on her own and disclosed the information voluntarily, she might have had a better result and opportunity with Duquesne.

   Employers have to rely on the element of honesty in employment applications and resumes. No employer has sufficient resources to verify the information contained in all the applications, or even the final pool selected for interviews in the case of a job or position. The termination of Ms. Green sent a strong signal to employees about the importance of honesty to and within the company.

7. If applicants are not honest in their backgrounds and experience, then individuals can be hired who are not qualified for positions and others who

1.12   Puffing in the Resume (cont'd)

really are qualified are precluded from those positions. Such a system makes achievement irrelevant for the statements about degrees are not distinguishing characteristics.   Everyone has the same credentials, allegedly, and the hiring process is not able to distinguish among applicants.

Legal Issues

If you are bidding on a contract and fail to disclose information about yourself or misstate or overstate your qualifications, there could be statutory penalties as well as an action for fraud or misrepresentation.
Your misrepresentations on your resume can be used against you later on as a justification for firing you.

1.13   The Glowing Recommendation

Answers and Key Discussion Items

1. Jake's dilemma is an interesting cross between ethical commitments, legal issues, and the liability of a firm for employee recommendations. Jake has agreed to be a reference, so he must answer the prospective employer's questions. Jake does have some good things to say about Bob--he is conscientious and a hard worker. The absence of information on his skills should alert an observant employer of gaps that should be checked with others.

2. Another dilemma will arise if the new employer calls Jake and asks for the information intentionally left out. It is at that point that you need to talk with Bob. This talk should have been conducted long before Bob went job hunting. It should have been conducted as part of Jake's responsibilities as a manager. Jake has the obligation to use his employer's resources wisely and allowing Bob's work efforts and habits to continue over the years was not an effective use of anyone's time or resources. Jake's loyalty to his friendship took priority over his loyalty to his employer.

3. Yes, Jake, like many of us, has failed to confront an uncomfortable situation head on. He needs to address the problem, which is more than the reference request.

4. Many glowing recommendations are given to be rid of employees. It is neither balanced nor ethical to do so. These recommendations harm both the employee and the new employer.

5. Not when employment/supervisory issues are involved. We often tell "white lies" to avoid offending a friend. We should not tell white lies about employees and their work.

Legal Issues

The area of recommendations from employers is fraught with legal pitfalls. As a result, many employers follow a policy of simply stating whether an employee would or would not be rehired. However, these policies do not preclude the personal types of references and recommendations Jake agreed to provide here. Jake should understand his liability for statements that are inaccurate (liability to Bob). There has been liability imposed for glowing recommendations for employees who later turn out to be disasters as well as slander/libel liability for poor references. Many states now have statutes that provide qualified immunity for employers who are giving references. So long as the reference is given in good faith and is factually based, the employer enjoys immunity from defamation. Employers should stick to factual types of disclosures and not engage in opinions to enjoy immunity.

1.14 The Unofficial Government Contract and the Account Sale

<u>Answers and Key Discussion Items</u>

1. This is a classic conflict of interest. The situation has arisen because you did not remove yourself from the negotiations and sale process from the outset. Your loyalty is to your employer and the information should be disclosed. The fact that the information is unofficial is irrelevant. You have already made the first mistake in handling the sale.

2. At this point, you should disclose everything and let the employer decide about the contract and your fate.

3. Yes, to avoid these problems and conflicts, someone else should have handled the sale from the outset.

<u>Legal Issues</u>

In some states, this type of self-dealing would be criminal.

1.15 Radar Detectors and the Law

Answers and Key Discussion Items

1. Radar detectors are indeed a means of facilitating violations of the law. The fact that "everyone speeds," "everyone has them," or "the speed limits aren't right or are unfair," does not change the illegal nature of the activity.

2. Suppose that someone is injured or killed because of your speeding, would you be morally responsible? Therefore, it is immoral to violate the laws. The laws were established for a purpose and we can question that purpose and work to change the laws but self-determination of inefficacy does not permit violations. The laws are positive law enacted in a utilitarian sense: the most good for the most people. There is a certain element of morality even in the speeding laws.

3. Radar detectors facilitate violations of the law. Radar detectors have no purpose beyond evasion of the law. Ask the students if they would be comfortable running a very profitable business that manufactures radar detectors and other similar devices.

4. Many students feel this way: speeding may be against the law, but it's an arbitrary law and there are no moral issues involved.

5. The license plate covers do indeed facilitate breaking the law. However, the sellers and manufacturers of these products maintain that they are not breaking the law any more than gun manufacturers and sellers break the law. What buyers do with their merchandise is up to the buyer. There is, however, a distinction in the analogy in that the guns have lawful uses whereas the license plate covers have no lawful use other than evasion of law enforcement through photo radar and traffic light cameras.

Legal Issues

As any student knows, speeding brings fines. The activity is illegal. Discussions will attempt to justify it, but until the laws change, it is unethical.

Special note

This topic will be a particularly sensitive one because "everyone does it."

1.16   The Ethics of Looking Busy

Answers and Key Discussion Items

1. Jane's focus should be:

   Am I giving an honest day's work for my pay?

   Am I being honest with my employer?

   Am I taking something that doesn't belong to me (my employer's time)?

   Is it fair?

   Is it balanced?

   How would Jane feel if someone she was paying to work for her behaved in this fashion?

2. Employees who need flexibility should request it and not engage in Jane's behavior (which is dishonest).   Flex-time is an option more and more employers make available.

3. Jane does not have enough work that she feels comfortable leaving for long stretches.   Jane may not progress as quickly in the organization without the necessary, "How can I help?" attitude as opposed to her current, "How much can I get away with?" attitude.

4. No one should ever say or do anything that is dishonest at the behest of a supervisor or co-employee. A proper response is "Jane, or Ms. Nugent, I'm a good worker who will do anything that I am asked, but please don't ask me to say or do anything that is less than honest."   When Jane's conduct is discovered (and it always is), Jane's secretary may go too.

5. Firm management should revisit the basis for evaluation: quality time vs. quantity time. As employers consider the impact on employee family life, stress, health, etc., long hours may not be the only key to success and should not be a basis for evaluation. Further, employees are finding ways to deceive the system. Hours spent (or perceived hours spent) are obviously not indicative of work as we see from Jane's antics.

1.17 The Employment Application That Haunts the Applicant

Answers and Key Discussion Items

1. Yes, under the clear policies of the company, Weissman should be terminated. The reality is that Crawford never would have known about the application if Weissman had not become involved in a dispute at the office, but Weissman did fail to disclose relevant information in the employment application process and Crawford needs to send a signal with respect to how it handles dishonest employees.

2. Yes, the application has a place for a signature and full disclosure of the fact that the failure to provide truthful information was grounds for termination.

3. Weissman had several ethical breaches: saying things you know are not true; giving or allowing false impressions; hiding information; taking unfair advantage (she had the information and Crawford did not)

Legal Issues

It is well established in employment law that employees can be fired for lying on their employment applications. That termination can occur at any time during the course of employment following the discovery of the misinformation on the application.

1.18   Travel Expenses: A Chance for Extra Income

Answers and Key Discussion Items

1. The phrases the employees use when confronted with excessive and unauthorized travel expenses are the classic rationalizations for taking things that don't belong to you. The travel expenses that are not actually travel are a form of stealing.

2. Employees risk claiming extra expenses with the hope of making a little extra money, because they feel they won't be caught, and they feel entitled to it when raises have not been forthcoming.

3. Employees who are honest are harmed in that they are not trusted; the company is harmed in that it has additional expenses and investors and customers are affected by those higher costs and possibly declining sales. The extra expenses also create lower taxes based upon fraudulent expenditures. Up and down the chain with respect to the company, there are many affected when travel claims are inflated and created.

1.19 Do Cheaters Prosper?

<u>Answers and Key Discussion Items</u>

1. No, the suggestions involve many ethical breaches from taking things that don't belong to you, to saying things you know are not true, to taking unfair advantage.

2. The publication of a book with methods for cheating demonstrates enormous "chutzpah." That the author did so under an anonymous name is indicative of the embarrassment the author would feel if these tips and suggestions were attributed to him. Also, he might not be able to rent a car again!

3. The suggestions cost the businesses involved money, but there is also a trickle-down effect in that those costs must be absorbed somewhere. Perhaps employees are not given a raise, perhaps insurance rates run higher for the fake claims, perhaps product costs increase. There are always "retail-level" impacts when individuals cheat businesses.

2.1 Ann Hopkins, Price Waterhouse and the Partnership

<u>Use Transparency 9 to show the choices in language made in the evaluation of Ann Hopkins.</u>

<u>Answers and Key Discussion Items</u>

1. The partnership evaluation system appears to be widely-dispersed, uncertain in criteria, and not policed for violations of equal employment laws. In fairness to Price Waterhouse though, there was a time when such decisions (those for partnerships) were considered immune to EEOC attack (they were not classified as employment decisions).

2. One of the intriguing aspects of the case is why none of the partners, particularly any of the other women, ever spoke up and objected to the language and bases for Hopkins's evaluation. The process of group think results from peer pressure being applied to such an extent that those forms of conduct and types of statements that would otherwise be wrong and offensive are ignored.

3. The subjectivity was troublesome only because it allowed sexism to enter into the decision-making process. There is nothing wrong with not awarding a partnership to someone who is obnoxious, alienates the staff and is offensive in manner. These types of professional decisions on life-long commitments to employment necessarily include personal elements. However, in this case, and in many other employment cases, those issues were not the focus of the evaluation. The focus of the evaluation was Ms. Hopkins's appearance and her role as a woman in the workplace. In developing a procedure for evaluating potential partners, the firm should consider criteria such as revenue generated, relationships with staff, work compatibility with other partners, client satisfaction and others that are relevant, gender-neutral and serve to incorporate the concerns about the partnership decision.

4. The concept of "mixed motives" was covered in the U.S. Supreme Court decision. There may have been legitimate concerns about Ms. Hopkins' partnership "fit", but they were manifested in gender-descriptive terms.

5. The firm would have to have a diverse workforce. Top executives would have to support diversity by their hires and promotions. Basing decisions on experience and qualifications would become the firm's set of standards.

<u>Legal Issues</u>

The partners had concerns about Ms. Hopkins' fit into the partnership and those concerns are legitimate. The violation of the Civil Rights laws (and specifically Title VII) came as those concerns were translated into gender-descriptive terms.

2.2 Handwriting Analysis and Employment

<u>Use Transparency 10 to show types of handwriting and the conclusions drawn by the experts on that writing.</u>

<u>Answers and Key Discussion Items</u>

1. Handwriting is so easily altered that questions about its accuracy exist. Also, it seems to be an imprecise science when compared with drug-screening tests. However, many managers see it as a way to discern personality traits and those traits that make, for example, a good salesperson.

2. Handwriting analysis appears to be no different than a personality test. Questions exist about those types of evaluations as well. There appear to be contradictions in the experts' analysis of the same handwriting. Also, applicants have the ability to change handwriting samples just as they have the ability to control answers on a personality test.

3. As the transparency shows, there is great disparity among experts on treatment of handwriting. The question that arises is how much value such analysis brings to the employment decision. Managers are perhaps better served relying on interviews, questions and work samples.

4. Privacy issues may exist but handwriting is not an invasion of the person. Handwriting is part of working and not a taking of something that would not otherwise be seen. If the analysis are accurate, then a great deal of information is available to an employer that would otherwise not be available. Presently, handwriting seems to be a little bit of wizardry that enjoys some success.

5. Legally, many firms have run into discrimination problems because tests not really related to employment skills serve to screen out certain races. Depending on the analysts, it is possible women could be screened out of certain jobs. A valid accusation of discrimination via disparate impact could be made especially given the discrepancies in handwriting analysis.

6. The analysis of handwriting is not a refined art or science. In cases such as this one, an employee or potential employee is confronted with enormously personal issues and may be forced into a situation of disclosure that violates the law. The problem need not be disclosed to the employer so long as the employee is not currently suffering. There are also privacy issues associated with confrontations with information gleaned through handwriting analysis.

2.3   Health and Genetic Screening

Answers and Key Discussion Items

1. The use of the results of genetic screening is perhaps the real concern in any employee testing of this sort. If the results are being used, as in Israel, to avoid unnecessary risk and exposure in the workplace based on genetic composition, it is helpful. If, on the other hand, the screening results are used to deny employment, deny health insurance coverage or refuse to hire on the grounds that the employee's children would require additional medical care because of genetic diseases, there would be an invasion of privacy.

2. The clash is between the ability of all of us to overcome inherent defects and the use of pre-screening to prevent giving us the opportunity to do so. The use for all employees seems overly broad and carries the potential of exclusion of employees not on the basis of qualifications, but inherent composition. If carried to its extreme, some people would be essentially not hireable because of their genetic composition.

3. DuPont's program appears to have been implemented to prevent illness, not as a tool of discrimination or arbitrarily. Concern of making employees ill is at the heart of it.

4. The screening on the basis of sickle-cell anemia could result in a disparate impact on particular races. Although screening might be intended to ensure safety and put high risk employees in other jobs, the effect may be to preclude certain groups from higher-paying jobs.

5. Yes, DuPont's goal appears to be protection of employees; minimizing illness. Unfortunately, statutory protections clash and DuPont may lose.

6. The ADA provides that employment cannot be denied or terminated strictly on the basis of illness if the employee is able (with reasonable accommodation) to do his or her job. DuPont thus could not simply exclude sickle cell anemia victims so long as they can do the job.

Legal Issues

The U.S. Supreme Court has already ruled that an employer may not use a woman's fertility or possible fetal exposure (and the resulting dangers or permanent damage) to exclude women from certain jobs that are higher-paying, but also higher in risk. The use of a genetic screening device that impacts a particular race would probably meet the same fate in a judicial challenge.

2.4   The Smoking Prohibition

<u>Answers and Key Discussion Items</u>

1. Many companies take a different approach and attempt to have employees make the voluntary choice to eliminate unhealthy activities through educational programs, incentives and additional health insurance coverage costs for those who do smoke.

2. The interests of the employee's privacy are at risk as they clash with the interests of the employer in keeping employees healthy and keeping the cost of health insurance down. A utilitarian approach says that in doing the most good for the most people, eliminating smokers reduces health coverage and ensures that more people will have coverage.

3. There is an interest in health costs, passive smoke and safety of other employees. However, the issue of rights is also present. The ban on off-the-job smoking is a violation of individual freedom. As pointed out by one legislator in the case: if you permit off-the-job control, where do you draw the line?

4. It is not discrimination to refuse to hire smokers. Title VII includes no category for protection for voluntary conduct that translates into exposure for other employees as well as additional health insurance costs for the employer and other employees.

5. The exclusions for hazardous activities are quite common. Again, the employer is trying to provide the best possible coverage at the lowest possible price and exclusion of these employees achieves that goal. Again, refusal to hire on these bases is also not discrimination. The employer does make an investment in an employee in training, benefits, etc. and implements policies such as this to ensure that there is a return on these employee investments.

   Many insurance policies that cover key individuals include clauses that prohibit these activities during the period of coverage. For example, film stars would carry large policies on them because of the costs involved if they are unable to complete a movie. These activities are prohibited during the course of the movie shoot to minimize risk.

2.5   DUI and Deliveries

Answers and Key Discussion Items

1. The employer is balancing the privacy rights of the employee with the rights of society. Safety on the roads is imperative as so many others' rights are affected when irresponsible drivers are driving.

   The students should recognize that in this case, the DUI screening is simply good business. Safety of the drivers affords the company a good reputation. If drivers are, in fact, under the influence, their errors are likely to injure others and cost the company a great deal in litigation and public relations in the event of the discovery of the employee's drug or alcohol abuse.

2. Random means a larger net. Announced means temporarily clean employees. Notice is more dignified, but not as effective as determent.

3. There are various approaches to testing. Some employers require all employees to be tested. Other employers only require employees who are involved in positions that affect public safety to be tested. Other employers require officers and those employees in safety positions to be tested. The officers are tested to show compliance and good faith.

4. Testing employees who are involved in an accident may not be a choice. Law enforcement agencies may do that for you. It would be best to test all the drivers, require it periodically and then perform random tests. Employees and potential employees should all be told clearly the policies and procedures on drug testing.

5. Drug-testing is similar to the invasion of privacy that occurs when we go through the screening devices at the airport. It is an invasion of privacy, but one we are willing to accept because of our overriding concern for safety.

6. Testing only suspicious drivers minimizes the invasion of privacy, but minimizes the deterrent effect of a testing program. You may not have a large enough net to catch offenders.

7. Many people differ on the action that should be taken in the event of a positive result on a drug screening. Many employers take the posture that it is a violation of company rules and there is immediate termination. These policies tend to dominate in employment situations where public safety is at issue (drivers). Other employers take the position of a warning and mandatory drug rehabilitation and education programs. Accuracy is ensured through follow-up testing or the ability of the employee to use an independent lab.

8. Counseling, retesting, rehab programs, reassignment, stress reduction

9. Two labs; employee's choice of labs; latest technology

2.5   DUI and Deliveries (cont'd)

10.   You should inform drivers of testing as a precondition of employment and your ongoing test. Being candid up front is fair and ethical.

2.6   Corporate Anthropology: Is the Boss Spying?

Answers and Key Discussion Items

1.   Many argue that spying is the only way the employer can monitor effective performance. Many maintain that electronic surveillance is just a more sophisticated means of having the supervisor walk around and observe employees at work. On the other hand, the electronic surveillance is relentless -- employees are never given the opportunity for a "let-up."

2.   Many argue that they are the same with one exception: an employee can see a supervisor walking around and respond. They can't "see" electronic monitoring. They don't know when they're being watched.

3.   The right to privacy while doing one's job has not been recognized. Employers have the right to observe, correct and monitor. The advance disclosure of the monitoring seems more fair to most employees. However, in an ethical sense, shouldn't an employee always be performing his/her job effectively? Isn't the employee accepting wages in exchange for doing what is asked by the employer? In other words, should it make any difference in the way an employee acts whether or not he/she is being observed?

4.   Employees are told of the monitoring and can thus assume they are always being observed. There are no surprises. Employees know their conduct is watched.

5.   The desk is slightly different. Some elements of private life are within the desk and the invasion here is not directly related to job performance. Observing an employee work at a desk is different from actually going through the desk when the employee is not there.

6.   The nature of the employee's work can make surveillance more or less necessary. Telephone work must be monitored in a specific way and those monitors give employers information about how long the calls take, whether more operators are needed and whether the operators are following company guidelines on information, courtesy, etc.

Point out that hotels and other service industries have used customer satisfaction surveys as a means of monitoring employees for years. If anything, those surveys are less objective since customers can recount encounters with employees in their own words without adding a different perspective. In-house observation at least collects the full information.

7.   Employers should at least adopt a policy of full disclosure. Employees should understand at the outset the privacy limitations that exist and then they can adjust their conduct accordingly. One of the key methods for eliminating ethical dilemmas is disclosure. Disclose in advance the use and existence of the technology and employees can adjust their privacy needs to that surveillance.

8.   A sign-off by employees on their understanding about the technology and

its privacy limitations would be very helpful in eliminating the employer's taking unfair advantage.

9.   Yes, the disclosure of accessibility is critical for employers and employees.

10.   The employer provides the equipment and the means for the use of such technology — it all belongs to the employer. The employer has the right to expect that employees are serving them during the work day. Further, so long as employees understand that ownership right and interest, it is fair to expect that employers could monitor employees.

11.   Full disclosure is always the best policy for any form of intrusion.

12.   Some claim they have left voice mails and e-mails when in fact they didn't. Further, technology does not permit the level of verification needed to ensure that others are not involved in industrial sabotage. Follow-up to technology messages can provide significant reassurance of their authenticity. A call to verify the message or e-mail can be good documentation of authenticity.

2.7   The Athlete Role Model

Answers and Key Discussion Items

1. The contract perhaps did not have a per se morals clause, but Mr. Irvin was signed with the idea that he would be a good representative for the companies in the sense of no public scandals.

2. Morality can be a condition for being a spokesperson if that condition is something that those who have hired the spokesperson desire. In other words, the company offering the endorsement is free to set its standards for its product and those with whom that product is associated.

3. It would be difficult to make the point that morality is implied in an endorsement contract. However, the idea of endorsements is to take the goodwill that the celebrity has and associate it with one's product. To the extent that the celebrity does not bring to mind talent or goodwill, but rather, a reputation for drug use, the whole purpose of the endorsement contract is defeated.

4. A criminal charge is perhaps as close to a universal standard for bad conduct that costs a company when a celebrity endorser is so charged. There is very little positive that comes to mind when the celebrity charged with a crime is associated with your product. All potential customers see is that your business is associated with criminal activity. The idea is to promote a positive image and goodwill, not criminal activity.

READINGS - SEXUAL HARASSMENT

A MATTER OF DEFINITION
Anita Hill

FEMINISTS AND THE CLINTON QUESTION
Gloria Steinem

1. According to the pieces, the significance of "no" in sexual harassment is that if the person making the advance stops after a "no," then it is not sexual harassment. If the person continues to make advances following a "no," then the conduct becomes sexual harassment.

2. According to the writings, one sexually offensive advance cannot constitute sexual harassment.

3. Some simple ethical tests could go a long way in helping to resolve the issue that the law seems to have so much difficulty coping with. How would you want to be treated? What if it were you on the other side? Would you want your conduct reported on the front page of the newspaper? What is the likely result of your sexual advances? What is your intent in making them? What if everyone behaved in this fashion? What would happen?

Discuss with the students the Paula Jones and Kathleen Willey cases and have them sort out, along with the readings, what a company should do with respect to sexual harassment.

2.8 *Seinfeld* in the Workplace

<u>Answers and Key Discussion Items</u>

1. Mackenzie assumed that he was discussing an appropriate subject because the topic had been presented on prime time television. Also, under the readings, Mackenzie only discussed the topic one time with the employee and then dropped the issue.

2. Regardless of the legal standard, the topic was not an appropriate one for the workplace. Professionalism would dictate that such a show should not be mentioned anymore than in passing that it was on and the topic was "provocative." The discussion injects far too much personal life into the workplace.

3. The award is a message from the jury about the silliness of employers when it comes to handling cases such as this. A simple discussion with employees about such topics and their prohibition would have remedied the situation.

2.9   Hooters: More Than a Waitress?

Answers and Key Discussion Items

1. It is obvious from Hooters' ads, the attire of the waitresses, the name and the T-shirts that the restaurant chain has a focus on sexual entendre. The whole restaurant theme seems to say to women, "Avoid this place if harassment is a problem." The issue is not whether knowledge is critical. Knowledge is obvious. The issue is whether Hooters and its theme should be regulated in some way.

2. Despite the theme, Hooters managers should ensure that harassment of workers does not occur.

3. Managers can set the restaurant tone by intervening when workers are uncomfortable with customer behavior and by a asking those who can't control themselves to leave.

4. Students will debate the issue whole-heartedly. A former student shared a dilemma: he needed hours for continuing education for his license renewal. The seminar that would give him the hours he needed in time for renewal was being held at a Hooters restaurant. He felt uncomfortable going but needed his continuing education hours. What would you do?

5. The relationship between Hooters and the church raises some family values issues for the church. While having the funds is wonderful, there is the issue of selling one's soul. The reality is that many of the church members and certainly children, could not go to Hooters because of concerns about propriety. Further, the words "Hooters" is associated with the church in all advertisements for the special event.

2.10 On-the-Job Fetal Injuries

Answers and Key Discussion Items

1. The policy was designed to protect women of child-bearing capability and their fetuses. The policy of Johnson Controls had the best intentions and was based on sound legal advice: avoid liability for fetal exposure in certain jobs. The difficulty was that no choice was given and the high-exposure jobs were the ones paying the most money.

2. Freedom of choice is a good alternative with the exception of possible problems for the fetus who is left with exposure but no choice. This lack of choice on the part of the baby may still spell future liability for Johnson Controls.

3. The issue here is one of balancing the mother's rights for equal employment with the child's rights of freedom from injury, damage, etc. The difficulty lies in dictating the conduct of the mother for the benefit of an individual who cannot speak, but may be injured. The legal decision focused on the rights of the mother.

4. As the director of human resources, faced with the implementation of the U.S. Supreme Court decision, I would quickly develop a disclosure statement and waiver. All workers would be given both. Exposure to lead can be dangerous for men as well. With universal coverage, the waivers and signatures are an employment requirement and not a requirement for women only (or women of child-bearing years).

5. Whether the U.S. Supreme Court made the correct decision in subordinating the rights of unborn children remains to be seen. In the opinion there is a footnote regarding the possibility of state litigation with respect to insurance coverage of such birth defects. State law might permit recovery against the company even though the U.S. Supreme Court was mandating that women be permitted to hold those jobs that might result in the liability issues.

Legal Issues

Many employers are affected by the *Johnson Controls* case. Hospitals with technicians and other personnel in x-ray and nuclear medicine, nuclear plant workers, and VDT workers would be affected. Any exclusionary policies must be eliminated.

2.11 Denny's: Discriminatory Service With a Smile

Answers and Key Discussion Items

1. The forms of discrimination that occurred at Denny's were blatant disparate treatment forms of discrimination. These obvious forms of discrimination have been eliminated in most firms because of the laws against discrimination. That these forms of blatant conduct still occurred is indicative of a failure to monitor operations at the restaurant level. It is also indicative of a lack of feedback from customers and employees about the practices.

2. Denny's costs were in the millions as well as the ongoing commitments and monitoring that must occur. There was also the damage to Denny's reputation just because of the extreme nature of the problems that occurred.

3. The problems could have been brought to Denny's attention long before litigation if an employee hotline were available and open to employees. This type of discrimination issue is precisely the kind of problem employees would hesitate to report and would be reluctant to go public with their disclosures. A hotline allows employees to get their concern reviewed without having to come forward.

2.12   Texaco: The Jelly Bean Diversity Fiasco

Answers and Key Discussion Items

1. Texaco employed the following people:

   Robert Ulrich - Treasurer
   J. David Keough - Senior Assistant Treasurer
   Richard A. Lundwall - senior coordinator for personnel services

   Texaco was facing a discrimination suit brought by 6 employees on behalf of 1500 Texaco employees. The suit alleged disparate treatment as well as disparate impact in the work place at Texaco. The EEOC had found problems with discrimination at Texaco.

   When discovery requests for documents were made, the three above-listed officers met (with a recording being kept by Lundwall) and discussed the suit and document production. While the tape was initially transcribed incorrectly, there were some offensive statements in the tape and the tape reflects an effort on the part of the men to not disclose some information.

   Following the printing of the taped conversations in the *New York Times*, Texaco settled the discrimination suit for $176 million and agreed to begin sensitivity training and other programs in order to remedy the problem. Texaco had had diversity training under a program that used the concept of jelly beans as a means of helping people to understand the differences among employees and working together.

   Ulrich and Lundwall were charged with criminal indictments for their plan to withhold documents. However, they were both acquitted.

2. Lundwall recorded the sessions secretly, but he had been assigned the task of taking minutes of the meeting. He should have asked if anyone minded if he recorded the sessions.

3. The initial portrayal of the executives' discussion was very harsh. However, the trial revealed that the executives received very little guidance from the lawyers on the case and were confused about their requirements to produce evidence and the mandatory disclosure of all information relevant to the case.

4. The purpose of affirmative action is to increase protected class representation in the work force and the purpose of diversity training is to help those who are new to a company in the sense of their backgrounds to have co-workers who understand their differences.

   However, it is important to note that some experts in the field have questioned the qualifications of diversity trainers and have wondered whether the training does not, in fact, create a more hostile environment because of its oversimplifications and generalizations, as in the case of the Texaco jelly beans analogy.

5. While Mr. Bijur quelled a public relations nightmare, he may have admitted to too much. Texaco was not as bad as the press reports would have led people to believe, nor were the executives actually saying the things that had been printed in the *Times*. Bijur settled without full information and that may be problematic for the shareholders. However, Bijur also did serve to head off a battle in the media that could have damaged Texaco more.

LEGAL ISSUES

Emphasize for the students that it is a business's obligation to turn over all documents and not pick and choose which documents are favorable. Good or bad, the evidence is given to the opposition. If executives are unclear, they should seek out legal advice.

2.13   Hunter Tylo: Pregnancy is Not a BFOQ

Answers and Key Discussion Items

1. The distinction in their circumstances is that Ms. Locklear was an established star and lead character whereas Ms. Tylo was brand new to the show. Otherwise, their circumstances were the same. They were pregnant actresses with jobs in television that did not involve being pregnant as part of the story line.

2. Mr. Spelling seems to think that not being pregnant is a requirement for being a vixen on television. The problem is that he had set a precedent with Ms. Locklear and managed to work around a pregnancy.

3. Mr. Spelling said that it would cost more to rewrite the scripts and shoot at different camera angles. Additional cost for accommodation is not a justification for discrimination.

LEGAL ISSUES

Under the Pregnancy Discrimination Act, employers cannot hire, fire or demote on the basis of pregnancy. Mr. Spelling admitted that pregnancy was the basis for termination in this case.

2.14 Rudy Granser: From Chief Chef to Bottlewasher

Answers and Key Discussion Items

1. The original employment-at-will doctrine was to give employers wide latitude in the firing of employees. Commerce required rapid-pace activity and decisions and the justification for the doctrine was not to have employers in court every time an employee was terminated. There was a recognition of the delicate nature of the employment relationship in the sense of trust, confidence and performance and the courts should not become a substitute for the judgment of the employer.

   On the other hand, some employers did use the power to unjustifiably punish employees who questioned authority or questioned practices in order to preserve their own business practices. The power, in essence, bought employee silence on business operations and practices, regardless of their legality.

2. The due process comes in the documented and systematic evaluation and termination procedures all employers should have. The employer should have evaluations that let the employee know how his or her job performance is. In the event problems develop, the employer should have a warning system in place that gives the opportunity for improvement and then proceeds to termination. These steps are a form of due process in that employees know the expectations and evaluations and when they have fallen short of both.

3. Extensive protections for employees do slow down business operations and changes.

4. Whistle-blower statutes were designed to provide protection for employees who disclose illegal activity on the part of their employers. That whistle-blowers are sometimes depicted as dysfunctional perhaps stems more from the fact that they had to go outside their companies for relief because they could find none from within — no one was listening within the company to the concerns they were raising.

Legal Issues

The doctrine of employment-at-will has been subject to significant judicial and legislative modification since about 1986. In many states, employees cannot be fired for reporting illegalities or safety issues for such termination would violate public policy. Other states recognize contract rights as built into employee manuals and other policies and procedures of the employer.

2.15   The Dilemmas in Job Hopping

<u>Answers and Key Discussion Points</u>

1. The problems with job-hopping are that these employees, even those not necessarily at the executive level, possess proprietary and competitively valuable information about their employers. To allow them to go elsewhere is allowing them to take what they have learned and transfer it to a competitor.

2. Employees do have the right to work and earn a living and some states will not enforce restrictive covenants because such covenants effectively prohibit an individual from working.

3. The information is critical for product development, operations and even the supply chain.

4. Those who hire job-hopping employees should understand that they are hiring someone who in all likelihood will move on and perhaps take information with them. There are risks associated with hiring away talent from competitors.

2.16 Beech-Nut and the No-Apple-Juice Apple Juice

Use Transparency 11 for a chronology of events.

Answers and Key Discussion Items

1. While no one was harmed by the apple juice, it was fraud to tell consumers it was apple juice and charge apple juice prices. Also, there was the possibility that a baby might have had an allergic reaction to the chemicals in the product. Parents need to have content information before giving the juice to the babies. Selling no-apple-juice apple juice was unfair to the buyers, the users and the competitors of Beech-Nut.

2. This was a company that had no avenues for employees to report problems they suspected and did not have the appropriate culture for responding to problems and questions that were pursued diligently by employees. LiCari made sure he had his facts straight and he did follow the lines of authority, the proper plan for a whistle-blower. The problems LiCari encountered were that nobody at any level wanted to listen to him. Even LiCari's circumstantial evidence should have been taken seriously and followed up on.

3. Circumstantial evidence is not conclusive evidence. Often whistle-blowers look foolish when they do not have full information. Here, the evidence was, however, quite strong.

4. Beech-Nut was facing tremendous competition and the need to keep prices down. The ease of the substitution and its low cost made the continuing dependence on a chemical concoction necessary.

5. LiCari is an honest and conscientious man who did everything he could and explored every avenue to try to help the company correct its problems. LiCari wrote anonymously to the FDA because of his conscience, but did not want to be involved in the process of investigating or have his name revealed to Beech-Nut. Discuss with the students the ethics of anonymous tips. Accuracy can be difficult to verify and follow-up is impossible. Should the person be willing to accept the consequences that follow from coming forward? Compare LiCari to Anita Hill and her allegations against Clarence Thomas. Should she have come forward while still employed by Judge Thomas?

6. LiCari's identity was revealed eventually but he wanted to remain anonymous to avoid the public scrutiny, stress, and hassle.

7. Hoyvald and Lavery are still subject to state charges that are pending. But, it is important for the students to realize that criminal conviction or not, these two men are now unemployable and will spend most of the money they earned on attorneys' fees in defending their cases. The criminal charges may be the least of their problems. There are no positive aspects to their running Beech-Nut during this time. Their careers are finished, personal disgrace (guilty or not) follows and shareholders, employers and customers will continue to resent their conduct.

2.16 Beech-Nut and the No-Apple-Juice Apple Juice (cont'd)

<u>Legal Issues</u>

The FDA requires full disclosure of all product contents on the label. It is a felony violation of federal law to mislead or mislabel intentionally. Also, the sale of apple juice with no apple juice constituted fraud.

2.17 New Era — If It Sounds Too Good to be True, It is too Good to be True

Answers to Discussion Questions

1. Mr. Meyer had so much difficulty convincing his colleagues because of the draw of the return on their investment and greed. They wanted to believe it was true that you could really earn this much money. They wanted to ignore the facts.

2. Mr. Meyer tried to do everything from within and follow the lines of authority in reporting the problems about which he had concerns.

3. Mr. Meyer had no job security at the time he began bringing this issue to the attention of his supervisors and colleagues. He was questioning something in which they had placed great trust.

4. The college administrators, charged with raising funds for the college, were so concerned about meeting their fund-raising goals that they did not want to hear from any naysayers, even if they made sense. The call from Mr. Bennett should have been a flag for those a Spring Arbor. If Bennett had nothing to fear, a quick examination of the records for his company should not have caused his anger and should have been welcomed.

5. The return of the money when the organizations did not have to return the money under law is an admirable act. They could have taken the money and been done with their problems with respect to New Era. However, they wished to sustain a good reputation.

2.18 Dow Corning and the Silicone Implants: Questions of Safety and Disclosure

<u>Use Transparency 12 to show the history and ownership of the silicone implant manufacturers.</u>

<u>Use Transparency 13 to show the chronology of events for Dow Corning.</u>

<u>Answers and Key Discussion Items</u>

1. Manuel Velasquez holds the test for moral responsibility to be: who had the ultimate decision-making authority for the product? The engineers, designers, and production employees who follow orders would not be morally responsible under the Velasquez test. However, Velasquez ignores the feelings of those who worked on the product. Whether they would or would not be held responsible on an accountability test will not change the fundamental personal feelings they will have about having worked on a product that injures many, often leaving permanent damage. The information on the 1975 study should have been disclosed -- people can then make a decision based on full disclosure.

2. For employees like Talcott, and LiCari in the Beech-Nut case, the failure of the company to take action and their anticipation of harm to others means that their resignations are necessary to alleviate the moral responsibility they will feel.

3. Ask the students to put themselves in Talcott's shoes and whether they would have done more or less. Remind them about the issues of their livelihood, peer pressure and company pressure so that they appreciate how difficult circumstances were.

4. Freedom to choose is a moral right. But choosing should be based on full information and accurate disclosure. In this case, there are differing views about the implants. Some women would very much like to have the choice because of their need for reconstructive surgery. They weigh the dangers with the self-esteem problems and want the option of the implants. Such an option is viable but there must be full information so that the choice is made with an accurate weighing of the risks.

5. The FDA not only has a moral responsibility, it is charged by Congress with the enforcement of the law. Those products that cause harm (as documented for the FDA), must be recalled. The FDA waited for too long a time in handling the problem and should have required warnings or a halt of future sales.

6. Dr. Rudy was attempting to get full information to physicians. But the problem was that the information needed to go directly to users so that full disclosure and freedom of choice were assured.

   Note: Ask the students if choice is most important in this case. Also ask them why companies are hesitant to respond to issues raised by employees with respect to safety. Explain to them issues of profitability and the pressures to increase sales.

Dow Corning declared bankruptcy in June 1995. The settlements remain in jeopardy as the Chapter 11 proceeding continues.

7. Swanson faced a personal and business ethical dilemma in that he worked for the company that was producing a product he was fairly certain was causing his wife's illness. Swanson's first step should have been, as a matter of loyalty to his company, to go to the officers and discuss the possibility and give them the opportunity to take voluntary action. If that action were not forthcoming, then Swanson had to face the moral and personal dilemma of continuing to work for a company doing something he believes to be wrong. He would then resign and take appropriate steps for bringing the issue to the attention of the public, something Swanson did eventually.

2.19 The Changing Time Cards

Answers and Key Discussion Items

1. The harm fell upon the taxpayers who eventually foot the bill but also upon other contractors who share in an indictment of dishonesty. The harm fell upon shareholders as GE works to regain its reputation.

2. Mr. Gravitt did a difficult but ethical thing in reporting the time card violations. He followed the correct steps in trying to remedy the problem and gathered his information carefully. He was in a culture that did not provide the opportunity for self-correction.

3. Mr. Gravitt did violate the privacy of another and company procedures in the methods he used for the collection of his data. Ask the students if the ends Gravitt was able to accomplish justified the means he used. Is it permissible to violate one rule in an attempt to remedy other violations?

4. Tepe's moral responsibility test follows that of Velasquez; those making the orders are responsible, not the soldiers who carry them out. However, this test fails to take into account the consciences of the soldiers and their recognition that something wrong is being done. Mr. Tepe's attitude is a means of ignoring wrongdoing.

5. That type of executive philosophy teaches employees that no questions can be asked and that you do what you're told regardless of what you think. Breaking the law becomes easy in such an amoral atmosphere.

6. Incentive programs which base compensation on revenue only are programs that invite employees to cheat, be dishonest and "do whatever it takes" to meet goals.

7. GE would need:

   (a)   a more open atmosphere
   (b)   different compensation system
   (c)   different management philosophy and attitude
   (d)   hot line
   (e)   statement of values
   (f)   ombudsperson office

Legal Issues

Under the new Federal Corporate Sentencing Guidelines, corporations can mitigate criminal penalties by demonstrating the presence of a code of ethics and training for employees in the area of ethical decisions. The companies can also mitigate criminal penalties by showing they had a hotline for employees to call and report wrongdoing. Further, the companies can reduce penalties by voluntary compliance. If they come forward with violations that are self-discovered, judges can take their self-reporting into account in sentencing. These guidelines make it

2.19 The Changing Time Cards (cont'd)

necessary for people such as Mr. Gravitt to be able to come forward and receive a response.

Also, Mr. Gravitt is the beneficiary of a federal law that permits reporting employees to recover portions of the amount they report is involved in wrongdoing. Legal incentives now exist at the federal level for ethical compliance.

2.20 The Extension of Benefits to Partners of Homosexual Employees

<u>Answers and Key Discussion Items</u>

1. The issue of covering same-sex domestic partnerships and not heterosexual couples who live together is currently the subject of a suit in federal district court. The argument a male employee who lives with a female partner makes is that he is discriminated against by the company because he is heterosexual.

2. Some employees have noted that they do not take advantage of the benefits because it means disclosure about their personal lives.

3. Lotus and other companies plunge themselves into a public and company debate when policies regarding "significant others" are adopted that specifically reference the "significant others." As the comments by employees demonstrate, people have profoundly different feelings about the morality of homosexuality. Other employees are concerned about the difficulties of having to disclose their personal relationships.

   Employees feel the way they feel. There is great emotion on both sides of the issue in Lotus, in other companies, among the public.

4. To adequately cope with the complex issues of "family" in today's society, Lotus and other companies should regroup to provide dependent coverage. Dependent coverage could include, for example, anyone who resides in your household who is not covered under another insurer's or work policy (exceptions could be made for full-time student-children who reside, temporarily, elsewhere). Not only does this definition resolve the problem, it would permit employees who have the responsibility of parental care to provide coverage for those parents. This type of definition is neutral and not as likely to stir the emotions expressed by employees in this case study. The coverage is provided in a generic as opposed to specific declaration.

5. There is a conflict for employees whose religious beliefs run contra to homosexuality and who believe that sanctioning unions such as same-sex partnerships is morally wrong. These employees will have difficulty adopting such a policy. In companies where employees have strong moral beliefs that run contra to such practices, employers have provided benefits only for married couples thus leaving the decisions as to what constitutes a marriage or permanent relationship to judicial or legislative definition.

2.21 Cheap Labor: Children, Sweat Shops and the Fifty-Hour Work Week

Answers and Key Discussion Items

1. The economic issues center around the comparisons between U.S. wages and wages in these countries. The discussion must begin from the value of a dollar in those countries and the going wages. The social discussion must center around the children and what is best, in the long run, for the economy of that nation. The ethical issue is that many U.S. firms are doing in a foreign country what would be illegal here and that is the use of child labor.

   The points that many economists make is that these countries that are developing must go through the same evolutionary process as was present in the United States before we had child labor laws. However, the ethical issue is whether U.S. companies have an obligation to enlighten these nations about the effects of child labor.

   While libertarian economics produces fascinating discussions, it does assume that both sides to the transaction have full information and the capability to contract. These jobs and wages are negotiated with those who are traditionally assumed unable to contract because of lack of experience and knowledge.

   One way to look at the view that the jobs support the families is to ask if the jobs are so good, then why don't the adults in the families do them? Why are the children forced into the jobs?

2. The legal issues of employing a 12-year-old are very different from the moral ones. The issue is no different from Union Carbide and Bhopal. Yes, there were in compliance with the law, but what they did was morally wrong. The same question is here and the answer is the same. Legally you can do it, morally you should not.

3. Some companies have actually improved the lives of children through school programs coupled with work at decent wages and for limited hours. The children are off the streets and are fed and educated.

4. How children are treated is also a question of ethics. Using the jobs as a means for them to get ahead and carefully policing the work efforts are critical parts of the ethical obligations imposed for employing children.

5. The stories involving this big shoe company and a big star hit home and made people realize what was happening with sweat shop labor. The reality hit home when famous icons were associated with it.

3.1   BCCI and the Role of Internal Auditors

Use Transparency 14 to show the complexity of BCCI and its various subsidiaries around the world.

Answers and Key Discussion Items

1. Yes, if management is engaged in fraud, it is possible. It is not, however, impossible to spot the issues and problems with piercing questions based on experience.

2. At a national meeting of internal auditors a speaker asked the question, "How does a BCCI happen with competent, international auditors auditing its books?" Her speech went on to explain that a BCCI happens because many people recognize what is happening but don't know how or fail to bring it to the attention of those who can take appropriate action. As a board member she reflected on how very possible it would be for members of the boards of BCCI subsidiaries not to realize the extent and nature of BCCI's activities if management had hidden information from the auditors or if the auditors were missing signals and failing to alert the board.

   In some instances auditors are misled by management and it is the position of AICPA and FASB that it is not the responsibility of auditors to detect management fraud unless the auditor specifically agrees to do so. Thus it would be possible for an auditor to issue a clean opinion in a BCCI case because the wrongdoing would be hidden from the auditors. There has been some pressure on auditors from the investment public, investment regulators and as a result of large settlements and verdicts against auditors in cases like BCCI to undertake detection of fraud. The clean opinion reflects the auditor's work and review of appropriate samples. No fraud or other misdeeds might be detected.

3. Various red flags are touted by plaintiffs' lawyers in cases against auditors as means of detecting fraud. One such flag would be a young senior management and a CEO and/or chairman who is a full generation older (as in the Charles Keating/Lincoln Savings and Loan case). Other red flags would include complex paper trails that are difficult to follow. Another red flag would be the denial of access to books and records of subsidiaries. Cash flow issues, rapid sequences of capital offerings and one-time gain recognitions to boost earnings would signal possible difficulties.

4. A member of the audit committee has very little choice because of SEC regulations. The information would have to be disclosed and action taken to eliminate the activities. In the event there is a refusal for action to be taken, the audit committee directors would be forced to resign.

5. Fraud can be detected generally by signals as noted above and by non-quantitative factors such as experience in human nature and personalities, an ability to detect evasiveness and the personal strength to note flattery as a means of avoiding detection.

3.1 BCCI and the Role of Internal Auditors (cont'd)

6. As subsequent indictments of both Clifford and Altman suggest, it seems unlikely that they could have held the positions they held and defended BCCI as much as they did in so many intricate financial dealings and not know of the nature of BCCI. They were serving as officers and directors of a subsidiary and defending the parent company in litigation. Further, they were the beneficiaries of loans that enabled them to make substantial profits in stock deals. Clifford and Altman had no incentives to report any problems in the BCCI operations or subsidiaries, although technically such reporting would have been their responsibility as board members.

7. A great deal of focus and discussion has been held regarding the need to avoid another BCCI. Its incorporation in Luxembourg and its large number of multinational subsidiaries made it difficult for any one nation's regulators to detect exactly how the finances of BCCI were being handled and used. Jurisdiction appeared to be deferred to so many countries that really no country was in charge, including the United States, and hence the problems were permitted to continue and BCCI was relatively unsupervised.

8. The tips were not a high priority. It was difficult to believe a bank this large could have the problems alleged in the tips. It was a function of not believing the tipsters enough to act. Also, the whistle-blowers could have supplied additional information.

3.2   Medical Billing Errors and Practices

Use Transparency 15 to show a summary of all the creative medical billing tactics.

Answers and Key Discussion Items

1. Given the nature of medical costs and the proposed reforms for medical care and insurance, Ms. Young would no doubt attract positive attention from consumers of medical care and insurers for her efforts. However, some physicians, labs and even some patients who benefit from code creeps, unbundling, exploding, etc. might be quite hostile toward her and her efforts. Ms. Young's motive is a noble one: be certain that there is accurate billing in all medical procedures.

2. Even if Ms. Young commissions a study and makes billing procedure corrections, she will not be able to change the behavior of physicians who submit insurance bills. For changes here, she may have to conduct seminars or demonstrate why accurate and moderate billings are the best practice for the medical community in the long run.

3. Everyone is harmed by the upcoding and other creative processes. Costs to insurers and hospitals are always passed along to the ultimate customer. We all pay for medical care and insurance when costs continue to rise because of these creative billing methods. Some patients are helped in terms of extra compensation but if their insurance was not written to cover a procedure, is it fair to obtain coverage through deceit?

4. Discuss with the students why there is a tolerance of error and expanded bills when an insurance company or another deep pocket is involved. Why is it less ethical to lie in a sales transaction than it is to lie in an insurance submission? Is it because the system is unfair? Is it because everyone does it? Is it because that's the way it has always been done?

5. Patients may not be complaining because they are unaware, or because they are temporary beneficiaries of this billing system. However, over the long term, this type of conduct will harm all consumers and providers in the medical care system. A new system of limitations may have to be adopted because of the uncontrollable costs submitted under this lenient system of reimbursement. Cost shifting is debated for its ethics and problems in economics. We cover the costs but what happens to supply and demand as a result?

3.3   Creative Billing

Answers and Key Discussion Points

1. Just because everyone is doing it does not make it right and just because no one is doing it does not make it wrong. The language of rationalization is rampant in the whole billing process. An entire consulting industry sprung up to service the notion of maximum billing. The concern about ethics arises because no one is being fair and open about actual medical costs and the result is a large impact on the health care system and the insurers providing for such.

2. The higher code may not be justified in a set of circumstances. The billing code should be based on actual treatment given and actual condition diagnosed, not what diagnosis and treatment will bring the most reimbursement.

3. There are many variations on the theories about the role of hospitals. Many hospitals were founded as non-profits with the very idea being to avoid business and the problems the motivation for profit might bring to the treatment of patients. On the other hand, many of the best-run hospitals are those that are involved in competition for profits and patients, the quality does go up without monopoly.

4. There is a process of rationalization that precedes both legal and ethical violations. Individuals smooth their consciences with each little step until eventually overbilling is a way of life. Overbilling can climb to a point of billing for services not actually performed. There is a slow wearing down of the conscience as well as an elimination of the bright line between right and wrong.

5. The whistle-blowers in this case were found because internal response mechanisms for their concerns were not there. Also, it should be noted that these whistle-blowers stand to receive 10 percent of anything Columbia is required to pay as a result of their tip-off on the violations. A finder's fee is available for cases such as this.

3.4   MiniScribe and the Auditors

<u>Use Transparency 16 to show the types of employee cooperation in the fraud at MiniScribe</u>.

<u>Answers and Key Discussion Items</u>

1. The MiniScribe case is an illustration of the types of extreme managers will go to when pressured for results as they were in the case with the threat of being fired or, at a minimum, experiencing personal humiliation in meetings. The signal from top management was to get results with no limitations on how to get those results.

2. Under the Velasquez test, Coopers & Lybrand was not morally responsible because its auditors had no control over the fraud committed by the management. Coopers & Lybrand was not a participant in the acts noted on Transparency 26.   They were duped themselves and would not be morally responsible.   Moral responsibility would require some knowledge on their part.   The auditors may have been negligent in failing to spot red flags regarding possible fraud, but oversight and mistakes do not equate with moral culpability. Moral culpability is different from financial culpability, and they were indeed held financially responsible for the losses.

3. It is troublesome that none of the employees came forward to question wrapping bricks as disk drives. However, the pressure that management felt from upper management may have been felt by the workers as well, and hence they were willing to do whatever was necessary to secure their employment. Again, the Velasquez standard would not hold them morally responsible because they were only following orders.

4. Assuming the internal auditors had access to all books and records and knew of the tactics in Transparency 26, they would be morally responsible because they had the authority to stop the activities.

5. Auditors, under AICPA and FASB, are not responsible for detecting fraud by management unless they agree to assume that responsibility. Management, as in this case, can withhold whatever information it chooses and change numbers in work papers and engage in various forms of deception to ensure that the auditors do not even have red flags to lead them to question management. It seems unfair to hold them liable when they were tricked. The message may be that auditors should be above being tricked.

3.5   Phar-Mor Earnings

Answers and Key Discussion Items

1. Conflicts of interest
   Taking things that don't belong to you
   Saying things that aren't true
   Giving or allowing false impressions
   Engaging in personal decadence
   Interpersonal and organizational abuse

2. Rapid growth
   Executives without accountability
   Executives with great spending discretion
   Auditors lacking sufficient access
   Earnings/growth pressure

3. Yes, this was an alter ego situation where the funds and property of the company were not seen as separate from individual control and funds. The officers felt the money could be spent, wherever and however.

4. Board should have been notified. Outside auditors should have been notified. Officers should have been threatened with outside notification.

5. Outside auditors or board members (audit committee). The existence of two sets of books means that fraud/lack of ethics is pervasive among executives. Internal reporting will not help.

6. Creditors
   Shareholders
   Employees of closed stores and their families
   Other stores (credibility problems when they attempt expansion)
   Communities where closed stores are located
   Suppliers
   Accounting firm
   Lawyers
   Insurers

3.6   The Ethics of Derivatives

<u>Use Transparency 17 to show extent of derivative losses.</u>

<u>Answers and Key Discussion Items</u>

1. a. Those affected by your decision:

     Shareholders
     Creditors
     Competition
     You
     Your career
     Your family
     Pension holders
     Pension fund managers
     Employees (retired and otherwise)

   b. Kant: How would you want to be treated? If it were your pension fund,
      would you want this risk and exposure? Probably not.

      Laura Nash: Could you disclose this to those affected? No, it would be
      uncomfortable for you to disclose the level of risk you were engaging in.

      Blanchard/Peale: Is it legal? At the time, yes. Is it balanced? No, it
      risks the pension fund to maximize earnings. One might not feel
      comfortable about the choice.

      Front page of the newspaper: Treasurer bets pension fund; Gibson loses in
      gamble of pension fund.

2. Many have theorized that for Citron (whose compensation was not determined by
   returns), it was an ego problem: earning as much as possible while minimizing
   in one's mind the astronomical risk and exposure if the investments did not
   work. For Procter & Gamble and Gibson, derivatives seemed an easy means for
   high returns.

3. Leeson's motivation was career progression, and his financial rewards were
   determined by his portfolio's return. The higher the return, the more he
   earned, and the greater his recognitions and promotions.

4. Often managers look the other way when returns are high and things are going
   well. They should, perhaps, ask questions, but fail to.

   In fact, managers should follow a philosophy: If it seems too good to be
   true, it probably is and that would be the time to ask questions.

5. The story shows that what many people thought was just a method for high
   finance hedging and leverage actually did make its way down into the retail
   level of investment and cost a great deal for two people who were unable to

3.6   The Ethics of Derivatives (cont'd)

evaluate the risk and sophistication of these instruments. There is no line between high finance and the common investor. The common investor's money is what fuels the high finance official's dealings. He is accountable to the small investor and should behave as such in a fiduciary manner. High risk types of ventures should be disclosed and should not be hidden beneath a blanket of security marketed to individuals as safe.

3.7   Overstated Earnings: Bausch & Lomb

<u>Answers and Key Discussion Points</u>

1. The culture at Bausch & Lomb became so obsessed with achievement of earnings and sales goals that it lost sight of encasing those achievements within certain basic ethical values such as honesty and fairness. This was a culture possessed with achievement of goals — to do whatever it takes to meet the numbers.

2. A 50% plus dip in earnings, dip in stock price and a long road back to recovery. There was also a shareholder suit over the problems.

3. The former employees had to go because they engaged in such egregious behavior with respect to meeting the numbers. The pressure was there to meet the numbers, but, employees do not have to follow orders and no one ordered them directly to cheat — they undertook to cheat because of pressure and would take the fall for that, even if the company created the pressure that produced those results.

4. Employees need to understand that the achievement of goals is within the bounds of the rules and the rules are no cheating. This limitation on goals is often not communicated clearly to the employees.

3.8   The Inside Scoop — Trading Stock on Inside Information

Answers and Key Discussion Items

1. At the heart of insider trading sanctions is the commitment that a market in which all cannot believe they are on a level playing field is a market doomed for failure. Free markets don't function without complete information and investors don't invest if they don't have trust and believe that their chance at success is the same as that of other investors, buyers and sellers alike.

2. They absolutely understood the law, they somehow felt themselves immune or that the law was not needed or that they would not be caught. The temptation of the large gains is often too much for many people.

3. "Everybody else does it," is not a defense under federal securities law. The law is there for the protection of investors. That enforcement is difficult and many are able to get away, at least temporarily, with it, does not mean that the involvement in these behaviors is ethical or legal.

4. Ms. Baridis was lured by money and power and the opportunity to get ahead. AS a compliance officer, she understood the law and risk. She believed she would get away with it because her name would not be involved in the actual trades. But, those whose names were involved were kind enough to share the information.

3.9   The Inside Tract: Dan Dorfman

Answers and Key Discussion Items

1. There is a conflict of interest in accepting benefits from someone who would
   like to see Mr. Dorfman promote stocks for him.   There is also taking
   advantage of a position as a market authority when viewers are not aware of
   his involvement and conflicts.

2. Moving stocks for friends when Mr. Dorfman was to occupy the position of
   impartial outside observer was wrong.   Accepting benefits from those whose
   offerings he could affect was a conflict.

3. There are the issues of defamation.   Just the disclosure of an investigation
   can be very damaging to an employee, particularly one such as Dorfman who
   operates in such a public eye.   The employer has an obligation to
   investigate, but it should issue cautions about assumptions and guilt and the
   reasons for the investigation.

3.10 The Ethics of Bankruptcy

Answers and Key Discussion Items
_____

1. At the time the bankruptcy code was written, there was a certain amount of
   disgrace associated with the declaration of bankruptcy. Bankruptcy was
   viewed by debtors and others alike as an absolute last resort when there were
   no other alternatives for there was a strong moral conviction about the
   repayment of one's debts. The issue of bankruptcy loopholes really did not
   arise until the 1980s when more consumers began declaring bankruptcy and
   began looking to maximize what they took with them following the bankruptcy.

   There was an assumption of honor built into the bankruptcy code. The
   examples in the reading demonstrate that bankruptcy is being used for other
   purposes — to avoid contract obligations.

   Another problem was that at the time the bankruptcy code was written, debt
   was more unusual and certainly at lower levels than today. Debt is now
   entered into with an attitude that the ability to repay or even the repayment
   is not an issue for bankruptcy is always there was a way out.

   Discuss with the students the moral obligation to repay a debt, apart from
   the legal obligation to repay. Discuss with them issues of fairness etc.

3.11   Product Dumping

Answers and Key Discussion Items

1. Is it legal to dump products? Yes, so long as the other country has not banned them. Is it balanced to dump products? No, you are selling products without a full disclosure of their hazards and their fate in your own country. How will this action be depicted in a newspaper? As it sounds: dumping bad products on those with little knowledge in countries with little consumer protection and no liability system for recovery for harms.

2. The inventory write-off or write-down needs to be analyzed over both the short term (20% income reduction), and the long term (damage to reputation; possible accidents in those countries and liability; public relations damages). The write-down can be explained as a one-time event. Wall Street and investors are sufficiently sophisticated to understand this.

3. In some cases, the evidence on safety is disputed. Some officials believe the product is safe and others do not. Perhaps selling the product internationally is possible with new disclosures attached about the debate regarding its safety. It is not the selling of the product itself that is unethical. It is the selling of the product without disclosure of its previous history here.

4. Full disclosure is a compromise on products with safety issues. If the problem of defect is known, and one still buys the product, there should not be an ethical problem. When the information is withheld, it is unfair and unethical. Further, the purpose of information is a free market.

3.12 The Taboo of Women in Management

Answers and Key Discussion Items

1. Burns & McCallister's policy may be one to help women succeed. If their proposals will not be reviewed if they present them, they are destined to fail in international work. B & M needs a compromise position. Women should be offered positions in the countries in which accounts can be lucrative, but should have the cultural drawbacks explained to them. B & M doesn't have two standards of operations. The reality is that they cannot change a society's culture by placing women in positions of negotiation and responsibility for accounts in these countries.

2. The issue of discrimination in foreign countries is resolved: U.S. firms can't discriminate against employees there.

3. The idea is to allow women to progress both nationally and internationally. Burns & McCallister's record is not a stand-still one. Women should be permitted to progress in Burns & McCallister's growth areas as well.

4. B & M can work to gradually change the culture. These changes may come about by having women present in their offices in these countries, having them work on proposals and having them have some contact with the client so that the barriers begin to erode. Change does not come about if B & M cannot successfully bid and stay in the country. Opinion is more so -- as firm progresses, women should enjoy an equal opportunity to join in on that progress and success (and earnings).

5. A statement, "if we don't do it, somebody else will," comes to mind. If we don't do business in his country without women, somebody else will do the business and we will have lost revenues. Again, the position that B & M takes may not require complete withdrawal, but simply a gradual indoctrination in these countries. As the borders come down in international trade, it will be important for all countries to accept the business culture and attitudes of others; including the fact that women are key players in business proposals and negotiations.

6. Many firms sacrifice earnings in international markets until ethical concerns are resolved in the areas of human rights, child labor, women's rights, etc.

3.13 The Adoption Agency and Señor Jose's Fees

Answers and Key Discussion Items

1. The payment to Señor Jose would be considered a bribe in all 50 states and under federal laws. This type of payment is illegal in the United States. This case deals with the fine line, as defined in the Foreign Corrupt Practices Act, between bribery to achieve a desired result and "grease payments" or those fees paid to just see a matter through the system, regardless of the results.

2. A grease payment may be perfectly legal in another country. The ethics of the payments are complicated by the fact that without them, business cannot be done. For example, in this case, there can be no adoption, certainly a noble pursuit, unless there is the payment. A question to ask the students is whether the end in this case, the successful adoption of the little girl, justifies the means used, the grease payment.

3. There are many parents who have gone through with adoptions requiring such payments. Children who would otherwise have lives in poor conditions are given the best opportunities in life. Many employees at agencies that arrange international adoptions feel that their work results justify the means needed to accomplish them. Ask the students if they agree with that posture.

4. Have the students personalize the example: Would you break the law to help a child?

5. Have the students personalize it: Would a government raid make you uncomfortable?

3.14   Facilitation or Bribery: Cultural and Ethical Disparities

Answers and Key Discussion Items

1. It is arguable that the conduct in all the offices violates the law. Money and/or benefits (directly or indirectly) are being given in exchange for favorable results.

2. No, a business should not adopt a culture-by-culture code of ethics. It is confusing to employees. Further, the company's potential for capitalism, investment and growth is undermined by systems of bribery.

3. None are ethical. Moreover, the conduct is probably illegal.

4. Simple standard: our U.S. code of ethics.

5. Yes, the variety in standards generally results in the firm migrating to the lowest standards.

6. The recent adoption by OPED of a code against bribery demonstrates that non-involvement in bribery is seen by many as a means of economic development as opposed to a restriction on it. US firms have done more business than ever since the passage of the FCPA. The magnificent part of the FCPA is the willingness of firms to report suspected bribery activity and the resulting enforcement that comes mainly from settlement of cases that both the country and the U.S. company find embarrassing. Businesses and governments alike are beginning to understand that long-term economic development and success are contingent upon mutual trust and definitive rights afforded not because of the arbitrary corruption payments.

A cover story for American Enterprise magazine in May noted that the Asian nations are asking businesses to return and begin operations under new regimes where bribery and corruption will not interfere with their commitments on everything from long-term leases to labor regulations in factories.

The FCPA is a means of establishing trust and an environment for investment and is now being recognized as a key to much of the US expansion in international business.

3.15 Electromagnetic Fields (EMF): Exposure for Workers and Customers

Use Transparency 18 to show chronology of events in this "field".

Answers and Key Discussion Items

1. The evidence is not conclusive at this point but there is sufficient question, as at a similar stage in the asbestos development, for additional precautions, education and further research.

2. The companies that should be concerned about the liability from EMF would be:

   electric utilities (for employees and customers)
   governmental entities that decide on placement of power lines
   manufacturers of electric equipment (warnings on use and fields)
   manufacturers of power lines and power line poles
   property owners with self-electrical generation
   military operations
   radio stations

3. Regulation in the future will focus on power-line sites, warnings on products, limits on EMF fields on products, limits on employee exposure to EMF, hour limitations in EMF fields.

4. Landlords and other property owners will have issues of value and liability with respect to the location of lines on or near their properties. The issue of EMF will affect the value of land near EMF fields.

5. Many utilities are following a policy of "prudent avoidance." That is, they are trying to control or limit exposure. If a line can be placed away from human contacts, it is done so. The location for facilities for employees is made away from substantial EMF fields. Many utilities are conducting long-term epidemiological studies of workers and those located near strong fields to determine health effects, if any.

6. Warnings would be imperative at this point on blankets and water beds. The evidence in this regard, particularly with respect to these products, is too strong to not take the precaution of furnishing a warning. Remind the students that there might be a hesitation in these cases as in asbestos because of the fear of a loss of earnings. Ask the students to predict the outcome of the companies over the long term if the warnings are not given. The result would be a steadily increasing stream of litigation and high, possibly destructive costs, for these companies.

7. Monitoring employees; rotating work duties; reconfiguring wires to minimize EMF.

8. Yes, reconfiguration is a low-cost preventive measure. It should be done.

Note: Raise with the students the ethics of plaintiff suits and whether product liability cases are filed too often regardless of the level of harm.

3.16 Domino's Pizza Delivers

<u>Answers and Key Discussion Items</u>

1. No, there are no guarantees with drivers. Incentives to deliver on time made speed and recklessness almost a part of the job.

2. Yes, the public outrage over safety sacrifices for pizza delivery was growing.

3. The jury verdict was a strong public message to Domino's: stop the focus on time at the expense of safety.

4. Have the students personalize the costs: job, verdicts, etc.

5. It is taking something that doesn't belong to you; saying things that are false; taking unfair advantage.

3.17   The Generics of Downsizing

<u>Use Transparency 19 to provide an overview of the extent of downsizing</u>

<u>Answers and Key Discussion Items</u>

1. Downsizing has an immediate and positive impact on stock price.

2. There are many reasons companies downsize. For some, it is a matter of technological change — there is new technology that replaces the need for as many employees. For others, the downsizing is the result of a merger and the resulting need for fewer employees to do tasks now combined. For others there are spin-offs of divisions and fewer employees are needed. Still others do not have a strategic reason other than cutting costs.

   There is as yet no evidence that downsizing serves to serve shareholders in any fashion either in terms of financial growth, dividends or better sales performance.

3. When there is a downsizing, employees have more work in many cases. There is also the impact of losing colleagues with whom they have worked for long periods. There is also the uncertainty that comes despite management reassurance. There is the fear that they too will be victims of downsizing.

4. The downsizings of the past were generally the result of automation of production processes. Machines were available to do what used to be done by employees. The replacement of man by machine was very common with the resulting lay-offs. Today, it is not always the case that there is a strict causal relationship or any relationship to automation. Downsizing is often used as a quick fix for disgruntled shareholders.

   The downsizings of the 1980s and 1990s have drawn a great deal of attention because managers, as opposed to line workers, were downsized. Indeed, downsizings seem to continue despite a relatively robust economy. For example, Motorola announced a 15,000 employee downsizing on June 4, 1998.

3.18 The Closure of the Stroh's Plant Upon Merger

Answers and Key Discussion Items

1. Stroh's may have been engaging in Albert Carr's business bluffing. They were doing the "right" thing but perhaps for the reason that the backlash from the closure might affect product sales in the state. The result of the placement program is a positive feeling in the state toward Stroh's.

2. The early announcement of a plant closure can have an impact on a company's stock in the marketplace. The shareholders' rights are affected by the protection of the employees and the community. Morale is also affected as employees prepare for outplacement or unemployment. Productivity declines during this period.

3. There is a balancing of employer, employee, shareholder and community interests in these plant closure cases. See the discussion of the various ethical views on closure on p. 89. At some point there comes a time when a local economy can no longer absorb the outplacement from plant closure and the community needs to focus on economic redevelopment efforts to change the focus of its economy as opposed to relying on departing employers to absorb the cost of their departure.

4. Yes, the outplacement program was a way to buy back a possibly alienated Detroit beer-drinking market.

3.19 GM Plant Closings and Efforts at Outplacement

Answers and Key Discussion Items

1. This case is distinguished from the previous plant closing cases because in this case the company had extracted promises from the government in exchange for its promises with respect to operations in the area. These promises result in a greater obligation on the part of the employer and less flexibility in terms of its business decisions because of its financial obligations and otherwise to the local and/or state governments.

2. Have the students focus on the right of a business to make decisions that will stop the losses it is experiencing. Have them evaluate whether this case is one in which the government and GM almost had a joint venture. Have them discuss whether the government knew there was always the risk that the product made at the plant might not sell.

3. Ask the students whether there should always be insulation for business plans and decisions that are not successful. Does ethics require that you take away the risk of doing business and have the shareholders absorb that risk for everyone, including employees and government entities involved with the business in a joint venture?

4. Some courts are beginning to require businesses to repay tax and other benefits if they pull out of a town, reneging on a plant operation agreement.

Legal Issues

The federal plant closing law requires advance notification of closure. There are no financial obligations associated with the law. The purpose of the law is to permit a time period for employee preparation for the lay-offs and closure.

3.20 Aaron Feuerstein and Malden Mills

Answers and Key Discussion Items

1. Mr. Feuerstein's conduct demonstrated that it is possible to consider employee well-being in a decision and still have a company make it through some difficult times. Mr. Feuerstein took his steps to protect employees while other companies were downsizings.

   Mr. Feuerstein indicated that he made the decision for his conscience and not on the basis of what others would have done in the circumstances.

   Point out to the students that Malden Mills had a set of circumstances in which employees would have understood had they not had a paycheck. The loss of pay or their jobs would have been the result of something beyond the owner's control, yet Mr. Feuerstein still stepped in.

2. The closure of the plant would have meant the complete collapse of the economy because there was no other means of support or business in the area.

3. Mr. Feuerstein did not have the publicly-held company syndrome in which he must be accountable to large and small shareholders and the outcry they often produce when they disagree with the CEO or resent the resulting impact on their earnings.

3.21 Herman Miller and Its Rain Forest Chairs

Answers and Key Discussion Items

1. The woods used for Miller's traditional Eames chair were part of the chair's distinction. The woods were also part of what Miller's carpenters were used to working with. However, Miller and Foley were looking at the environmental impact of the use of those woods and behaving in a socially responsible manner. Further, Foley may have been ahead of his time. It is likely that there would be future restrictions on imports of the woods and Miller would be forced to make changes at that point. Foley may also be hopeful that the voluntary change is something that helps the company in a public relations and marketing sense.

2. It was troublesome to the board of directors that Foley made his "environmental" decisions with costs attached at a time when the company's earnings were off. However, the board was looking at the short-term profit picture and Foley was anticipating Miller being around for a long time and coping with environmental concerns before being forced to do so by regulation. Further, Foley's actions did pay off as sales increased and Miller gained national recognition for its responsible positions.

3. Albert Carr, a business ethicist, maintains that businesses take socially responsible and ethical actions only when it is in their best interests to do so. The appearance of the decision may be noble, as in this case, an environmentalist company, but the bottom line in the decisions is the bottom line. Carr would support the decisions because they brought the company financial results.

4. Miller made the decision to do all that was technologically possible and not just comply with the law. Positive law as a standard for ethical behavior is not always sufficient. Miller did as much as it could and probably earned the respect of local and national regulators as well as its customers and potential customers.

5. The issue here is: is it wrong to publicize the fact that you are doing the right thing? is such publicity in the interest of the shareholders, employees, creditors, etc. Yes. The advantage of behaving as a responsible company is being able to tell about it. There is nothing wrong with detailing the program. The company made ethical choices and has the right to let it be known.

6. Yes, Miller has changed from high dollar items into lower-priced lines that still have a quasi custom look to them. Herman Miller has realized that a business must still have a focus beyond environmentalism and a strategy for earnings.

3.22 Green Marketing as a Business Bluff

Answers and Key Discussion Items

1. Milton Friedman would support green marketing. It is a decision that is in the best interests of the shareholders that just happens to be ethical. To the extent that we prevent people from doing beneficial things because they don't have the right reason, we are preventing businesses from making rational choices. The most good is done for the most people regardless of motivation.

2. No. The response of the market to a company that makes correct choices is to be anticipated. The fact that the market responds to an ethical choice should not prevent the company from making that choice. We are assuming a certain level of honesty in the company's green marketing; that in fact their tuna is dolphin-free and their detergents are biodegradable. Companies should not be permitted to benefit from dishonest claims that capitalize on environmental consciousness.

3. To the extent companies are not truly committed to environmental issues and make claims that they are, they are being dishonest. If they have truly made the commitment to the environment and environmentally conscious products, their marketing can focus on these issues as well as quality, service and other marketing tools.

4. This question focuses on doing the right thing for the wrong reason. If the result is that firms are environmentally conscious and goals are accomplished without legislation or regulation, should we prevent firms from doing something simply because they are not noble?

3.23 Exxon and Alaska

Use Transparency 20 to give a summary of the extent of damage done by the oil spill.

Answers and Key Discussion Items

1. Exxon's attitude about the oil spill was very much criticized by government officials, local residents and the media. Exxon did not recognize the magnitude of harm, was not appreciative of the urgency of the clean-up work and seemed reluctant to commit the resources necessary for a good job. Other subsequent spills demonstrated Exxon's attitude that clean-up efforts or even prevention efforts were not a high company priority.

2. Cutting back on staff and maintenance was a means of reducing costs. Over the short run, these decisions saved the company money.

3. Hazelwood bears some moral responsibility for the accident because he was drinking. Just as someone who drinks, drives an automobile and injures someone in an accident is held accountable under DUI laws and civilly liable in tort, Hazelwood is accountable for his individual action in drinking and then reporting for duty. Exxon's policies may have caused the excessive drinking, but Hazelwood made the choice to drink and drive, so to speak.

4. Exxon management also bears some moral responsibility for the spill. The cutbacks in staff caused undue pressure on the crews. An error in operating the ship or in personal judgment (drinking) was bound to occur in such demanding circumstances. Maintenance procedures and the structure of the boat itself all contributed to the accident and its extent. These decisions regarding personnel and maintenance were made by Exxon management.

5. Exxon needs a commitment to environmentally-conscious operations. Following this accident, many oil firms began upgrading their ships with double-hull protection so that an accident would pierce only one layer of the tanker and a spill would not automatically occur. Exxon needs to base its decisions on long-term issues with respect to its operations as opposed to short-term cost-cutting measures that ignore the environmental and personnel impact. Exxon also needs to understand public expectations with respect to its product and the need to raise its environmental consciousness.

6. No, follow-up articles have cited Exxon's conduct as a means for creating a public relations nightmare and losing regulatory and customer good will.

7. The secret deal on punitive damages really took away from the jury's authority and made the trial a bit of a sham. These secret agreements inevitably backfire on the company when they are made public, as was the case here. The company is better off with a public settlement or the results of a jury verdict as opposed to these partial, but undisclosed deal.

8. While the claim for insurance may be bona fide, the insurers can make more

money in interest by fighting the claim than they can by just paying it. However, the reality is that those making the claim may truly be in need of the funds and unable to function as they wait for the claim payment. There are ethical issues underlying the decision to postpone payment of what is often acknowledged as a valid claim in the name of making more returns while fighting the claim.

3.24 The Death of the Great Disposable Diaper Dilemma

<u>Use Transparency 21 to show lists of the pros and cons of disposables.</u>

<u>Answers and Key Discussion Items</u>

1. Arthur D. Little does have a conflict of interest in its work. The largest maker of disposable diapers is sponsoring its work. There will be a question regarding its credibility because of the source of funding. P & G should have found alternative ways of having a study conducted. Arthur Little should have been more conscientious about accepting the assignment and developed ways to ensure autonomy. No matter how effective the study is, the question of Arthur Little's independence will always cloud the result.

2. The increase in costs should be measured not over the short run, but the long run. The hospital may be making a decision that will be made for them if regulation continues. The decision may assist regulators is seeing that self-regulation is sufficient.

3. It is important to note that businesses must still sell products. If people want disposables, you can't sell them cloth. This is an environmental issue where the commitment is just not there. Conviction disappears when messy diapers appear.

4. That there are often environmental issues raised for which the scientific evidence is not present. That consumers have definitive preferences in certain areas that take priority even over the most strident protests. Businesses should be prepared with their own information to answer charges from groups protesting their products.

5. The environmentalists seemed to lose some credibility by not acknowledging that there was other relevant information in comparing the disposables with cloth diapers. They did not seem to be forthcoming with information and lost the debate as a result.

3.25 J.C. Penney and Its Wealthy Buyer

Answers and Key Discussion Items

1. Taking things that don't belong to you
   Personal decadence
   Conflicts of interest
   False impressions
   Interorganizational abuse

2. Those harmed include:

   shareholders of Penney's
   Penney's customers
   other buyers
   other vendors, suppliers, manufacturer's reps
   Penney's employees
   Locklear's family(is)

3. Again, he was doing well. Why rock the boat? Why question? Locklear was doing amazingly well given his salary level. His lifestyle far exceeded his earnings from the company.

4. It is an "everybody does it" philosophy; doesn't make it ethical.

5. Yes, both have engaged in act; both are unfair to others.

6. The advantages: no line-drawing; no benefits; all quid pro quo is removed.

7. Poor products; pricing issues; bad choices in lines; product liability.

8. Mr. Locklear acknowledged that it was his personal life that was fueling his taking the kickbacks. He became accustomed to a lifestyle and had to feed the lifestyle with cash beyond his salary.

   Mr. Locklear's minister makes an incisive remark in that many good people who do fine things in the community lose sight of their values in the business world. It's as if they see their lives as compartmentalized and their work life separate in an ethical sense from their behavior with their families and communities.

3.26 Cars for Cars: Honda Executives' Allocation System

<u>Answers and Key Discussion Items</u>

1. Quid pro quo; self-interested executives; lack of honesty; lack of loyalty; lack of commitment.

2. The money and goods were economic rents that belonged to Honda. They should have gone to Honda.

3. Because they were fiduciaries who breached their duties of loyalty to the company. Their judgment was impaired.

4. You probably would lose your job for such a confrontation, but given what went on, you will lose your job anyway AND testify. Confront the individuals. Take a position. Remind them of their legal responsibilities and liabilities.

5. The lawyer is observing something that is usually true in cases such as this where the corruption is widespread throughout an organization. Many people know, but the activity becomes part of the culture and no one speaks up to discuss the problems with the conduct. The question in this case is whether management endorsed the behavior through inaction in the face of so much blatant activity.

4.1 Joe Camel: The Cartoon Character Who Sold Cigarettes and Nearly Felled an Industry

Answers and Key Discussion Items

1. The cartoon character makes Camel cigarettes and all cigarettes more attractive to young people than they would otherwise be. The character is charming, wears his baseball cap as they do (backwards) and makes a lasting impression on young people. Smoking is depicted, via Joe, as something charming.

   RJR is in the business to sell cigarettes. Suggest to the students that perhaps RJR should sponsor some types of education programs designed to discourage young people from smoking. Would this work or would it just be tokenism that would never counter the efficacy of Joe Camel?

   The executive needs to make a decision as to whether it is comfortable with the impact of the campaign. If the company's ethics are in question because of its ads, the executive is equally in question for developing it.

   There are times when executives must decide whether they are able to continue with a company or need to move on in order to satisfy their consciences.

2. There are many pension funds (Harvard included) that have made the decision not to hold investments in cigarette companies. These decisions are based on the fact that their focus on health and well-being cannot be reconciled with an investment in a product that has been established as detrimental to health and, in many cases, deadly. Ask the students if they would personally hold tobacco company stocks. Point out to them that it may just be a matter of time before the stocks of these companies begin to decline with the increasing focus on health and studies linking tobacco use to disease. RJR recently spun off its stock; investors can own a choice of RJR food stock or RJR tobacco stock.

3. A positive association with a logo is a positive association with the product. A positive image makes use of the product more likely. It is a weak argument to say that the identifiability of the product does not translate into additional use of the product.

4. Self-censorship can reverse a regulatory trend. By limiting the use of cartoons on cigarette ads, producers could avoid what will inevitably come: government regulation of cartoon/cigarette ads.

5. Discuss with the students whether the studies were even necessary. Discuss the problems with attracting young people to cigarettes. Did those who are concerned wait too long to speak out?

81

4.2   The Sexist Beer Ads

Answers and Key Discussion Items

1. Ads with attractive women in them have two things in common: (1) they are very common; and (2) they are very effective. An issue for the students to discuss is whether there are other ads that are equally or more effective that may not emphasize sexuality. Review for the students some of the most effective ads over the last 30 years: "I can't believe I ate the whole thing." (Alka-Seltzer); "Where's the beef?" (Wendy's); Little Caesar's Pizza ads today; Coca-Cola's "I'd like to teach the world to sing,"; Oreo cookies; Rex the Beer Dog; etc. None of these ads involved a focus on sexuality but were effective in both the selling and award-winning senses. Successful ads do not require a focus on sexuality.

2. Regulation of sexism in ads would be difficult if not impossible because of definitional problems. This area of responsibility is truly an ethical and self-regulation one. The Canadian guidelines have faced definitional and application difficulties. Even if the regulations are put into place, enforcement become arbitrary and difficult.

3. Nudity in alcohol and other advertising available to the general public is inappropriate. Again, the advertisers and agencies need to focus on successful ads, not sexual ads.

4. The idea in advertising is not to have ads that are objectionable or generally unobjectionable. The idea for ads is to sell products. Those who are offended by the ads are not going to buy the product. The disturbing trend in advertising is to assume that sexuality is a prerequisite to a successful ad. History and experience tell us differently and companies need to focus on successful ads that sell products.

5. The First Amendment does provide protection for free speech, but commercial speech is regulated for content in terms of deception and fraud. Commercial speech for certain products is also regulated because of the sensitive nature of the ad content, as with liquor and prescription drugs.

Legal Issues

Advertising does enjoy some First Amendment protection. Regulation is permitted to prevent deception, misrepresentation and disparagement of competitors. However, absent these problems, ad content is a matter of taste, customer appeal and goals of the advertiser. This form of broad First Amendment protection is appropriate because regulation of other factors could prove to be arbitrary and difficult to define.

4.3   Alcohol Advertising: The College Focus

Answers and Key Discussion Items

1. The brewery officer needs to consider that there can be tremendous backlash in the adult market for its focus on college-age drinking. Also, the officer should consider the possibility of increases in the drinking age because of irresponsible advertising. Also, the officer should accept the social responsibility of not having the company take advantage of the lack of wisdom and discretion that accompanies youthful drinking. The issues of moral responsibility arise when young people cause accidents as a result of drinking.

2. The ads could have a more general focus, but the spring break campaigns are directed at college-age drinking. There are certain portions of the advertising that would not hold appeal for a general audience. The additional focus is not the issues. The problem is the unusual appeal for college students and their temptation to overdo it.

3. The government certainly has precedent for censoring ads completely and also controlling content. Cigarettes are no longer advertised on television. The possibility for alcohol ad bans clearly exists because of the same harm argument made with respect to smoking. The standards for controlling youth appeal might be difficult for the government to define and a ban might be an easier regulatory control.

4. Companies often undertake responsibility campaigns to counter the effect of their ads in a general sense. The campaigns are pointed to as being socially responsible. But many experts maintain there is comparatively little time and money spent on responsible drinking in comparison to the general ad campaigns of the companies.

5. All breweries deny that the ads are designed to encourage underage people to drink. However, the ads are geared toward young people, feature young people and represent the alleged intrigue that accompanies drinking.

4.4   The Obligation to Screen?   The Obligation to Reject? *Soldier of Fortune*
Classifieds

<u>Use Transparency 22 to highlight the types of questionable ads from *SOF*.</u>

<u>Answers and Key Discussion Items</u>

1. A policy many firms have adopted with respect to classified ads is that no questionable or ambiguous ads are accepted. Background checks on all ads are too expensive. But you could screen out by type of ads.

2. The conflicting moral standards in the case are the First Amendment rights of publication and the issues of responsibility with respect to those publication rights. There are also physical difficulties of trying to screen all the ads and those who place them.

3. There are conflicting loyalties in making the decision with respect to *SOF* ads. There is the loyalty to your employer and the conflict with the moral standard of not having the ads bring about harm to innocent people who become victims of the connections made through the ads.

4. *SOF* made the decision to run the ad and ads like it even knowing that there were previous criminal investigations resulting from ad connections. It was a risk *SOF* agreed to assume. Although <u>SOF</u> had no direct knowledge of any problems with the ad or those associated with it, the nature and character of the ad and the magazine make such events likely. *SOF* is not held to any legal liability in the case but does have some moral responsibility for what occurred.

5. The court's decision is a utilitarian one. The court is trying to balance the need for advertisements with the rights of individuals to be safe from the harms that can occur when connections are made through the ads. The court acknowledges the risk but finds there is no effective way to screen for that risk. The utilitarian analysis fails to take into account the natural law concept of the value of human life and the concept of rights.

   Utilitarianism often dictates who will recover and who will not. We can impose burdens of protections in some cases but not in others. For example, in Arizona, water and utility companies are exempt from liability for injuries or deaths caused by people falling into the state's man-made water canals. Those same deaths or injuries that result in private swimming pools or ponds would be actionable. However, the water and those utilities are the lifeblood of Arizona and have been given additional protection in the interest of doing the most good for the most people.

6. The Sandra Black murder makes the power of the ads very clear. It shows that people who would not otherwise become involved in harming others become involved in such because of the connections the ads bring. *SOF* has had presented to them, through the Sandra Black murder, a much more vivid picture of the power of their ads. The ad policy should at least be changed to require a screening or refusal of ads similar to the Hearn ad.

4.4 **The Obligation to Screen? The Obligation to Reject?** *Soldier of Fortune Classifieds* (cont'd)

7. We have made the decision to impose liability when the conduct is foreseeable, preventable or outrageous enough. We make distinctions based on a balancing of interests: liability vs. injury and danger.

8. Yes, as suggested in answer 1, it avoids the heavy cost of screening but eliminates worries about connections and liability.

4.5 Aggressive Marketing of Prescription Drugs: Forms of Direct Sales

Answers and Key Discussion Items - Part I

1. The increased sales goes to the Laura Nash questions: What is your intent in doing this? What are the likely results? The campaign may have been intended from the outset as a marketing ploy.

2. In a way the donations suppress criticism; it's hard to go after a donor or not at least look at the donor's product.

3. The recipients of these gifts need policies on contributions to help them maintain their independence.

Answers and Key Discussion Items - Part II

1. Users of prescription drugs need medical advice -- ads cannot provide that information.

2. Yes, ads on hair loss, etc. appeal to a "we'll try anything regardless" group.

3. Patients come in demanding the drug, not seeking medical advice or a determination of their condition and whether the drug would work.

4. Yes, as in other industries, too much with too little disclosure leads to a ban on ads.

4.6   Ragu Thick and Zesty

Answers and Key Discussion Items

1. Ragu is an aggressive competitor, but Ragu has crossed the line and appropriated the efforts of Hunt's. The appropriation of "Thick and Zesty" and the attempts to confuse the two sauces with the use of similar ad photos is not comparison or aggressive advertising; it is appropriation of an idea and an attempt to palm off one product as another or at least create confusion in the consumer market.

2. Ragu has violated the moral standards of honesty. Its product is being touted as the same as Hunt's. Indeed, Ragu is borrowing the Hunt's ad theme and other similarities to make its product the same in appearance. Ragu is appropriating the efforts of a competitor.

3. No ad executive should feel comfortable with the new Ragu name because the name is an appropriation of Hunt's work and ideas. It is just wrong to use the name.

4. No, product confusion is not an appropriate method of competition. Palming off, an attempt to use another's good product and name to sell your own product, is a tort and Hunt's would be permitted to recover damages for Ragu's actions. The amazing thing about Ragu's poor ethical choices is that they were made at a time when Ragu enjoyed a monopoly in the market. Hunt's was a new entry in a market in which Ragu enjoyed a 65% share of the bottled sauce market.

5. Ragu is always free to compete with a better product. However, instead of distinguishing its product or developing a better one, Ragu chose to rely on the work of its competitor and compete through confusion. The choice was dishonest and only a temporary measure. Ragu will need to refine its product to compete.

Legal Issues

The tort of palming off is the use of confusion in advertising and labeling to take advantage of another's good name and make sales because of that. That tort has occurred with Ragu's conduct in this case.

4.7   The Little Intermittent Windshield and Its Little Inventor

<u>Answers and Key Discussion Items</u>

1. The decision to go forward with an idea because the person who had the idea is a "little guy" and probably would not go forward with litigation is an unethical choice. The company would not want to have its ideas appropriated like this so it is treating others differently than it would like to be treated. Also, the approach is not balanced. It was a taking of someone else's idea and property and it was wrong.

2. The intermittent system was an original idea, a helpful addition to an auto, and a means of distinguishing one's product in a very competitive business.

3. Many small inventors are learning to file their ideas with independent third parties before presenting them to large corporations. This pre-filing enables them to establish that they did indeed have the idea and that the company later appropriated it. In one case, an inventor videotaped his presentation to the company to provide documentation in case the idea was used. It is a sad commentary on U.S. businesses that a small inventor risks circumvention when an idea is presented to a large company trying to avoid paying for the idea and the work in its development.

4. An executive could not correct the past decision to bypass Kearns, but could make the decision to treat him fairly now and offer to settle with him as opposed to carrying through with the litigation with the hope that he would drop out eventually. A settlement is the honest thing to do based on the poor decisions in the past to appropriate Kearns' ideas and work.

<u>Legal Issues</u>

It is infringement to use another's idea without compensation. The issue in this case was whether the idea was obvious and would have been developed independently by the car manufacturers' engineers. Apparently, the courts have found the idea would not have been developed as quickly as the car manufacturers alleged and Kearns expedited the process for them.

4.8   V-A-N-N-A: It Belongs to Me

Answers and Key Discussion Items

1. Yes, Vanna's image, a role she has made famous, has been used to commercial advantage without her consent and without compensation.

2. Samsung is enjoying the attention an ad that plays on Vanna and "Wheel of Fortune" will get.

3. Satire is on "Saturday Night Live". This satire is used to sell products which makes it different (more of an appropriation).

4. Yes, permission, which as the case decision subsequently demonstrated, was needed. Both ethically and legally, Ms. White should have been asked. Ms. White is also entitled to damages.

Note: The ninth circuit ruled in Ms. White's favor.

4.9   Unhappy Campers and Copyrights

Answers and Key Discussion Items

1. Copyright laws are self-enforcing. ASCAP may seem as if it is picking on campers, but it is simply trying to preserve the copyrights on the songs. They could fall into public domain without such protection.

2. The songs fall into public domain and they lose their copyright protection.

3. The use of the songs by the children at these camps, cancer camps and otherwise, is something that is helpful to them and the disallowance evokes a great deal of emotion on the part of the public against ASCAP and possibly the songs. ASCAP is dependent upon play and use of the songs for value in their copyright.

4. The camps could pay a nominal fee for a certain number of uses and then the ASCAP needs would be satisfied. Or ASCAP could be paid and then donate the funds back to the camps.

5. Donate the fee back to the camp. Collect the same fees as for other uses, but donate it back to the camp.

4.10 Caterers and the Duplication of Overhead Recovery

<u>Answers and Key Discussion Items</u>

1. All firms assign a percentage of overhead as part of their costs in service contracts such as these catering contracts. The issue is whether the overhead assessment is a fair estimate of the actual overhead costs. The computer time is another common contract cost in a service contract; the issue is the fairness of those computer charges. Not passing along the 15% discount is an example of one billing practice where Cindy is being dishonest in that she is not reflecting the actual cost of the soda. Billing for soda when it was not actually furnished is dishonest and wrong. Hoping the customer will catch it does not mitigate the fact that it is dishonest.

2. All of the billing practices from the overhead and computer charges to the soda issue are unethical. In Cindy's defense, these types of practices are very common in the food vendor business, but just because everyone else does it does not mean that the practices are ethical. Cindy's approach is not balanced and, although she is successful now, she may be setting a pattern of billing that could cost her customers or, at a minimum, cost her credibility with her customers. Once a customer discovers these types of errors in billing (and they do through their internal audit functions), they are suspicious in the future and all bills will be carefully scrutinized if they continue to use Cindy at all. Cindy's attitude is very short-sighted. Her successful business does not entitle her to be dishonest.

3. Cindy is correct. It is standard industry practice for food vendors to overbill. Unfortunately industry practice does not make it ethical or a wise business choice.

4. As noted above, Cindy could lose customers. She is viewing the situation incorrectly. Why doesn't she cut her prices by billing honestly and perhaps attract more volume? She has independent success and does not need to rely on these tactics.

5. Vera could make the suggestion in number 4. She should also explain the function and role of internal auditors in the customer firms and the consequences to Cindy of discovery of the billing practices. Vera could put together some data with the help of professors to make her case for an ethical billing system.

4.11 Pharmaceuticals: Ethical Pricing of Life-Saving Cures

Answers and Key Discussion Items

1. Pharmaceutical firms must be sensitive to the life-saving/life-giving nature of their industry. As such, the ability to charge and obtain higher prices should not be used in a monopolistic way. Public outcry could force government pricing or price controls.

2. The shareholders want a return, but they also want the company to continue. Good pharmaceutical CEOs learn to balance short-term and long-term goals. Temporary high short-term prices and profits might bring on destructive price regulations.

3. Yes, effective self-regulation could halt regulatory process and steps.

4. Yes, government pricing can't address issues of why pricing is high, exceptions, etc. Inflexible regulation contributes to market withdrawals, etc.

5. To the extent those staging the campaigns stand to make money from their proposal to buy and sell the drugs in larger doses, then there is a conflict interest in the ad campaigns.

   Campaigns from the companies themselves serve to create demand as well for innovative treatments.

4.12 Salomon Brothers and Bond Pricing

<u>Use Transparency 23 to illustrate how Salomon was able to control the U.S. Treasury's bond market.</u>

<u>Answers and Key Discussion Items</u>

1. There was documented harm in the Salomon case. Many who had anticipated being able to cover their purchases were unable to do so. Bond traders and their clients suffered tremendous financial losses. Also, the general integrity of the bond market suffered because Salomon cornered the market. There was question as to whether it was a level playing field.

2. Competition, opportunity, ease of infiltration, pressure for earnings.

3. Much was written about the sufficiency of the Salomon Brother penalty. Many said criminal charges should have been brought and the penalty was insufficient. Others, as noted in the materials, viewed it as nearly half the penalty paid by Drexel Burnham for its ongoing involvement in the junk bond market that involved much more in terms of dollars and investor losses.

4. The failure to disclose the practices by anyone within Salomon who was familiar with them is typical of organizational misconduct. Employees are aware of the wrongdoing but the peer pressure, the strength of group think, the feeling that everyone else does it and the need to retain a job all contribute to the lack of disclosure at either the internal or external levels.

5. Michael Irelan is a good illustration of how unethical behavior does affect individuals even though it seemed to the Salomon traders that their conduct was detached and remote. His reputation has suffered permanent damage and his professional life is destroyed.

6. Salomon is paying the costs for ethical violations. Charles Williams had to be brought in because of the climate at Salomon and the need for a strong public statement to correct past misdeeds. Firms with an ethical culture can work to prevent misdeeds and avoid having to hire expensive officers to correct the past and its poor choices.

7. Yes, Buffet is making a case for the "front page of the newspaper" test.

8. No, hindsight always demonstrates how obviously wrong choices and actions (and lack of actions) can be.

4.13 Archer Daniels Midland: A Giant in Grain

Answers and Key Discussion Items

1. The criminal violations that occurred would include everything from violations of the antitrust laws under the Sherman Act for price fixing, mail fraud, wire fraud and conspiracy.

   The ethical violations are taking things that don't belong to you (market share), saying things you know are not true, taking unfair advantage, violating the rules.

2. The comment in on the culture of ADM and the inability of the board to control the activities of the officers that should have been controlled. In other words, the fine is being paid by the shareholders who relied on the board to put in place competent officers and then provide adequate supervision for their activities.

3. Some of the officers are responsible for the conduct that led to the plea. Companies often follow the pattern of settling because of the negative publicity that results from the trial and the cost of fighting the battle in a court.

4. Mr. Whitacre was caught between a rock and a hard place. He knew the illegal conduct was occurring and he had no choice but to go to the government, but it meant he became involved in catching his fellow officers in their illegal acts.

5. The fine was substantial and will affect ADM for years to come. It was more than a slap on the wrist. One question for the students to debate is whether fines ever really punish businesses or there is a need for individual officers to go to jail in order to bring the lessons of violations home.

4.14 Slotting: Facilitation, Costs or Bribery

Answers and Key Discussion Items

1. Some see slotting fees as a means of shifting the risk of product failure back to the manufacturer. The manufacturer has to absorb the retailers' risk of shelving or carrying a new product.

2. Because slotting fees are not set by any rates and vary from product to product and store to store, the temptation for employees to take the money or extra and keep it for themselves is tremendous. This type of under-the-table payment is a sure-fire way to encourage corruption among employees.

3. Exposing the fees and the payment schedule to the light of day could return the concept to one of risk allocation instead of maximization in an unknown environment that breeds corruption among those managing the store.

4. The issues in ethics are taking unfair advantage, hiding information, some half-truths about the nature of the fees, and , in general the creation of a market not based on full information.

4.15 Mr. Gates: Genius and Fierce Competitor

<u>Answers and Key Discussion Items</u>

1. The issues in the antitrust case surround the questions of whether Microsoft has monopoly power. If just personal computers are used, then Microsoft has 90% of the computers with its software on them. If the entire computer industry is used as a measure, then Microsoft is a small player.

   Another issue is whether Microsoft obtained its position because of superior products or because it tied all of its sales; i.e., the computer manufacturers could not have Windows 95 if they installed any other company's software.

2. With tying sales, the seller forces its product on buyers who may desire one of the seller's products, but not all of them. In order to get the product they desire, they have to buy the product they don't want.

3. The ability of new market entrants to compete when Microsoft won't sell unless it has exclusive rights on the software to be installed on computer manufacturers.

5.1   Intel and Pentium: What to Do When the Chips are Down

Answers and Key Discussion Items

1. Ethically <u>and</u> legally, Intel should have disclosed the flaw. The inventory should have been used for those who were not concerned about the flaw and would buy for a discount. Intel was gambling with its reputation, trust, consumer confidence, buyer faith, etc.

2. Yes, and now looking back most Intel executives and experts agree that an immediate recall would have been best.

3. No, the product was flawed. Legally, whether you needed it for math computations or not, the product was flawed.

4. Consumer trust was sacrificed. Intel will take years to shake not that they made a mistake, but the fall-out from the way they handled the mistake.

5. Business history would be persuasive in your meeting with Grove. You would offer the following:

   Tylenol and its miraculous recovery following a recall;
   Jack-in-the-Box and its E-Coli disaster for not responding quickly enough;
   Exxon and its PR problems from the appearance of a lack of remorse;
   Dow Corning and its bankruptcy over product flaws that may not truly be there;
   Johns-Manville and its bankruptcy from liability for asbestos damages;
   A.H. Robins and its bankruptcy for the flawed Dalkon Shield; and Ford and the Pinto fiasco.

   Point out that the failure to spend a little to correct resulted in financial and PR disasters for these firms.

6. Not a life-threatening product issue, so you might stay to try to change things. Document your position.

7. The issue of computer component manufacturer liability for flaws will be a topic of legislative discussion.

8. See the list above. Add to it Sears, ATVs, EMF and VDTs. Many refer to the 5-part plan as "Watergate PR" named after the burglary of Democratic National Headquarters by men tied to the Nixon White House. It is a common pattern and it is important to emphasize to the students: IT DOESN'T WORK!

9. Intel faces the same sorts of questions now facing Microsoft. Are they dominate because they are good or are they dominant because of threats and other predatory practices. Intel's antitrust case continues.

Legal Issues

There was warranty protection under the UCC for customers.

5.2   Hidden Car Rental Fees

Answers and Key Discussion Items

1. The policies with respect to CDW are dishonest. The customers should be informed of the possibility of other protections. The charges for CDW should be explained up front. The car rental companies' policies with respect to CDW were deceptive enough to bring about litigation and regulation. A voluntary change would be the balanced and ethical thing to do.

2. Advertising need not spell out CDW charges but could include a phrase to the effect that there could be additional charges. Other industries do it ("tax and license not included" for the car industry). The point in this case and many others like it is that either the companies can make the disclosures ethically and voluntarily or they can be required to do so through regulation.

3. The agents should be instructed to be certain the customers understand that CDW is not required. Nor should the agents do anything to mislead the customers into thinking that they should purchase CDW. The agents will not know whether the coverage is necessary for a particular customer. But they can be instructed to say, "You may have coverage through another source such as your car insurance, but that is impossible for me to tell you."

4. Many companies fail to see that by choosing an ethical path, they may be able to develop a market niche. For example, a company that was able to advertise a flat rate (CDW included) would probably win the hearts of many customers. The change could help in a competitive sense. Such changes also might prevent detailed regulation on disclosures and, as was noted, FTC actions for deception.

5. Yes, the disclosure of car seat, mileage and gas charges. Rates on additional drivers. Rates on younger drivers. Deposits and accident payments. To the extent a firm makes changes voluntarily, it is able to keep going when regulation inevitably arrives. Further, it builds trust of its customers and an ethical culture within the firm.

6. Enterprise took a different approach that consumers seemed to relate to. It's innovation has enabled it to capture the market. The disclosure of full fees seem to be something consumers appreciate.

Legal Issues

The car rental firms have probably violated FTC standards in advertising. The car rental prices are a form of bait and switch because the lower prices advertised don't actually exist due to additional charges for CDW, gas, mileage, etc.

5.3   Thinning Diet Industry

Answers and Key Discussion Items

1. The ethical constraints you might feel as a diet counselor would include the information you have that the weight doesn't stay off in most of the cases. The client is paying money for something that will not work permanently. In some cases there has been damage to health as a result of these programs. As a weight counselor you should provide the information for the client to check with a physician periodically and to consider a long-term maintenance plan.

2. Most people do just want to lose weight quickly for personal reasons or because of a special event. Perhaps it is human nature to return to old habits such as the eating habits that existed prior to entering the diet program. Ask the students if most people don't understand that risk going into a diet program. Do the programs need to explain that the percentage of permanent success is low? The FTC guidelines require companies to disclose their clients' average weight loss and not simply highlight their best success stories in advertising. The additional disclosures require a statement to the effect that not everyone loses as much and that permanent weight loss figures would be different.

3. The diet industry capitalizes on human nature. There is a tendency to overeat and a need to lose weight quickly when the motivation strikes. Ask the students if it is wrong to take advantage of human nature.

4. The FTC believes the ads are misleading and made the changes noted above so that everyone is aware of the actual weight losses and the problems with permanency of those losses.

   The FTC regulations and disclosures are simply the result of companies taking advantage of human nature. The companies went too far in their ads and approaches and regulation was required to impose ethical standards in advertising and operations.

5. Weight Watchers is adopting an ethical posture that will quite possibly give it a market niche given the ethical void in the industry that prompted the FTC regulatory crackdown.

6. The diet industry will always have risks when products beyond just eating less and exercise are touted. The risks with every product have come out with the only variable being the time it takes for the problems to emerge.

7. The conflict on the study will be the sponsorship by those with an interest in selling the drug. The credibility of the study will be questioned given the self-interest in its favorable outcome.

5.4   The Sure Sale of the Paper Bags

Answers and Key Discussion Items

1. There was an element of honesty and reliance in the parties' ongoing relationship. The failure to purchase the remaining bags changed a multi-decade pattern of behavior for the two parties. If that pattern was going to change, there should have been some notice given. There was an obligation of honesty and fair dealing between the parties and those moral standards were violated.

2. Yes, the parties had a pattern of conduct on which they both (justifiably) relied.

3. Mayer was saying that the company would honor its commitments as it had done in the past. There was no cause for concern with respect to the bags.

4. There were no alternative uses for the bags and the pattern was to have sufficient bags on hand. There was no resolution other than buying the bags.

5. Even though there was not a formal contract covering the bags or the holding of the bags in inventory, a pattern of behavior and reliance had been established. If that pattern was to be broken, there needed to be notice to allow both sides room for planning. Ethical obligations arose here well beyond the legal obligations of a contract.

Legal Issues

A pattern of dealing between two parties can become the parties' standard of performance. Any deviation from that pattern requires notice.

5.5   The Cluttered Apple Powder

Answers and Key Discussion Items

1. The parties thought they understood the terms of their agreement. But they were selling and buying two different things. Tree Top was selling standard industry apple powder. But Schulze and Burch was buying apple powder that would work in its processing machines and not clog up the equipment with stems and other items traditionally found in industry apple powder.

2. Arbitration should really not be the issue here. The issue should be the intent of the parties and their good faith in performing. The issue is whether Tree Top should have furnished clutter-free apple powder. The issue was really not negotiated. However, Tree Top should examine the issue over the long term. If the case is settled between the two, Schulze and Burch will probably continue as a long-term and loyal customer. Litigation will produce costs and arbitration will produce a settlement, but the relationship of the parties will be lost.

3. The product did ruin the equipment and is about to ruin the relationship. Ask the students in a case such as this whether it matters who is right or wrong. Shouldn't the desire be to have a satisfied customer, not a customer who is forced to bear the costs of a misunderstanding because of a legal interpretation?

4. Tree Top's reputation and a possible long-term source of apple powder purchases are being lost in the legal battle. So often litigation is used as a means of resolving business disputes that are better resolved by the parties in a way that preserves their relationship (ethically).

5. Tree Top must ask: Regardless of my legal obligations, do I want to continue to do business with this customer? Do I want to preserve the relationship? How would I want to be treated? Is my approach balanced? Will I be as comfortable with my decision over the long term as I am now?

Legal Issues

Tree Top probably did all that it was legally required to do under the contract. It did not agree to furnish a particular type of apple powder. However, the legal resolution may not be the ethical resolution. Is it balanced? How does it make me feel? Will I feel as good about this over the long run?

5.6   Sears and High-Cost Auto Repairs

Answers and Key Discussion Items

1. The employees were under an incentive system that indeed gave them every incentive to sell more than a customer or car needed. Their judgment was affected by the bonuses and rewards built into the Sears compensation system.

2. Repairs for safety reasons are not unethical recommendations. Repairs recommended when the brakes are fine or the service will not be needed for some time are unethical. The case revealed the fact that cars that had just been repaired were being re-repaired at the recommendation of the service advisors. These recommendations were unethical and illegal.

3. Sears reputation has been damaged. Its earnings were down for the quarter following the announcement of the California investigation. Sears is currently reeling from an attempted re-focus of its efforts. The company suffered tremendous public setbacks because of the repair scandal.

4. Brennan acknowledged both legal and moral responsibility for the repairs. Sears has agreed to compensate the victims and Brennan accepts responsibility for the compensation system that led to poor ethical judgments on the parts of the service advisors.

5. The motivation for the overcharges is irrelevant. They were wrong whether recommended dishonestly or in the interest of incentives. Reasons are not relevant when the result is that the customer was taken advantage of.

6. Honesty. Fair treatment. Correct conduct in the future, changing the company's ethical culture and incentive system if necessary.

7. Abuses. Incentives tied solely to sales and revenues motivate employees to cut ethical corners.

8. The ongoing problems with Sears that seem to erupt every few years evidence a culture that does not value customer trust. There is a constant desire to push the envelope and see how much Sears can gain through questionable approaches that are either in violation of the law or skirt the law so closely that Sears looks as if it is a desperate retailer as opposed to a store with a strategy and set of goals. Further, the incidents indicate a lack of appreciation for basic ethical values of honesty, fairness and trust.

5.7   Magazine Contests: The Disclosure of Odds

Answers and Key Discussion Items

1. The way the letters read would lead an unsophisticated individual to believe they were really in line for the prize. The letters also seemed to mislead about whether subscriptions were necessary. It was unclear who was a finalist in the letters that were sent. It would be impossible to tell how many people were actually involved.

   There is an ethical issue here of taking unfair advantage of people who are not sophisticated enough to see the finely tuned language used. Also, the letters left the average reader with a false impression.

2. The role of regulators here is to provide the guidance in language so that those who cannot discern as easily are not deceived. The standard among attorneys generals in the states varies. Some use the standard of actual deceit — was someone actually deceived by the letter? Others use the standard of reasonable person deceit — would an average person reading this letter be deceived by it? Their role is to have the language redrafted so that the deceit is eliminated.

3. The companies have taken unfair advantage of those who do not have the skill of discernment. Further, they are selling their products (magazines) through the use of this deceit.

5.8 Tylenol: The Product Safety

Answers and Key Discussion Items

1. The key is to find out if the studies are correct. Depending on findings there, you might want to issue warnings and offer physicians and pharmacists information on the problem. The important thing is to follow the PR rules covered in the Intel/Pentium case (5.1).

2. The product is a good one. It is needed and can be used effectively. That there are other things that shouldn't be mixed with it does not take away from the product. The information should just be disclosed.

3. Have the students discuss the following issues as they address the question of warnings:

   a. Consumer trust
   b. Company reputation
   c. Physical harm to customers
   d. Long-term reputation of the company
   e. Public relations issues
   f. Honesty

5.9   Ford and Its Pinto

<u>Use Transparencies 24 and 25 to show the costs analysis for the redesign of the Pinto.</u>

<u>Use Transparency 26 -- it is a summary of the Ford internal memo on the value of human life as used in Ford's evaluation as to whether to redesign the Pinto.</u>

Answers and Key Discussion Items

1. $18.66.

2. Management's position was that the "fixes" would take too long. Ford needed a small car out on the market to compete with the foreign car manufacturers. Further, the fixes were not worth the additional costs given the analysis that had been done on accidents and the cost to Ford of the accidents and the compensation for victims.

3. Mr. Copp, under the Velasquez test, was one who carried out orders, but did not have the ultimate decision-making authority with respect to the Pinto. He would thus not be held morally responsible. However, Mr. Copp did possess certain strengths by virtue of his position in which he could have revealed the information or stood firm with respect to the redesigns.

4. No, there was no violation of any safety standards or other laws. It was simply an ethical decision to leave the design as it was.

5. There was tremendous demand at the time for small, fuel efficient cars. Ford was trying to deliver the car as quickly as possible. But, using one of the Laura Nash questions, it is difficult to believe that the buyers would have wanted the car that quickly had they known of the defect in design with respect to crashes.

6. All autos are dangerous and we all assume some risks. But, as was decided many years ago in the *MacPherson* case, we only assume a reasonable risk in accidents. We do not assume risks that manufacturers had knowledge of and could have corrected or minimized.

7. Copp, as noted above, had valuable information and could have used that information to change events either inside or outside the company.

8. The resurgence in popularity of the car should cause Ford to take some actions with respect to warnings. Particularly given the nature of stock-car racing, warnings about the gas tank and its possible rupture should be given again.

9. The ad that Ford ran represents a complete turn-around from the days of the Pinto. Ford's ad sets out all the questions, concerns and background. There

5.9   Ford and Its Pinto (cont'd)

is a number for more information. There is full disclosure even though this
product safety issue did not even affect all vehicles as did the Pinto design
problem. Ford's reaction to the issue was immediate and its offer universal.
The contrast is dramatic.

5.10 A Toy to Die For

Answers and Key Discussion Items

1. Larami needs to realize that its toy carries potential dangers. The marketing of the toy may need to be changed. The design of the toy may need to be changed. Larami may have to develop ways to prevent or discourage the use of liquids other than water in the gun. A suggestion would be a type of plastic that disintegrates when any harmful chemicals are inserted. Another suggestion would be the marketing of a disappearing ink that would give buyers the thrill of a fired shot without harm to the individual or clothing.

2. A moratorium might be appropriate until Larami can develop alternatives. Larami needs to see the consequences of misuse of the toy. Such misuse could lead to costly lawsuits and tremendous damage in terms of public reputation. The desire to continue with sales as usual may be fueled by the felt need to capitalize on a very popular trend. However, often the ethical choice makes things better for the firm. For example, a moratorium could (because of supply and demand) make the product more in demand by the time Larami reintroduces its safer, more colorful model.

3. Larami may want to restrict marketing or perhaps provide neighborhood interaction in certain areas. Sponsoring a safety event or contest may be the best way to discourage the types of dangerous behaviors that are beginning. Contests that are safe and challenging could serve to turn the use and image of the product around.

4. Some toy stores did make the decision to pull the guns. Some would argue that absent illegality, the guns can be sold. A compromise might be appropriate where the store sells the guns but undertakes a warning program or sells them only to young people who are accompanied by an adult for the purchase.

5. Larami apparently had no knowledge of the potential misuse of the product. In this first case, there would be no moral responsibility. After this point, however, Larami does have knowledge of the potential dangers of its product and absent mitigation would be responsible for future injuries.

5.11 Nestlé Infant Formula

Answers and Key Discussion Items

1. Nestlé, as an unassailable proposition, had a brilliant marketing program for infant formula. However, social responsibility and the moral responsibility for the right of these young children to life, dictated that Nestlé take other factors into account before using the marketing program. Once the boycotts began, the harm to children was obvious. It was morally wrong to continue the program unchanged. An executive with authority to do so should have changed the program.

2. Nestlé has suffered a twenty-year taint on its reputation because of the decisions made in the infant formula marketing program.

3. A marketing program that satisfies not only WHO and AAP but the ethical constraints as well is one that begins with the premise that in these third world nations, mother's milk is best and should always be the first choice. "If you cannot nurse . . . " is the next line in a marketing program that would be socially responsible. Also, a marketing program must involve some education because mothers need to understand the risks they run of drying up if formula is used.

4. Those who made the decision to go forward with the program and were aware of the cultural, physical and educational problems that would produce watered-down formula and malnourished babies are morally responsible for the deaths and developmental problems of those children.

5. The moratorium is voluntary but it is only a matter of time before regulation is imposed that would prevent distribution of samples. The potential for harm is great when the samples are used and the mother's milk dries up or decreases. The lack of knowledge about lactation can cost infants' lives. The moratorium is not required by positive law, but it is mandated by ethical constraints.

6. A discharge pack from a hospital with formula sends a signal of hospital approval. There is no disagreement among the experts about breast milk being best. As a hospital administrator, you may be making rationalization easier and actually be affording the opportunity for formula.

7. Some ads do read "Breast is best." Many companies are exercising great ethical discretion in the marketing of their products. Such an approach has the additional business benefit of building trust among mothers.

5.12 The Tobacco Industry

Answers and Key Discussion Items

1. Mr. Bible is stating, in an indirect way, that the product they sell is not
   necessarily safe, but it is as safe as it can be made and that the company
   does have a responsibility to let the public know of the dangers of the
   product. That duty may be more along the lines of a legal duty compliance.
   In other words, from a product liability perspective, the cigarette he makes
   is no more dangerous than any other cigarette and there are adequate warnings
   on the package to let people know of the dangers of the product.

2. The strategies for "Uptown" and "Dakota" are targeted toward specific and
   vulnerable groups. Their success rate is evidence of the target success.
   The strategy is to appeal to groups that seem to be most vulnerable to
   adopting the smoking habit. This type of strategy is no different from
   marketing BMWs to lawyers (they seem to be vulnerable) with the exception
   that the product sold has been linked to various types of lung diseases and
   cancer.

3. Freedom of choice is a moral value too. Cars are dangerous, but we still
   sell them. Have the students compare and contrast other potentially harmful
   products with tobacco such as alcohol, sugar, lard.

4. Harvard, Johns Hopkins, NYU, and Sara Lee have taken the position that they
   do not wish to profit from a product that brings so much harm to its users.
   Universities with medical schools must be particularly sensitive to health
   issues. They are not required to divest but it seems inconsistent to have a
   commitment to health care while earning on investments in products linked to
   so much of the health care problems. Ask the students if there aren't other
   similar products. What about the danger of autos? What about butter?
   Products such as potato chips?

   The statement of Harvard read as follows: "We have made the decision that in
   spite of its dangers, tobacco should still be available and be legal and that
   there should be freedom to choose." Some U.S. surgeon generals have
   advocated the elimination of advertising to stop some of the teenage
   association with smoking, its ads, and characters (like Joe Camel).
   Restrictions or bans on advertising have been accomplished before (TV ban on
   cigarettes) and could easily be adopted for other media forms.

5. Have the students contrast the testimony statements with the provisions of
   the settlement agreement. What happened to make the difference in the
   philosophies? Do you think the executives believe what they testified to in
   1994? Why did Liggett break rank?

6. The freedom of choice is a principle of American government and has been
   manifest in everything from abortion rights to debates on health care. The
   issue some see in advertising is that the product is made available and
   consumers can choose whether to buy it. However, the focus of the concern
   appears to be that the ads attract those without the discernment skills for

choosing or seeing potential harm: teen-agers. The thrust of the settlement is preventing the choice before the age of understanding and accountability.

7. Taxes on tobacco would cut back on sales and there will be an impact on growers and all those they employ as well as on the communities in which tobacco is grown and produced into cigarettes. This industry is a large part of the economy in the South. Have the students discuss how those economic interests influence decisions about tobacco. Have the students discuss the notion of balancing economic interests against the resulting harm. Remind them of those who divested themselves of tobacco stocks — tobacco stocks were performing well.

8. Passive smoke represents an interesting dilemma because it is not an issue of choice. If we allow smoking, we are requiring those who do not smoke to subject themselves to a documented risks. There is a certain infringement of rights involved when passive smoke is considered. Freedom of choice cannot violate the rights of others.

5.13 ATVs: Danger on Wheels

Answers and Key Discussion Items

1. The product is either too dangerous or the nature of the product causes a lapse in judgment for the people using the product. It appears that the three-wheel product cannot carry sufficient warnings or require sufficient responsibility for guaranteed safe use.

2. The companies must do more than comply with the bans. They must be certain that ATV owners of the three-wheel model have knowledge about the ban and that the appropriate warnings and information be given to them. There is potential liability for the companies beyond their ethical obligations.

3. The sales efforts for the four-wheel models are different from the previous three-wheel sales. The four-wheel vehicles are more stable, warnings are increased and appropriate limitations on age and speed maximums make the vehicle what it was intended to be: a vehicle for enjoying the terrain but not hot-dogging.

4. There are some who would have supported a recall. But there are the rights of the individual owners who would elect to keep their vehicles. Freedom of choice is an issue in the recall. Perhaps more effective than a recall would be a recall of the customers only for the purpose of training or warning.

5. The cost of a recall (in this case requiring replacement of three-wheel vehicles with four-wheel vehicles) would have been astronomical. On the other hand, the cost of civil liability for accidents on the three-wheel vehicle may exceed the costs of the recall. As a compromise, although not required by positive law, the companies might want to consider a substantial trade-in allowance for a new four-wheel vehicle. Again, this would be costly to the companies but would it be as costly as compensation for the certain injuries that will occur with the three-wheel vehicles?

5.14 Tylenol: The Product Rescue

Answers and Key Discussion Items

1. The risk was very small that there would be any further Tylenol poisonings.

2. No, the shareholders' interests were examined for the long-term. In the short-term, the shareholders had to accept a write-off that was substantial. But, as history has shown, the write-off helped restore consumer confidence and restored Tylenol to its previous market share and then some. Ethical choices are not mutually exclusive. Ethical choices benefit both customers and shareholders.

3. Most did continue with their capsule sales, assuming that the public wanted those sales. Again, the firms would miss the opportunity for a market niche. The caplets would be what consumers were looking for and would feel comfortable with.

4. Burke's decision was one for Tylenol's future. It was a difficult decision in terms of present costs but it ensured that Tylenol could return to the market position it once held. The interests of consumers and shareholders were the same: make a good product and be certain that it is safe. The formula translated into what consumers want and hence profit for the shareholders.

5. The decision to abandon the capsule makes Tylenol the odd market entry. Unfamiliarity can cause a drop in the market share. In this case the caplet was the answer to consumer fears and the down side of not having what the customer wanted was minimized.

6. In this case, as in many others, taking care of the moral responsibility of producing a safe product, was the same as ensuring long-term survival and earnings for the company. The balancing is not difficult once a manager establishes that ethical choices are often the same as good financial or marketing choices.

7. Yes, the manufacturers should have made the decision to do the tamper-proof packaging on their own. However, they followed the prisoners' dilemma notion: you are always better off doing nothing.

8. With the Tylenol case, Johnson & Johnson did follow its credo. However, its more recent response on the liver issue has not been as forthcoming or as consistent with its credo.

Note: In June 1995, the FDA announced that companies could elect not to have tamper-proof bottles. Apparently the bottles were adult-proof as well.

5.15 Preventable Potholes

Answers and Key Discussion Items

1. Ask for the students' view on doing something cheaper than another company knowing the product won't last as long. Isn't there a need for cheaper alternatives in markets? For example, many people buy Yugoslavian Hugos knowing of reliability problems, but it is very cheap and provides them with transportation for at least a few years.

2. Quality in service and product is an ethical component of a business. The lack of quality will cause a business to lose customers and eventually end the business. The lack of quality is costly in a financial, ethical and survival sense.

3. No, it would not be difficult to run a business by underbidding and sacrificing quality. It is done all the time. Many businesses survive, at least temporarily, by underbidding and them scrimping on the product or service. The cost is non-renewal of the contract and a message to others in the industry regarding the workmanship or service.

4. Yes. He could offer to do a stretch of road to demonstrate the difference in the lasting quality and let the work flow in after this graphic demonstration.

5. Moral responsibility for accidents caused by poorly maintained roads is a tough causal connection to make because of the other factors that enter into accidents. It could be argued that accidents and property damage to cars and personal injuries caused by potholes would be attributed to the firms who do shoddy workmanship and are aware of the road risks. The link is more difficult to establish.

5.16 Generic Consulting

Answers and Key Discussion Items

1. The only sustainable advantage a company has is its reputation. With the revelation of these two very similar reports, Towers Perrin has tarnished its reputation because it looks as if they are issuing the same reports regardless of the company and regardless of their "diagnosis." It looks as if all companies are paying for the same report issued over and over again. Towers Perrin looks as if it has cheated its clients.

2. Yes, there will be a certain amount of distrust of Towers Perrin in this area and its competitors will be able to capitalize on the problem because they will provide assurance of custom programs as opposed to the generic advice rendered by Towers Perrin.

5.17 Credit Card and Buying Privacy

Answers and Key Discussion Items

1. Customers whose names are sold without their knowledge have had their privacy violated. There may not be a positive law against such sales of lists and names, but there is the moral constraint of privacy.

2. The credit reporting agency has an even greater obligation of privacy because the information it has is so sensitive and cannot be disclosed without the permission of the debtor. It is more wrong for credit reporting agencies to sell the lists than the creditors.

3. There are those who would not be offended by the sale of their names in a list. Indeed, some would like to have their names on certain mailing lists. Their preferences need not be ignored but this waiver of the right of privacy should be done voluntarily and with full knowledge.

4. No, the lists can be sold without violating the law. However, positive law standards are not the sole measure of ethical behavior.

5. The firms should take a proactive position and ask those on their lists their preferences with respect to the sale of their names in list firm to certain marketers. The ability to choose takes away the ethical issues of violating privacy.

6.1   Ice-T, The *Body Count* Album, and Shareholder Uprising

Answers and Key Discussion Items

1. It is free speech, but the sensationalism of it all does make money. Freedoms also bring responsibilities -- some discretion must be used to enjoy the First Amendment protections we have.

2. No, and in fact, the head of Time Warner's record division was terminated in June 1995. Levin should have been more sensitive to public backlash and to institutional investors' concerns.

3. Time Warner does not want to be seen as a censor. Perhaps it is not morally responsible for the artists' works. But Time Warner <u>is</u> responsible to its shareholders for earnings, stock value, etc.

4. Yes, any screening of speech is carefully watched and controlled in a constitutional sense as a slippery slope.

5. Shareholder objections <u>should</u> influence corporate conduct. As Milton Friedman phrases it, managers of the corporation are simply agents of the company and are accountable to them. If you can't sell shares, there is no company.

6. The termination of the executives associated with the decisions for this product demonstrates, at least indirectly, Time Warner's message that the company cannot have these types of controversies. Although Time Warner may have stood on a soap box and preached First Amendment rights, its bottom line dictated different conduct which was that those who cause these types of difficulties with products cannot remain with the company. There was no protection for the executives responsible for the public and shareholder outcry.

6.2 Compensation-Fueled Dishonesty: Fraud to Get Results

Answers and Key Discussion Items

1. It has been said that there are two reasons for dishonesty: need and opportunity. The opportunities for dishonesty are available and the high stakes/high pay atmosphere makes many Wall Street employees feel the need to make more and more money. The compensation system of a company does set its ethical tone: how much people make and how they make it are two forces that influence workplace conduct.

2. In many situations like Jett's at Kidder, Peabody, supervisors want to believe in super performers. They do not ask the hard questions. The advice many ignore in unusually high earnings periods is: if it sounds too good to be true, it probably is.

3. Firing those who question practices; fear of losses and reporting them; under reporting to cover future losses. Earnings were everything.

4. They were fired so no one would rock the boat. No one wanted to believe anything was wrong and everyone was enjoying high earnings individually based on Jett's and Kidder's supposed performance.

5. Never questioning is "That's the way it's always been done." Firms need to have an "always question" attitude, whether there are high earnings or losses. Not questioning creates an ethical culture that says earnings count, how you got there is irrelevant.

6. A hotline; an ombudsperson; more emphasis on the corporate compliance program; all would help. The programs at Kidder seemed to be symbolic; name only. The obvious commitment of the CEO and board would also help.

7. Jett, his family, friends
   Kidder investors
   Kidder employees and their families
   GE investors
   GE employees
   All who do business with Kidder and GE

   There is an economic ripple effect of all who lost money and jobs as a result of Jett's deceit.

6.3   Levels of Executive Compensation: How Much Should the Boss Make?

Use Transparency 27 to show a chart of various CEOs' pay.

Answers and Key Discussion Items

1. There are two schools of thought on executive compensation. The first
   school, an economics-based one, is that CEOs should be paid whatever the
   market will bear. A second school of thought maintains that CEOs are paid
   too much and their pay should be tied to the wages of the employees and the
   performance of the company.

2. The argument has been made that large CEO salaries are subsidized with taxes
   because they are deductible. There have been Congressional proposals to
   place a cap on the amount of CEO pay that would be deductible.

3 and 4. Many follow the philosophy that CEO pay should be tied to maximums
        above worker compensation and that the payment should not go up unless
        the company's financial health is improved.

5. Currently the compensation committee of the board of directors of a company
   establishes officer pay. Their independence has been called into question in
   recent cases since these directors are often doing business with the company.

6. Institutional investors have been demanding more say in board matters and
   have raised objections about CEO pay. However, there are some questions
   about having outside investors set the management pay incentives in a
   company. These investors would then be involved in micro-managing the
   company which is not the role of either the board or the shareholders. The
   issue arises also at what point do the shareholders simply sell their shares
   and move onto other companies that pay officers within reasonable bounds?
   Traditionally, the market has functioned as shareholders move from stock to
   stock depending upon the performance of the company. Shouldn't these
   investors express their dissatisfaction with the pay system via the market,
   with sales?

7. Yes, these directors are not independent and have conflicts of interest in
   maintaining the happiness and presence of existing management.

8. Yes, there would be interference but it is bound to come.

6.4   The Boy Scouts of America, U.S. West, and Gay Rights

Answers and Key Discussion Items

1. U.S. West was simply contributing to a longstanding organization that promotes the values of honesty, patriotism and integrity. The BSA policy is one example of many policies many organizations have that might not be consistent with corporate policies. The issue becomes will donations be made on the basis of the donee organization's goals and accomplishments or on its policies?

2. Freedom of choice in philanthropic giving is an important standard whether it is a corporation or an individual. A corporation runs the risk, however, of offending customers through its choices of donees. Milton Friedman would say that the corporation should engage in philanthropy only to the extent that such contributions help the company make more money. To the extent that customers are lost through philanthropic giving, the giving should stop.

3. Public outcry may not restrict corporate giving but it may eliminate it because of the company's fear of alienating customers and receiving adverse publicity about its donees.

4. Levi Strauss is experiencing the backlash from the withdrawal of funding. On issues such as the BSA ban on homosexuals, companies cannot win. There are as many customers that would support the ban as there are customers who would object. The result is that the giving or not giving alienates customers. The company is then not serving its main purpose which is to earn a profit and the philanthropy must be abandoned to avoid the controversy.

6.5   Dayton-Hudson and Its Contributions to Planned Parenthood

Answers and Key Discussion Items

1. No. In both this case and the U.S. West case the companies cannot win. They have encountered issues in which public opinion differs and public outcry on both sides is strong.

2. On issues this sensitive, tying marketing to contributions is a fatal mistake. Under Friedman's notion, the company's voluntary giving is costing it customers and should be avoided.

3. If the contributions are consistent with the firms' values, they may not be consistent with a group of customers' values (as in the Levi's/BSA dilemma). These donations are lose/lose propositions and need to be avoided. The downside is the impact on organizations that rely on corporate funding for survival.

4. The ethics of the situation are that attacks be answered or the firm loses customers and money; a violation of its duties to its investors.

6.6 Giving and Spending the United Way

Answers and Key Discussion Items

1. In light of the purpose of the United Way, the nature of its donors and the problems of too many needs and too little funds, Aramony's salary and expenses were not balanced and did not take into account how the $12,000 per year wage earner would feel about these levels of expenses as he/she makes a $500 per year payroll contribution.

2. The Board was responsible for the supervision of the expenses and had the authority to halt the expenditures.

3. Aramony may have been behaving as other CEOs of large multi-national organizations behave, but his distinction came from being the head of a charitable organization as opposed to a for-profit corporation.

4. Compensation in for-profit corporations should be whatever the market is. Salary, benefits and perks should be set along the lines of industry. CEOs of non-profits must be particularly sensitive to their fish bowl existence and recognize their vulnerability on the issues of salary and perks. People don't want to donate funds to organizations that they perceive spend lavishly.

5. Chao faced and faces the decline in donations, the tarnished reputation of United Way, public outcry and local chapter uprisings and withdrawal from the national United Way. In short, Chao faces the task of restoring a non-profit's reputation lost through questionable spending. Her task is a fund-raiser's nightmare.

6.7   The Chicago Inner-City School Experiment

Answers and Key Discussion Items

1. Yes, Friedman would support their actions so long as the CEOs could show that there would be a return to them in their businesses, which would be better-trained employees and a savings in training costs.

2. The comments from the shareholder should be addressed with information about training costs, the inadequacy of the public school systems and the business's need for adequately trained workers. The sponsorship of the school should be addressed as a quantitative issue; one that will produce higher returns for the company over the long run.

6.8   The Rock Music Warning Labels

Answers and Key Discussion Items

1. There are not controls on how the albums are distributed or sold. Young, impressionable teenagers have access to them. Without the appropriate levels of wisdom and discernment, their activities and attitudes may be influenced by very popular groups whose attitudes and beliefs may not reflect ethical values. These lyrics sometimes cause the adoption of behaviors that would otherwise be foreign to the young people. Rock groups have significant power to influence young people and the use of explicit lyrics is an abuse of that power (when there are no warnings about content and the ability of parents to screen).

2. So long as the labels are universal, all those who have objections to the lyrics appear ready, willing and able to accept the voluntary compromise. The only drawback would be the unwillingness of the artists or the record companies to participate.

3. The songs with explicit lyrics often do well. The question is whether you are willing to assume moral responsibility for the consequences of the lyrics, as in the Reno case where there is a suicide.

4. As a record producer, you would probably be unable to do much more than to put on the labels. Asking that the albums be set apart in stores may actually fuel the sales as opposed to controlling them. If you decide to produce the records, there is little control that can come once they are "out there."

5. If you are aware of the suggestive nature of the lyrics and the influence that rock music stars can have on young people and their particular vulnerability, there would be some moral responsibility. The courts have not held record producers or the groups legally liable but the question of moral responsibility is one of prior knowledge.

6.9   The Mommy Doll

Answers and Key Discussion Items

1. The concern about that doll is that it would glorify, encourage and make look
   glamorous teenage pregnancies because the doll looks so young and the "ease
   of delivery" so appealing.

2. Some see the doll as a means of educating children about the birth process
   and family responsibilities. There is a father doll to go with the mother
   and child.

3. Parents always have the ultimate control over what comes into the home but
   friends will still have the dolls and conversations, questions and some
   idolizing will occur.

   Note: Have the students consider the latest concern about the talking Barbie
         doll that says, "Math is tough." The concern is a characterization of
         women, i.e. that they can't do math. Ask the students whether
         objections have gone too far or the toys have gone too far.

6.10 The Toys Parents and Teachers Hate

Answers and Key Discussion Items

1. The toys represent socially irresponsible behavior. They are a brilliant product line with great potential that disregards the ethical issues and long-term implications of marketing such a line of toys. The possibilities of boycotts of Kenner and the backlash from the sales have not been adequately reviewed.

2. If the toys are manufactured, the failure of store owners to sell them can still spell their demise. On the other hand, often the refusal to sell the toys translates into added sales.

3. The ads are something that could be the subject of future regulation since children's television ads have already been subjected to certain minimum FTC standards. Good choices by station managers will ensure that future regulations are kept to a minimum. Toys such as this involve line-drawing. Someone has to be willing to draw the line when we have crossed into the anti-social arena. If everyone goes along with the toy, we have only made a toy manufacturer rich from a poor ethical and socially irresponsible decision.

6.11 Beavis, Butt-head, and MTV

Answers and Key Discussion Items

1. MTV, by placing the program on in prime time without warning to parents, shares some responsibility for the mishaps.

2. As noted in the *Mortal Kombat* case, parents do have a responsibility to supervise, but the standards of society decline as more and more is tolerated, despite parent's ability to say "No".

3. MTV did a great service with the program move and disclaimer, but the question can still be raised, "Why do we need this program?"

4. Have the students discuss why the program is popular. What is its purpose?

5. "The proud sponsor of `Beavis and Butt-head'" is not a noble label. Sponsors risk boycotts on these types of controversial programs. Beyond the ethics of sponsorship is the risk of loss of sales and earnings from a boycott.

6.12 Shock Jock: Howard Stern

Answers and Key Discussion Items

1. Infinity may hang its hat on First Amendment issues, but it is still in business. It must be able to sell air time, it can't face boycotts and it can't risk astronomical fines. To that extent it has a business obligation to monitor and control Stern. An ethical responsibility for those you employ exists as well.

2. Yes, and Simon & Schuster has some restraint. The First Amendment does not mean that every manuscript must be published. Social, moral and financial considerations are part of every publication decision.

3. The shareholders are probably very pleased with Howard Stern. However, do the shareholders and management recognize the short term focus of this one-time publication and short-lived radio figure? Can they recover? Can they focus on strengths?

4. Have the students debate the merits of a Sternless world.

6.13 Retailers and Weapons: Self-Imposed Bans

Answers and Key Discussion Items

1. Although the decisions by these two major retailers may have been prompted by the potential liability for selling guns, there are other reasons that could have played into the ban. For example, some customers are happier if weapons are not sold in the stores in which they shop. Also, the chains enjoyed a great deal of free publicity from their decisions. The moral responsibility for another's death because of the sale of a murder weapon could also be a great relief to the store in a public relations sense.

2. The realistic-looking toy guns created problems for law enforcement officials. Although the employers (municipalities and so forth) of the police officers involved in shooting the youngsters with the toy weapons would be first in the liability line, it is possible that in the scheme of deep pockets and product liability, the families and victims could return to the retailers and manufacturers of the realistic-looking toys.

3. Yes, the decision earned all the stores a great deal of positive publicity. In a nation that faces the problem of weapon use, it was a terrific story to see a retailer respond by doing what it could do to cut down on the possibility of senseless deaths. It was an ethical and moral choice for the retailers, but it also brought them great economic benefits in terms of publicity and customer appreciation.

4. Have the students discuss the issue and what information they would want: how much business is involved? what is the potential liability? are we creating an additional societal problem with the realistic-looking guns?

5. Guns are still a legal product; the issue is whether it is ethical to continue to sell such weapons. Guns can be used for lawful activities such as hunting. A ban on selling guns is an easy way to avoid the complexities of the paperwork as well as the liability for the failure to adequately screen gun purchasers. Another choice would be to screen carefully all potential purchasers, honor waiting periods, be careful on screening applicants etc. Some retailers, such as Sears, felt they could not do an adequate job on the paperwork and abandoned selling weapons so they did not make a mistake.

6.14 "It May Be Immoral, But Not Illegal.   The Bottom Line is Money."

Answers and Key Discussion Items

1. The Daniels follow a positive law standard. If what they are doing does not violate the law, then it is okay to do. The Daniels do not consider moral issues in their business.

2. They make the argument that no retailer can control what is done with a product purchased at a store and that no one can anticipate every act performed with a good purchased from a merchant.

3. The Daniels have indeed found a market niche and are doing quite well within that Niche. There are still protected rights for gun purchases and the Daniels believe their role is part of making sure the guns are always available despite current trends away from permitting gun sales.

4. Have the students review some of the quotes from the Daniels and decide whether they are there to fulfill the Second Amendment or for profit and gain.

6.15 E. Coli, Jack-in-the-Box and Cooking Temperatures

<u>Answers and Key Discussion Items</u>

1. Jack-in-the-Box did not follow the formula for handling corporate and national crises:

   a. Be forthcoming with information;
   b. Respond immediately;
   c. Recall, recall, recall;
   d. Do not blame others;
   e. Do not say it is not a big issue;
   f. Do not attempt to cover-up; and
   g. Do not discredit the media or the victims.

2. The change should have been made voluntarily and sooner as an ethical choice because of the potential loss of human life and certainly illness and also because of the relatively low cost of implementing the temperature increase as opposed to paying out for the loss of life and illness as well as the long-term damage to the chain for the bacteria-induced illnesses.

3. The misplacement of the memos tells us that compliance with the law was not systematic at Jack-in-the-Box. The company should have made regulatory compliance a top priority.

4. Yes, the harm to individuals is so extensive and there is a great potential for loss of life. The cooking temperature decision was absolutely a moral decision. It was treated, however, as an expense and time situation.

5. Jack-in-the-Box tried to make things right with those who were harmed. The praise from an adversary indicates that the chain tried to do "the right thing." Even those who were harmed felt comfortable about what was done for them, which should go a long way to restoring the chain's reputation. Sales have declined and the chain is trying to recover. Despite a new advertising campaign, the chain continues to struggle.

6.16 "Dateline NBC": Pick Up GM from the GM Pickup Story

Answers and Key Discussion Items

1. The explosion devices made the story much more compelling and more interesting to watch. It made a good teaser for the story to see the exploding pickup.

2. It is significant that outsiders disclosed the embellishment because the culture at NBC was such that no one there would have disclosed that there was a staging of the accident. The culture in the news organization was such that either no one saw a problem with the embellishment or such that no one would dare to bring the problem to the attention of those who were in charge.

3. It was the appearance of the accident that was emotional and upsetting. Even if the rockets did not cause the explosion, the depiction of what happens to the trucks in accidents was not accurate.

4. Yes, the firm was involved in the litigation of the case for plaintiffs. It was in the firm's best interests to have the accident look as awful as it possibly could.

5. Have the students review the pressure you would feel if you noticed the rockets and felt it was wrong. Ask them who they would approach first. What would they say? How would they follow up? Would they discuss standards of fairness? Would they discuss the implications for NBC and Dateline if the rockets were disclosed publicly?

7.1   A Club in My Name

Answers and Key Discussion Items

1. The funds from the settlement were intended to help children in the state. They were not intended to be used to develop name recognition for elected officials. The donations were not made the attorney generals from their pockets -- they were from a lawsuit settlement.

2. Is it bad form to use charity to develop name recognition? Although much good comes from what it done, the introduction of political benefit into a good cause is an appearance of impropriety.

3. The front page of the newspaper test would have helped. Gaining mileage from a donation for which other attorneys general are not raises questions about motive and propriety. It is a terrific topic for newspaper mileage.

7.2   The Fireman and His Family

Answers and Key Discussion Items

1. Conflict of interest in hiring family members for city contract; taking things that don't belong to you (pay and storage place for free); hiding information; taking unfair advantage

2. The front-page-of-the-newspaper test would have helped. The disclosure of this information should have been particularly anticipated because the breaches were so obvious. Would he have wanted his business to be treated in this way by an employee?

7.3   The Censured and Resigning Council Member

Answers and Key Discussion Items

1. Interpersonal abuse
   Conflict of interest
   Giving or allowing false impression
   Organizational abuse (pressuring city employees for signatures)

2. Mr. Stapley's conduct in some instances would intimidate city employees. In all instances, however, his conduct set a very poor example for the city employees because anyone of his breaches would have violated the city code and probably cost the employee his or her job. Mr. Stapley was setting a very poor tone at the top for the employees to follow.

3. Yes, Mr. Stapley's presence in law enforcement and judicial proceedings would have a chilling effect on their proceeding to completion because of his position and authority. Because he holds hiring and firing power over many involved, their independent judgment would be affected.

4. No, employees in fact said nothing during the entire tenure of Mr. Stapley. There was significant fear of retaliation. It was not until Mr. Stapley's departure that the city employees expressed their concerns and suggested that a code of ethics be developed for elected and appointed officials so that they were not placed in the same pressure situations again. The city has developed such a code and the code addresses many of the problems created during Mr. Stapley's tenure.

7.4   IRS Employees and Sensitive Data

Answers and Key Discussion Items

1. The ethical breach here is divulging information that should not be divulged
   or taking unfair advantage of taxpayers who assume that their tax information
   will be treated confidentially.

2. The law is not the only standard for their is a standard of professionalism
   here as well as a standard of morality. The temptation to peek when
   information is so accessible would be tremendous. It is still not ethical.
   It should not be done. The long-term personal, professional and business
   damage is too great.

3. If the litigation was for private purposes, then the snooping was more
   egregious than just "snooping for fun." If the use of the records was for
   preparing for a tax case, the employee is within his or her authority. Using
   such data for litigation advantage is an unnecessary breach of ethics for the
   laws of discovery will provide the information without the unauthorized use
   of the data by IRS employees. A document request from the opposing side will
   produce the same information.

7.5   Stanford University and Government Overhead

Answers and Key Discussion Items

1. Mr. Kennedy's attitudes did evolve as the case evolved. His initial statements conclude that whatever was done was insignificant and therefore justified. His last statement (March 23, 1991) is one that recognizes that while the accounting practices may have been legal, they were not necessarily ethical.

   Mr. Kennedy also resigned as a result of the Stanford problem. He became so identified with the problem that he needed to leave to restore Stanford's credibility. Mr. Kennedy's initial reaction to the accounting issues and his attitude of "little amounts not being issues" cost him deeply in the crisis. It became more than just unethical booking of costs; it became the unethical booking of costs and justification of it by a president who saw little wrong in a scenario that outraged others.

2. This case is an illustration of practices that were legal. It is also an illustration of practices that had "always been done this way" by Stanford and other universities. Accounting overhead was a nebulous concept that was used to maximize the government funds to the university.

3. Casper has set an ethical tone for Stanford by saying that everyone must observe, question and evaluate what is being done. He is suggesting that "the way things have always been done" be questioned. He is suggesting an open, honest and above-board atmosphere.

7.6   The Degrees-for-Grants Program

Use Transparency 28 to show similarities in writings and contract work.

Answers and Key Discussion Items

1. To the extent that the degrees were not earned, those students who actually earned their degrees are harmed. Also, those who rely on this academic measure of learning will assume that the steps required for the award of these degrees were followed. The University's credibility is also harmed as a result.

2. An employee who noted the similarities should first clarify the situation. Perhaps the degree work and the contract go hand-in-hand. Perhaps the university is benefitting from the work of the students and not vice-versa. Any employee raising ethical issues should be certain about the facts. The immediate supervisor is the first step. If there are no results, then the employee should turn to an independent party within the university or the next immediate supervisor and keep progressing until a response or clarification is obtained.

3. It would be very tempting to be able to earn a degree with relative ease. However, the degree holder would always be glancing back to be certain no one exposes the true nature of the degree and the work for that degree.

4. The Institute and the University appeared to be so inextricably intertwined that the contracts for the Institute were bound to have some effect on the relationships and the quid pro quo that resulted from the contract decision-makers also pursuing degrees.

5. This situation was more than just a quid pro quo. A university was stating that a degree had been earned when, in fact, the degree seemed to be no more than a work product. The certification of an individual as having earned a degree is a public declaration of competence. The institution's reputation is at stake when degrees are awarded without requisite course and graduation work being completed.

7.7   Casino Leases and the County Supervisor

Answers and Key Discussion Items

1. Yes, when she has matters pending before the Board, it is a direct conflict to be soliciting space for her business at the places of business of those who have the matters pending. Even if she intended nothing and even if she remained completely detached, the appearance of impropriety is just too great and undermines the public trust.

2. The business solicitations should be handled by a third party, preferably with the third party acting as a non-disclosed agent. In other words, those who are soliciting the space for the daiquiri franchise should not disclose that Ms. Atkinson Gates in a principal in the business.

3. Mr. Adelson concluded that he was denied his application because he would not do business with Atkinson Gates. There would be few other conclusions that anyone could draw in the situation.

4. She may be a silent partner, but she did not remain silent and therein lies the conflict. A silent partner cannot be involved in the day-to-day business for then he or she ceases to be a silent partner.

7.8   Bids, Employees and Conflicts

<u>Answers and Key Discussion Items</u>

1. There is an inherent conflict of interest in having the spouse involved in any way with even the paperwork on the contract. The state employee should have disclosed her affiliation and she should have been immediately isolated from the process in all ways.

2. No one said anything because of fear, because of working relationships, because of an unwillingness to rock the boat when things seem to be progressing.

3. There will be long-term implications for this flaw in the process. Even if nothing improper occurred, i.e. Intergroup deserved the contract, this information has been made public and there is a distrust on the part of state employees. Intergroup will be looked at more carefully next time and competitors will be given a better chance in order to compensate for this problem.

7.9 Orange County: Derivative Capital of the U.S.

Answers and Key Discussion Items

1. Government has a greater interest in the public trust and is a fiduciary for public funds and the public. Their investment interests should be more conservative.

2. County employees
   All those who had funds in the account from personal injury victims to wards of the state to school districts
   Families of employees
   School children
   Teachers
   School programs and suppliers
   Airports, parks and other public facilities
   Taxpayers
   Bond traders in general
   Accountants, lawyers and investment bankers who handled the portfolio and the investments

3. Immediately after the bankruptcy, there were articles on how investors were now nervous about any other municipal bonds. Municipalities had to change their portfolios or offer assurances that they were not in the same situation as Orange County. The cost of municipal bonds went up.

4. No. You would not expose your funds to the leverage and risk that Citron exposed the Orange County funds to.

5. Yes, those who invested assumed the standard conservative government approach to investment, not this form of leveraged gambling.

6. Yes, the brokers should at least be brought in to answer questions about how candid they were about the risk and whether they advised the leveraged position and offered any advice on the potential for earnings and the problems in terms of risk. Merrill Lynch settled in June 1998 with Orange County for its role in the case.

7.10 Cars and Conflicts

Answers and Key Discussion Items

1. Mrs. Wilcox could have used any of the ethical models. The newspaper test would have helped her to see how the public perceived the ongoing use of the car. She also could have asked if it were her business and her business vehicles, would she want her employees using them in this fashion.

2. The employees within the government agency do not have role models to set the standard for their behavior and the tone at the top permeates throughout the organization so that employees begin to take the same ethical shortcuts that they see being taken by those who are elected and in charge. If conduct is not important to those who are in charge, why should it be important to me? This rationalization is used in corrupt organizations as employees seek to take advantage of the same things they witness their leaders taking advantage of.

True/False Questions

F   1.   A conflict of interest is unethical only if those involved actually change their decision based on the benefits to be derived.

T   2.   An illegal act is an unethical act.

T   3.   Using positive law as an ethical standard means simply compliance with the law.

F   4.   Those firms with higher compliance with the law earn less than those with greater numbers of violations.

T   5.   The element of balance in the Blanchard/Peale ethical model requires an examination of the issue from the perspective of the affected party.

T   6.   A valid ethical barometer is the reaction of family and friends outside the business setting to your proposed decision.

F   7.   An agreement by an agent to accept a 10% commission from a seller who will sell goods to the agent's employer is ethical so long as the agent would have chosen that seller anyway.

T   8.   A real estate agent who recommends a management firm to an apartment complex buyer without disclosing that the agent owns 50% of the firm has committed an ethical violation.

F   9.   A commercial broker who accepts fees from both the seller and the buyer of the business without disclosure to either has not committed an ethical violation if both parties are happy with the transaction.

T   10.   A member of the city council who is employed by a waste management firm would have a conflict of interest in voting on the city's award of a contract for the handling of the city's waste.

F   11.   A physician conducting a study on a new prescription drug manufactured by a firm in which he is a 10% shareholder does not have a conflict of interest so long as his stock ownership is disclosed in his report on the drug.

T   12.   A physical fitness expert retained by a fitness magazine to evaluate walking shoes has a conflict of interest if she has an endorsement contract with one of the shoe companies that manufactures the shoes she will be evaluating.

F   13.   Giving preferential treatment in contract bidding to the daughter of a member of the company board is not a conflict of interest.

T   14. Physician referrals of patients to laboratories for work-ups when the physicians own all or part of the labs, but do not disclose such, is a conflict of interest.

F   15. A major donation by one of your long-term suppliers to a non-profit organization run by your spouse should not create perception problems so long as your purchasing decisions are based on the merits.

F   16. Having loan applicants pay for the expenses of bank officer travel for purposes of evaluating collateral is not a conflict of interest.

T   17. Purchasing agents accepting a pleasure trip from a supplier when no bids are pending is still an ethical violation.

T   18. Payments of royalties from drug sales by a pharmaceutical firm to the university where a researcher conducting studies has validated the firm's claims is a conflict of interest.

F   19. Hiring an employee from a competitor firm who has brought with her proprietary information is ethical so long as the employee has not breached an employment contract with that competitor.

F   20. Leaking proprietary information to the media is not an ethical breach.

T   21. The failure to disclose that your college degree was withheld because of outstanding parking fines and violations is unethical.

F   22. Taking information from a confidential file accidentally left on your desk is not unethical.

T   23. The failure to speak out when an ethical or legal lapse occurs within your firm is in itself an ethical violation.

F   24. Lie detector tests can be properly used as employment-screening devices.

F   25. Drug testing for employees who handle deliveries for a company is unconstitutional.

F   26. Employers can prevent women of child-bearing years from working in positions where exposure to risks could harm a fetus.

T   27. Employers could be held liable for injuries to fetuses experienced as their mothers worked in jobs where, with full knowledge, they were exposed to known fetal hazards and risks.

T   28. The employment-at-will doctrine contains an exception for whistle-blowers.

F   29. The duty of loyalty between employee and employer makes whistle-blowing unethical per se.

T 30. The sale of a product with known, but undisclosed dangers, is unethical.

T 31. Removing records from the workplace to prevent access by regulators on a pre-announced inspection is both illegal and unethical.

F 32. The Equal Pay Act follows a comparable worth theory.

T 33. "Everyone else does it," is a signal of an ethical pitfall.

F 34. "The lawyers have okayed this," is a signal that the decision/action is legal and ethical.

T 35. Labeling infertility surgery as "diagnostic surgery" in order to allow the patient to recover the costs from an insurer is unethical.

T 36. The failure to follow U.S. safety standards in foreign operations constitutes an ethical lapse.

F 37. Product dumping does not present ethical problems in those countries without product liability recovery systems.

T 38. Selling component parts that could be used to construct weapons to a nation against which an embargo on direct weapons sales is in place would be an ethical breach.

F 39. "Grease" or "facilitation payments," which are legal under the Foreign Corrupt Practices Act can be considered ethical.

T 40. A company executive exerting pressure on a scientist and her university to delay disclosure of study results harmful to the company and its products would be unethical.

F 41. Downsizing itself is unethical.

F 42. Compliance with the Worker Adjustment and Retraining Notification Act meets the standards for ethical conduct in downsizing.

T 43. Ethical choices often prove costly to firms in the short term.

T 44. Ethical advertising requires an examination of unintended impact and effects of ad content.

T 45. It is unethical to introduce a product with deceptively similar packaging to that of a major competitor.

F 46. An industry practice that permits bill-padding is ethical.

F 47. Taking advantage of a party in a contract situation due to the party's inexperience, and not due to any lack of disclosure on your part, is ethical.

T 48. The failure to disclose relevant information about a product or service is unethical.

T 49. Long-term relationships create ethical and legal obligations between the parties through conduct and accommodations.

T 50. The failure to correct a known defect in a product is both an ethical lapse and a basis for a negligence claim.

T 51. A decision not to sell realistic-looking toy guns is an example of an ethical choice not mandated by law.

F 52. The failure of an auditor to disclose the possible obsolescence of a firm's major product is a judgment call and not an ethical issue.

F 53. Decisions on corporate charitable contributions carry no ethical implications.

F 54. Corporate takeovers and mergers are unethical per se.

T 55. Executive compensation disclosures include information about conflicts of interest between directors and CEOs.

T 56. If I worked in purchasing in my company, it would be unethical for me to accept season tickets for my city's NBA team from the company that has supplied catering for the company's training sessions.

F 57. If I discover that a fellow employee is reporting falsely his overtime hours, it is best for me to say nothing and ignore the situation.

F 58. If I discovered that I unintentionally violated a federal environmental regulation, I should just wait and see if anything happens before taking any action.

F 59. If my supervisor asked me to cover for him by lying about his whereabouts, I should agree to do it but remind him that I can't make it a habit.

T 60. Your company's policy on company vehicles is that no family members may use them or ride in them. It would be unethical to use a company car to drive you and your spouse to a movie.

T 61. You are taking a graduate level course in management that will help you in performing your duties at work. Each week you must submit case analyses to your professor. Using work time to complete the analyses would be unethical.

T 62. With respect to #61, using your work computer and paper to complete the case analyses would be unethical.

T 63. Attending a class on company time would be unethical.

F   64.   A supplier has just been awarded a large contract by your company. As an employee in purchasing, you were largely responsible for awarding that supplier the contract. The supplier's sales representative has just called and would like to take you to lunch to thank you for the support. Going to lunch with the sale representative does not present any ethical problems.

F   65.   Accepting gifts from suppliers and vendors is not a problem so long as no bid decisions are pending.

F   66.   You are a building inspector for the county. A friend of yours is a plumbing contractor. Under county regulations, all steps in plumbing construction from the initial dig to the final installation of sink and bathroom fixtures requires an inspection sign-off. Your plumbing contractor friend has just called and wants to take you to dinner for your birthday at a five-star restaurant. Because you are friends anyway, the dinner presents no ethical problems.

T   67.   Your company has several outdated computers sitting in a storage closet that no one is using. You have taken one home and set it up for personal use. This is unethical conduct.

T   68.   You work for a school district as a facilities coordinator. You drive to the various schools in the district and supervise construction and remodeling and assess various building needs. When you are traveling around to the various schools, you use a district vehicle that is clearly marked as such. One day you stop at the country club and have lunch before heading to the next school since the country club is on the way. You also stop at the bank drive-thru teller to do some personal banking business. Both the lunch and the bank stop are ethical breaches.

F   69.   Your supervisor has told you that he wants to "get rid of Jane." Jane is a Hispanic female co-worker who is very bright and capable and hardworking. Your supervisor has asked you to document everything Jane does and says that will help build a case for termination. You should do as your supervisor tells you.

T   70.   Alice is a co-worker who is going through a divorce and has two small children. Alice's husband is not paying the child support the temporary court order requires. As a result, Alice is broke until she can get her court hearing. Alice has been able, through diverting checks returned to the company, to take about $2200 from the company to "temporarily help her cover her bills," as she has explained to you. You must report Alice's embezzlement.

T   71.   The mayor owns property next to one of the proposed sites for the city's new baseball stadium. The mayor has a conflict of interest and should not vote on the location of the stadium when the city council takes action on the site.

F   72.   Although you are not part of your company's engineering group, you have discovered a major flaw in the company's new paper-thin solar calculator. The calculator adds when the subtract button is pressed if there are more than 3 figures to the right of the decimal point. Since it is not your area, you should do and say nothing.

F   73.   With respect to #72, it is not necessary for the company to take any action to correct the problem or refund money for those who already own the new calculator.

T   74.   You are in marketing for one of the three U.S. auto manufacturers. You have just received a notice from your seat belt buckle supplier that the buckles shipped to you and used in the cars made between June 94 and September 94 are defective. The defect means that the buckles will come undone if pressure is placed on the belts at any speed over 10 miles per hour. You must encourage your firm to issue a recall.

T   75.   Alice is a secretary in your department. Alice is also a member of the American Guild of Organists. Alice has been placed in charge of the Guild's national convention. Each time you pass by Alice's desk or go to her to have some work done, you notice she is on the phone discussing or working on the convention. Alice's work on the convention during work hours is an ethical violation.

F   76.   Your supervisor has had a calendar with pictures of naked women on the inside panel of his desk for several months. A secretary spotted the calendar and commented to your supervisor that it was not appropriate for an office. Your supervisor took down the calendar and has asked you to back him up if any complaints are filed. He has asked you to say that you never saw the calendar. It would not be unethical for you to do as your supervisor requests because he has removed the calendar.

T   77.   A newspaper reporter is interviewing you about your experiences in working for a member of Congress. You have indicated you have information about his private life but will not share it. The reporter responds, "Tell me, just between you and me." You share the information and a quote from you on the private life of the member of Congress appears in the newspaper the next day. The reporter was unethical in violating a trust.

F   78.   It would not be unethical for you to accept two employment offers in case one fell through.

F   79.   It would not be unethical to continue interviewing for positions after you have already accepted employment with a particular firm.

F   80.   Selling products banned from sale in the United States in other countries is not an ethical violation.

T   81.   You work for a construction firm that is submitting a bid for the construction of a new company headquarters building for Smithco. A friend you have known since high school works in Smithco's capital budgeting area and has full knowledge of all the bids from all firms. It would be unethical for your friend to share that information with you before you submitted your bid.

T   82.   With respect to #81, it would be unethical for you to hire your friend to get him to bring the information to your company.

T   83.   Your unit has not been able to meet its sales goals for your quarter. Your assistant has suggested that you ship out enough goods to meet the quarterly goals by simply overshipping quantities on customer orders. When the goods are returned, you would simply take the returns in the next quarter after you have had more of an opportunity to meet goals. Your assistant's suggestion is a breach of ethics.

T   84.   With respect to #83, suppose you learn that other divisions within the company have always engaged in this form of earnings shifting. The practice is still an ethical breach.

F   85.   With respect to #83, a customer who agreed to help you with your shifting would not be engaged in unethical behavior.

F   86.   Your college of business is sponsoring a case competition. All teams must watch the other teams compete. The order of presentation is by luck of a draw. The team that is the last to present left during one of the presentations, went to the computer room and redid its Powerpoint slides and restructured its presentation based on what other teams had presented. This team has done nothing wrong.

F   87.   Ethical codes for companies cannot apply internationally.

F   88.   Bribes to government officials are only unethical if the culture of a country does not believe they are unethical.

T   89.   Intentional breach of a contract carries a legal remedy, but it is also unethical.

T   90.   Conduct may comply with the law but still be unethical.

T   91.   The failure to disclose material information in negotiations is an ethical breach.

T   92.   Following positive law is not the full extent of ethics.

F   93.   It is not your responsibility to report a co-worker who leaves the office early each day without taking time off.

F   94.   Using things of minimal value that belong to your employer for personal reasons (such as paper, paper clips, pens) is not an ethical violation.

T 95. You should disclose to your employer if a relative of yours has submitted a bid for work with your company.

T 96. It is an ethical violation to disclose personnel information about your co-workers even to your family.

F 97. If you are fired from your job, you can use any information you gained while employed to help your next employer.

F 98. You need not disclose in your employment application those positions you held which will not result in good feedback about you if your supervisors there are contacted.

F 99. Violation of company rules is not considered an ethical violation.

T 100. Employee hotlines exist to help employees who feel they cannot communicate concerns through the lines of authority.

F 101. A false impression, unlike lying, is not an ethical violation.

T 102. A county commissioner who makes decisions on construction permits and zoning exceptions and approaches a hotel builder to lease space for her clothing store in his new hotel while his application for zoning and construction are pending has done nothing unethical.

T 103. Albert Carr likens business to a poker game.

F 104. The "Parable of the Sadhu" is an essay in support of the theory of survival of the fittest.

F 105. Violation of company rules would not be considered an ethical violation.

Multiple Choice

1. Which of the following phrases does <u>not</u> signal a potential ethical pitfall?

    a. "That's the way it's always been done."
    b. "If we don't do it, someone else will."
    c. "Your job is to be a team player, not ask questions."
    <u>d. All of the above signal an ethical pitfall.</u>

2. Which of the following is not an element of the Laura Nash's model for evaluating ethical dilemmas?

    <u>a. Is it legal?</u>
    b. How would I feel if I were on the other side of the fence?
    c. How will my actions be perceived?
    d. Could I discuss my decision with my boss, CEO, family, friends?

3. Under the Blanchard/Peale model, which of the following statements is correct?

    a. If it's legal, it's ethical.
    b. If it's illegal, it's unethical.
    c. If it's balanced, even if it is illegal, it is ethical.
    d. None of the above.

4. Which of the following statements is correct with respect to the correlation between ethical practices and earnings?

    a. There is no correlation between ethical practices and earnings.
    b. There is a short-term correlation between higher earnings and ethical practices.
    c. There is a long-term correlation between higher earnings and ethical practices.
    d. There is both a short-term and long-term correlation between lower earnings and ethical practices.

5. Ben Small, a sole practitioner, has just decided to form a law partnership with his lifetime friend, Harvey Steptoe. They agree to name the firm Steptoe and Small and to split all profits. Ben is also a director for a publicly-traded telecommunications firm, NewVector, Inc. Ben has just learned that Harvey is lead counsel is a lawsuit against NewVector. Ben continues to serve as a board member and participates in sensitive discussions about the lawsuit. Ben does not disclose that Steptoe is his partner. Ben's feeling is that he and Harvey are as honest as the day is long and neither would compromise their duties to NewVector and client, respectively.

    a. Ben has a conflict of interest and must either resign as a director or leave the partnership.
    b. The pledge of both Ben and Harvey is sufficient to cover the ethical issues on conflict.
    c. It is Harvey's obligation to take action, not Ben's.
    d. None of the above.

6. Randy White is the executive director of a non-profit preschool for special needs children. Part of Randy's responsibilities include fundraising for the preschool. Because of his experience and success in operating specialty pre-schools, Randy is sought after as a consultant at locations around the country to assist in the start-up and operation of such facilities. Randy does so quite frequently. Randy does not take vacation time for this work, and his consultant fees (which range from $750 - $1500 per day) are kept by him as personal income. Randy uses his secretary at the preschool to book his travel arrangements and prepare his consultant reports and bills for these outside engagements.

    a. Randy's activities are ethical so long as disclosed.
    b. Randy is using the time and resources of his employer in an unethical manner.
    c. Randy's activities are ethical whether disclosed or undisclosed.
    d. There is no conflict of interest in Randy's activities.

7. Beth Williams is an exercise physiologist who serves as an expert consultant for Women's Walkers, Inc., a shoe company specializing in manufacturing walking shoes for women. Dr. Williams is paid an annual consulting fee along with additional fees for drafting reports and making media and public appearances for the company. *Executive Woman*, a national magazine, has asked Dr. Williams to serve as one of three experts on a panel that will evaluate the full market range of women's walking shoes. Dr. Williams will be paid a consulting fee by *Executive Woman* as well.

    a. <u>Dr. Williams has a conflict of interest and should decline the *Executive Woman* offer.</u>
    b. Dr. Williams can participate in the *Executive Woman* panel so long as her affiliation with Women's Walkers is disclosed.
    c. Dr. Williams can participate in the *Executive Woman* panel if she waives her fee.
    d. Dr. Williams is an academic with no conflict of interest and can participate in the *Executive Woman* panel.

8. Which of the following is not a conflict of interest?

    a. A doctor's referral of a patient to an x-ray lab that he owns for a full work-up without disclosing his ownership interest.
    b. A purchasing agent's failure to disclose a 22% ownership interest in a supplier that would be chosen anyway.
    c. A bank officer's solicitation of a charitable contribution for a non-profit organization of which he is a member from a customer with a large line of credit up for renewal in 30 days.
    d. <u>All of the above are conflicts of interest.</u>

9. Jeff Sanders, head of finance for Components, Inc. has just interviewed Laura Dern, an employee from the finance department of InChip, Components' chief competitor. Laura has explained that she has been passed over one too many times for a promotion at InChip and is thus in the job market. As Laura is leaving she whispers to Jeff, "Look, I have no contract at InChip that obligates me in anyway. I can begin immediately. Further, I have been able to obtain copies of our newest computer chip designs. You'll have them before InChip even begins production."

    a. Jeff should hire Laura on the spot without any worries about ethical breaches since Laura is not under contract.
    b. Jeff's hiring of Laura may constitute an ethical breach, but would not constitute illegal conduct.
    c. <u>Jeff should not hire Laura, and must analyze the issue of whether to disclose Laura's conduct to InChip.</u>
    d. Jeff should not hire Laura and need not worry about Laura's conduct and its impact on InChip.

10. An application for graduate school admission at Arizona State University includes the following request for information:

Please list all institutions attended since graduation from high school.

Marie Davis, a returning student, is applying for admissions to the Masters in Architecture program. Marie attended the University of Arizona for one semester in 1976. Marie had a substance abuse problem and did not attend many of her classes. She left the University of Arizona before classes ended that semester. She did not take her final exams and earned 15 credit hours of "E" for that semester. After 8 years, the policy of the University of Arizona is to expunge the records of non-matriculating students. Marie's record was expunged in December 1994.

a. Marie need not disclose her attendance at the University of Arizona.
b. _Marie should disclose her attendance at the University of Arizona._
c. Since Marie did not matriculate according to the University, she did not attend the University of Arizona.
d. None of the above.

11. A radar detector:

a. if purchased legally, is not an unethical device.
b. if used only in those states in which they are permitted is an ethical device.
c. is a legal and ethical tool for circumventing speed limits.
d. _None of the above._

12. The sale of a product with a known defect or with knowledge of its potentially harmful impact on users:

a. is illegal.
b. is unethical.
c. exposes the manufacturer to strict and negligent product liability.
d. _Both b and c._

13. Which of the following employment tests would be illegal?

a. _Pre-employment lie detector screening_
b. Drug testing for delivery van drivers
c. Handwriting analysis
d. All of the above are illegal.

14. Which of the following is an exception to the employment at will doctrine?

a. More than 10 years employment
b. A recent evaluation of performance that is generally favorable
c. _Whistle-blowing activity by the employee_
d. All of the above.

15. Which of the following would be both legal and ethical acts in an international operations?

    a. Offering to pay a regulator for a favorable inspection report
    b. Offering to pay a police officer for not writing a ticket
    c. Offering to pay a government employee extra to speed up phone service connections
    d. None of the above.

16. You work in the finance division of a NYSE company. You have just learned that your supervisor has been using information on quarterly returns, prior to the time they are made public, to trade in the company's stock. You:

    a. need not do anything because the SEC will eventually uncover his activities.
    b. need not do anything because only officers are prohibited from trading on inside information.
    c. must confront the supervisor.
    d. must report the activity in some way.

17. You have witnessed one of your co-workers engaged in behavior that constitutes sexual harassment of one of the department secretaries. The secretary has spoken with you about the behavior and her concerns. She has also said, "Let me handle it." It seems that she is not able to handle it because the behavior has continued. You should:

    a. talk with her again.
    b. report the behavior.
    c. talk with your co-worker.
    d. Any of the above.

18. You are a sales associate with a large department store chain. You have noticed that a fellow sales associate has been taking high-ticket items home with her. You have checked the sales records and she has not been paying for the items. You should:

    a. ignore the conduct because it is not your business.
    b. ignore the conduct because she will be caught eventually.
    c. confront her with your knowledge.
    d. report her conduct to the police.

19. A professor for one of your courses has assigned reading materials from various publications. He tells you that the materials are on reserve and that each student should go and copy the materials individually. He notes that for him to copy the materials for students and then sell them or distribute them would be a violation of copyright law. The professor's conduct:

    a. is unethical and violates copyright law as well.
    b. is something everyone does and is accepted behavior.
    c. does not really harm anyone.
    d. is acceptable in an academic setting.

20. You had quite a night last night of partying. Because of excessive drinking, you are unable to get to work today. When you call your supervisor you:

    a. should just say you have the flu.
    b. should just say you are sick.
    c. should disclose the prior night's activity.
    d. None of the above.

21. You are at lunch when you notice one of your firm's delivery drivers sitting at the bar in the restaurant. The driver is having shots of tequila over the course of the lunch hour. He then returns to his truck in the parking lot and resumes deliveries. You:

    a. should stop the driver.
    b. should report the driver.
    c. should take the keys to the truck.
    d. should do all of the above.

Short Answer/Essay

1. Dr. Phil Hayes has received an offer of full funding for his research on a new drug manufactured by Eli Mentin. The drug would be a competitor for Prozac without the questioned side-effects of possible violent behavior. Eli Mentin has, however, attached a condition to the funding. That condition is that Dr. Hayes may not publish his findings until Eli Mentin executives and its attorneys have had the opportunity to review them.

   List the ethical issues Dr. Hayes faces with this offer.

   SUGGESTED ANSWER:

   Dr. Hayes is creating a conflict of interest for himself and possible sacrificing the perceived independence of his work.

   Eli Mentin is compromising the integrity of Hayes' research and potentially withholding information about the product and its safety.

   Eli Mentin's approach is not one of candor and compromises the ethical values of honesty, fairness and safety.

2. Data Processing, Inc. is a service firm that performs word processing functions for law firms, corporations and government agencies. Their facilities consist of 120 office units with a word processor in each unit. Their facilities were formerly a shoe manufacturing plant, and all of the office units are located in one large room. Over the past 14 months, 7 of the 120 word processors have been diagnosed with breast cancer. In six of the seven cases diagnosed, there is no family history of breast cancer. Jane Quinn, the owner and CEO of data processing, has seen a cluster study that links employment as a word processor to a higher rate of breast cancer. Ms. Quinn does not disclose the study to her employees and takes no further action. Discuss the ethical issues.

SUGGESTED ANSWER:

Ms. Quinn has knowledge of a potential harm and is withholding information.

Doing nothing does not solve the problem or minimize risk. At a minimum an investigation is warranted. Safety, fairness, honesty, balance and long-term survival of the employees and the firm are at issue.

3. National Medical Enterprises, Inc. (NME) is a multinational health care enterprise with 143 hospitals on four continents. NME was started by Richard K. Eamer, a tax attorney, in the 1960s. Eamer's development of NME was possible because of the implementation of the Medicare and Medicaid programs. He saw the programs as opportunities for a virtual guarantee of profits.

He began by acquiring six hospitals. He paid for these hospitals with promises to the physicians on staff of stock in his company. After the six hospitals were acquired, Eamer did a $25 million national stock offering and gave the physicians shares of stock in NME.

Eamer adopted a decentralized structure for the company. Hospital managers were simply given a financial goal and complete autonomy in their operations. Eamer traveled a great deal and used a company plane to get to NME-owned condominiums in London and Aspen. While Eamer was not a hands-on manager, he set very clear goals for NME managers. Achievement of established goals was rewarded. Under NME's pay structure, it was possible for managers to double their pay by meeting goals. Eamer was harsh when goals were not met. In meetings he would refer to those executives who had failed to meet established goals as "morons."

Eamer's managerial style paid off in the form of earnings growth of 15% per year through 1985. But, in 1986, earnings growth was off, down to 3%. When informed by his managers of the decline in earnings growth, Eamer announced that NME would now focus on operating and acquiring psychiatric, substance-abuse and rehabilitation hospitals. NME had 62 psychiatric hospitals in 1986, but by 1991, that number had grown to 86. Further, NME occupancy rates for its psychiatric hospitals were 25% higher than any of its competitors. NME maintained an occupancy rate of 84%.

The director of NME's Fair Oaks Hospital in New Jersey, testified at a Congressional hearing that NME executives circulated information on how to maximize insurance payments. Strategies included longer stays and additional tests.

NME's intake manual specified as a goal that one of every two people who came to the hospital for a psychological assessment would be hospitalized. Some adolescent patients were billed for as many as 10 therapy sessions per day. A memo from one senior officer to the various NME hospitals stated that the length of a patient's stay would be determined "not by the patient's individual medical needs, but on the insurance or payor mix."

A controller for an NME hospital in Texas testified that probation officers, clergymen and officers in corporation employee-assistance offices were offered up to $2,000 in referral or "bounty hunter fees" for referring patients to NME. The controller also testified that he was required to make "cold calls" on facilities for purposes of soliciting referrals. He indicated that one of his cold calls was to a nursery school.

Former executives of NME have provided information showing that physicians were given 50-year leases for $1 per year by NME and then referred their patients exclusively to NME hospitals. Many of these physician-occupied buildings operated at a loss. Both Medicare and Medicaid regulations prohibit payment of referrals fees to physicians.

By 1991, occupancy rates at NME psychiatric hospitals were down to 52%. Eamer began selling of the psychiatric hospitals and announced to shareholders than NME would return its focus to its core 35 general hospitals. In announcing the refocus to shareholder, Eamer noted, "Our focus is on the patient. We know everything else will follow."

a. What type of ethical culture existed at NME? Why?

b. What does NME need to change?

c. Do you think NME's strategies with respect to the psychiatric hospitals were ethical?

d. Evaluate the ethics of clergymen, counselors, and probation officers accepting referral fees.

SUGGESTED ANSWERS:

a. NME had a culture very much focused on earnings. Bonuses were tied to financial goals and achievement of occupancy rates. The quality of care and the needs of the patients were strictly sub-issues to the issue of earnings. It was also a culture that came as close to breaking the law as one can. The rent subsidies to physicians were arguable violations of the law. Further, the tolerance for less-than-goal performance was non-existent. In fact, managers were treated as "morons" for not achieving their goals. The focus in this company's culture was so much on earnings growth that the message came across as "earnings at any cost."

b. NME needs to change its "earnings at any cost" approach. Eamer may also need to be replaced as at least a symbol of the company's refocus. Its admissions policies, referral practices and discharge standards need to be set with a focus on the law and patients' needs as opposed to financial goals exclusively.

c. No, NME's standards could not survive the front page of the newspaper test. NME's approach was earnings at any cost. The approach was not balanced and, in some cases, bordered on illegality. NME treated hospitalization for psychiatric needs as a potential sales market to be tapped through sales calls and referrals.

d. The members of the clergy, the counselors and the probation officers have conflicts of interest. They are to be acting in the best interests of their clients and by accepting referral fees they have an interest in seeing as many of them hospitalized as possible. Further, they would have an interest in their patients going to a certain hospital as opposed to a referral to the facility that would be best for the patient.

4. Susan Wade is the president of the Illinois Hospice Organization (IHO). IHO is a state organization affiliated with a national non-profit organization, the National Hospice Organization. Both the state and national organizations have members from both for-profit and non-profits hospices. Susan Wade is the director of a non-profit hospice in Illinois. A Chicago newspaper has printed a story about hospices and what they do. Susan was interviewed extensively for the piece. In one quote in the article, Susan expressed her concerns about for-profit hospices. "It has become the sort of franchise of the decade. They're not all bad, but I think the original spirit of hospice is becoming very adulterated. There's one time in a person's life when he shouldn't be looked at as a number, as a piece of an actuarial problem. If your first and last priority is making money, it flies in the face of what hospice is all about. It's the end of the health-care chain. It's the place of last hope for patients. Dollars should not be the issue here."

A chief operating officer of a for-profit hospice has written to Susan complaining that her remarks are libelous and misinform the public about for-profit hospices.

a. Does Ms. Wade have a conflict of interest?

b. Is Ms. Wade properly executing her role as the president of the state organization?

SUGGESTED ANSWERS:

a. Ms. Wade has a conflict of interest in the sense that as president of the state organization she represents all members and should not speak favorably of one type of member and unfavorably about another type. It is not, however, the traditional type of conflict of interest in which she benefits. Ms. Wade works for a non-profit institution and discussing the problem of for-profit will not change whether she has a job. The remarks could have an impact on how many patients her hospice has, but because of the non-profit nature, there is no financial gain to her.

b. As an elected representative, Susan should represent all members and not divide the organization or question the motives of some members. Perhaps her issues that she raised for the newspaper stories could be topics of seminars and debates for the members. But she should not be in a position, because of her role as president, to use opportunities with the media to lessen the standing of some members of the organization.

5. James and Jennifer Stolpa and their five-month old son, Clayton, were stranded outdoors in a snowstorm for 8 days. They were rescued after James left Jennifer and Clayton in a cave and hiked 30 miles in subfreezing temperatures to get help.

    During the time they were stranded, the Stolpas ate Doritos-brand corn chips that they had with them in their car. When they were rescued and taken to the Washoe Medical Center for treatment of severe frostbite, they were visited by boxing champ, George Foreman. Mr. Foreman is a spokesperson for Doritos. His visit to the Stolpas earned national press and television coverage that emphasized the Doritos consumption.

    If you were an executive with Doritos, would you have sent Mr. Foreman to the hospital?

    SUGGESTED ANSWER:

    The issues here are that of privacy and propriety. The chip maker would be capitalizing on the injuries and suffering of a family with a fairly peripheral fact that they happened to have Doritos in the car. The family can consent to Mr. Foreman's appearance and the cameras rolling, but it is a fairly intense situation for them. The added sales from eating the same chips the stranded family did may not be as significant as the marketing folks may believe.

6. Henry Rauzi, the controller for Sunbeam, issued an offer to Linda Croce for an entry-level accounting position at Sunbeam at a salary of $34,000 per year. Ms. Croce accepted the offer and gave notice to her employer. When then-CEO of Sunbeam, Paul Kazarian, was informed of the offer, he demanded that Mr. Rauzi rescind it because Kazarian had not approved it prior to it being made. Mr. Rauzi called Ms. Croce at 10:00 P.M. three days before she was scheduled to being work and told her of Mr. Kazarian's action. Ms. Croce had no job and remained unemployed for several months while she searched for a new job.

    Evaluate the legality and ethics of Sunbeam's officer's actions with respect to Ms. Croce.

    SUGGESTED ANSWER:

    Apart from the obvious legal difficulty that Ms. Croce had a contract because she had already accepted the offer, there is the ethical dilemma, even without such formality, of reneging on one's word. There was a meeting of the minds and Ms. Croce relied on the promise in quitting her other job. The fact that an internal error in reporting lines was made should not affect the extension of the offer to Ms. Croce. Ms. Croce had no way of knowing that there were limitations on Mr. Rauzi's authority. Certainly she had no way of knowing that he could not issue an offer. Sunbeam's actions with respect to Ms. Croce were unfair, unbalanced and unethical.

7. In 1991, James McElveen fell 30 feet from a waterfall and broke his back. He was employed by a small business and had no medical insurance. His

lifetime friend, Benny Milligan, was with him when the fall occurred. Benny took James to the emergency room. Moved by his friend's severe injuries and pain and suffering and realizing that James did not have insurance, Benny switched IDs with James in the hospital emergency room. James required surgery to fuse his back to avoid what doctors said would have been certain paralysis. The cost of the surgery and hospitalization was $41,107.45. Neither James, employed as a mechanic, nor Benny, employed as a painter, could have paid for the surgery and follow-up care. Benny's employer's insurance paid for the surgery because the hospital took the information from Benny's ID found in James' pockets.

While Benny was contemplating telling his employer, someone notified the insurance company of the switch. Benny, James, and Benny's wife, Tammy Milligan were charged and convicted of mail fraud, wire fraud and conspiracy. Tammy, because of the Milligans' three young daughters, is serving her sentence through home confinement, Benny is serving 9 months and James is serving 7 months. All three were serve three years on probation and pay restitution.

Benny states, "I know what I did was wrong. But I look back on it, and I feel that I had to do it at the time. I don't feel like I'm a criminal in the sense of rapers, muggers and murderers." Benny said he did not understand that a hospital has an obligation to treat someone who is dying. Friends testified that as they were racing James to the hospital they told Benny that hospitals in the area had routinely refused to provide medical treatment.

Benny said he wanted to tell his employer, but he was afraid he would be fired and then be stuck with the bill. Tammy adds that the government is right to demand restitution but wrong to imprison them. James asked the judge if he could go to prison for all three of them, "I would be lost without my friendship with Benny. I probably would be dead."

a. Benny and James committed an illegal act. Was it unethical?

b. What punishment is appropriate in the case?

c. If you were Benny's employer, what would you have done?

SUGGESTED ANSWERS:

a. It was wrong and illegal to defraud the insurance company. It was taking the costs of the medical care, something that did not belong to James. Although the case evokes a great deal of sympathy, we all pay the cost when someone who is not insured enjoys payment by an insurer. The harm comes in the form of higher payments for all of us. Benny, James and Tammy all had to lie and sign sworn statements that were untrue in order for James' surgery to be covered under Benny' insurance. They committed their acts in the name of something very important, but it was wrong.

Benny defined the problem incorrectly: it was either switch IDs or have his friend suffer. In fact, there were alternatives, but Benny did not think them through. James would have received his emergency treatment at the first hospital. If the surgery was not something necessary to preserve his life, he would have been transferred to another hospital, such as a county hospital, where care is provided without regard to whether the individual has insurance. No one was asking questions about the care. They made assumptions and committed fraud to be certain there was medical care.

b. While the fact that there was lying and fraud involved cannot be changed, the circumstances, as well as Benny's misunderstanding about the availability of medical care, should have some impact on the punishment for the three individuals. It is proper and fair to require reimbursement. However, Benny's lack of criminal intent should be considered as a factor in determining whether jail time is appropriate. Some other form of punishment such as restitution along with community service or the funding of a program of medical insurance coverage for those without would seem to suit the situation better than imprisonment.

c. Benny's employer probably had little choice but to report the problem because the impact on its insurance costs was perhaps tremendous because of the extensive nature of the injury and care. The employer could not be expected to lie to the insurer about Benny's presence at work after such major surgery. In short, the employer could not be asked to participate in the fraud. However, the employer could have served as a character witness if Benny was a good and stable employee. Further, the employer might have been more understanding about Benny's motivations. On the other hand, from the employer's perspective, it is difficult to send a strong message to employees about insurance fraud if Benny is retained.

8. Althea Caldwell is the director of Arizona's Department of Health Services (DHS). DHS is charged the administration of the state's behavioral health system and is responsible for contracting with private providers for millions of dollars of mental health care each year for eligible patients.

Ms. Caldwell accepted a $20,000 per year director position for a hospital group corporation. One of the hospitals in the group was one to which state contracts for mental health treatment had been awarded.

One month after accepting the position, Ms. Caldwell asked the state's attorney general for an opinion as to whether she had a conflict of interest.

Does Ms. Caldwell have a conflict of interest?

SUGGESTED ANSWER:

Ms. Caldwell has a classic textbook conflict of interest. You cannot be the state official responsible for awarding conflicts AND the director of a company that owns one of the facilities bidding for those contracts. The $20,000 is a quid pro quo -- a position awarded with compensation with the hope of gaining an edge in the state agency's award of contracts.

160

9. Stanford University medical researchers conducted a study on the correlation between the use of fertility drugs and ovarian cancer. Their study, published in the *American Journal of Epidemiology*, concludes that the use of the fertility drugs, Pergonal and Serophene, may increase the risk of ovarian cancer by three times. The lead author of the studies, Professor Alice Whittemore, stated, "Our finding in regard to fertility drugs is by no means certain. It is based on very small numbers and is really very tenuous."

    FDA Commissioner David Kessler would like the infertility drug manufacturers to disclose the study findings and offer a warning on the drug packages. He notes, "Even though the epidemiology study is still preliminary, women have a right to know what is known. We're not looking to make more of this than there is."

    If you were a manufacturer of one of the drugs, would you voluntarily disclose the study information?

    SUGGESTED ANSWER:

    Given the history of asbestos, the breast implants, the Dalkon shield and other products covered in the text, it is not difficult to spot a similar pattern here. Although the law may not require disclosure, the ethical tests of balance and "how would you want to be treated?" point manufacturers in the direction of disclosure. Full market information requires that buyers make choices based on full disclosure. Without the study information, making those decisions becomes one-sided. The drug firm has more information that is not available to their purchasers. Further, the history of the cases mentioned demonstrates that firms are always better off financially if they make the disclosure and allow the market to function than if they withhold the information and must later defend product liability suits. The disclosure should be made not only from an ethical perspective but also from a financial and litigation perspective.

10. Raymond Randall is an attorney with the Federal Trade Commission. A 19-year veteran with the agency, Mr. Randall was known as a good trial attorney. The FTC charged William Farley, the chairman of Fruit of the Loom, Inc., with violations of the reporting provisions of the Hart-Scott-Rodino Act, when he purchased shares of West Point-Pepperell Corporations prior to a Fruit of the Loom takeover bid. The Hart-Scott-Rodino Act requires investors to notify the government when their holdings in a firm pass $15 million.

    The FTC sought a fine of $10,000 per day against Mr. Farley, for a total of $910,000. Mr. Farley did notify the FTC once Fruit of the Loom made its decision to acquire West Point-Pepperell. Randall was assigned the Farley case. The FTC took a position of refusing to disclose to Farley and his attorneys documents relating to the case. Mr. Randall felt that the documents pointed to weaknesses in the FTC case and supported Mr. Farley's point that he notified the FTC once the takeover position was announced. Mr. Randall leaked the documents to Mr. Farley's lawyer.

Mr. Farley's lawyers were concerned that they should not be in possession of government documents returned the documents and resigned from the case because they had seen the documents. Mr. Farley's new attorneys went to court demanding production of the documents. The documents were ordered produced by the court. When the FTC refused to produce them, the case against Mr. Farley was dismissed by a federal district judge.

a. Did Mr. Randall do the right thing in disclosing the documents to Farley's attorneys?

b. Did Mr. Farley's lawyers do the right thing in returning the documents to the FTC?

SUGGESTED ANSWERS:

a. Mr. Randall was engaged in a form of civil disobedience. He knew that the documents were government property and enjoyed the protection of the courts, but he also felt that Mr. Farley was being prosecuted without sufficient evidence. Mr. Randall's principles, values and ethics took control of the situation and he sent the documents as a means of allowing Mr. Farley access to the information. It is important to note that Mr. Randall's action should have been his last choice. Did he go to those within the agency and attempt to resolve the problem? He should also consider his loyalty to his employer and his responsibilities as an attorney before taking the action that he did which was a form of civil disobedience.

b. Mr. Farley's attorneys acted with the utmost integrity in returning the documents and resigning from the case. They made some difficult choices and not only followed the law but then resigned from the case because they had seen things they were not permitted to see. Their forthright actions probably helped Mr. Farley with the court and provided great credibility for Mr. Farley and his new attorneys as they successfully pursued the dismissal.

11. Joseph Horne Company, a Pittsburgh department store chain, was the target of a management leveraged buyout in 1986 and was suffering with the resultant $160 million in debt.

Horne executives were relieved when, in 1988, Dillard Department Stores, Inc., and mall developer Edward J. DeBartolo agreed to buy Horne's stock for $74 million and to assume the 1986 buyout debt.

As part of the deal, Dillard's installed data lines and computers in Horne's fourteen stores to prepare for the consolidation. With the stores hooked into its Little Rock, Arkansas, headquarters, Dillard's assumed control of Horne's merchandise purchasing.

Dillard's executives wanted financial and purchasing control because the contract price was contingent upon a finding that Horne's financial statements were accurate. Horne's CEO, Robert A. O'Connell, voiced his concerns to E. Ray Kemp, Dillard's vice chairman, about the extent and speed of Dillard's assumption of control. Kemp told O'Connell, "Trust me,

162

it would take an act of God for this deal not to go through."

Dillard's had been acquiring department stores like Horne's all over the country, adding 196 stores in five years. From 1987-1991 Dillard's earnings had gained 20 percent through its strategy of taking over financially troubled firms.

In 1990, however, Dillard's deal with Horne's fell through, and Horne sued Dillard's and DeBartolo for breach of contract and fraud. Horne's suit alleged that Dillard's plan in taking over the buying and data was to decrease the value of Horne's to get a bargain price.

Experts in the industry indicate that Horne demonstrated inexperience by allowing Dillard's rapid infiltration. The contract provided that Horne could veto any proposal for Dillard activity in Horne's business.

Between the time the contract was negotiated and Dillard's cancellation of the agreement, Dillard's executives found that some Horne accounting practices were questionable. But some industry experts and Horne executives said Dillard's often "nickels and dimes" sellers to bring down the price.

Horne's suit also alleged that Dillard's told 500 employees that their jobs would be gone after the takeover. Thirty percent of those employees quit before Dillard's and DeBartolo withdrew. Because Dillard's took over merchandise buying, Horne maintained, merchandise deliveries were late and the wrong merchandise was ordered for critical periods, such as the holiday season.

A Pittsburgh National Bank officer testified in his deposition in the suit that a Dillard's executive told him in 1988 that Dillard's might wait until Horne's bankruptcy to buy the company. Dillard's denies the statement and the plan. Dillard's and Horne's settled the suit in 1992.

a. Were the damages Horne's experienced just a consequence of a failed business deal?

b. Did Dillard's take advantage of a debt-ridden company?

c. What financial-disclosure obligations do takeover targets have?

d. Did Dillard's have any special obligations because of its access to Horne's data and buying power?

e. Is it unethical to take advantage of a naive party in a commercial transaction?

SUGGESTED ANSWERS:

a. Horne's damages were something more than a failed takeover. Horne's, perhaps naively, allowed too much infiltration of its organization and experienced too much loss of authority along with too poor management of its orders and merchandise. Dillard's perhaps because of its

163

experience, may have gone too far in conducting its due diligence and may have become too involved in Horne's operations.

b. Dillard's is a large company with extensive experience in takeovers. Horne's is a local company with no experience in takeovers. Dillard's was able to take over the books as part of its due diligence examination, but was also able to assume a management role prior to the actual takeover. Horne's was probably naive in terms of the extent to which Dillard's could take over in performing its due diligence. Horne's was anxious to have the takeover and may have been willing to do more than it was required to do with respect to the books, records and management control.

c. Horne's did have to surrender access to its books and records, but did not have to surrender management control of purchasing and other functions. The due diligence portion of a takeover is a means by which the offeror (Dillard's) can examine the books and records to verify the financial information furnished by the takeover target (Horne's).

d. Dillard's had a duty of trust imposed by its experience and the tentative nature of the takeover. It was not proper to take over the functioning of Horne's nor interfere with its management structure until the deal was completed. Due diligence does not authorize assumption of responsibility for management of the firm. While Horne's could have objected to Dillard's conduct at any time, it apparently was not experienced enough to know that such conduct was unusual prior to closure.

e. Many business people argue that they hire experts: lawyers, accountants, to do just that -- find the technicalities to minimize cost and maximize returns. From an ethical perspective, the long-term views should be: how long do I want this relationship to last? What will my reputation in the industry be?

12. Lee Iacocca, chairman and CEO of Chrysler Corporation, announced on January 27, 1988, that the automaker would be closing its Kenosha, Wisconsin, plant. Iacocca and his board of directors were under significant pressure from shareholders due to Chrysler's continuing poor financial performance. Chrysler had acquired the Kenosha plant when it purchased American Motors Corporation in 1987. In his announcement, Iacocca blamed national trade policy for Chrysler's declining sales and resultant earnings problems.

At the Kenosha plant, which manufactured the Dodge Omni and the Plymouth Horizon, 5,500 of the 6,500 workers were to be laid off and production moved to a Detroit plant. Kenosha, a city of 77,000 on the shores of Lake Michigan, depended heavily on Chrysler's presence.

The announcement of the closing came at a critical time. Chrysler was negotiating to renew its contract with the United Auto Workers (UAW). Also, the Kenosha plant carried a history of union financial assistance. The UAW had loaned American Motors over $60 million to keep the Kenosha plant running, and Chrysler had assumed the loan obligations as part of the acquisition. Also, Wisconsin had paid $5 million for job training at the Kenosha plant in 1987 after Chrysler promised that the plant would build Omnis and Horizons for at least five more years.

Peter Pfaff, a member of the UAW Local 72 of Kenosha and an employee at the plant since 1972, said: "I was there. We've got it on tape and in writing. They said they'd stay. Greenwald (then Chrysler Motors chairman) keeps saying Chrysler never said that, but I was there when he said it."

The Kenosha local threatened to delay negotiations on renewing the national contract with 64,000 workers. After the threat, Iacocca announced that Chrysler would establish a $20 million trust fund to aid the 5,500 Kenosha workers through housing payments and educational funding. This fund would be in addition to severance pay, extended unemployment benefits, and repayment of the UAW loans. While denying that Chrysler was setting a precedent, Iacocca declared it had a "moral obligation" to Kenosha.

Wisconsin threatened to sue Chrysler over the job training program but agreed to hold off in exchange for Iacocca's promise to extend production at the plant for several months into the fall of 1988.

Iacocca stated that Chrysler was "guilty as hell of being cockeyed optimists. Blame us for being dumb managers, for spending $200 million to put two old cars (the Chrysler Fifth Avenue and the Dodge Diplomat) in an eighty-six-year-old plant, but please don't call me a liar when I've got to close it sooner than I thought." Iacocca sought congressional support for converting the Kenosha plant to defense work by Chrysler.

Chrysler and the UAW negotiated a contract that provided additional unemployment benefits for the 5,500 laid-off workers and more job security for the 1,000 workers who would transfer to other Chrysler operations. Ultimately, the plant closing resulted in 3,700 layoffs.

By mid-1990, Kenosha was enjoying unprecedented economic growth. At a July 1990 ceremony in which engineers detonated explosives to destroy the 250-foot-high smokestack of the Chrysler plant, dignitaries and former workers cheered. Kenosha resident T. R. Garcia said at the blasting, "I think it's about time they got rid of it. What we need to do is develop the lake front, and this thing is the last to leave." City planner Ray Forgianni, Jr., added, "The community's image is probably the best it's been in 100 years. The closing was almost like a catalyst. The handwriting was on the wall—the economy needed to diversify."

a. Did Chrysler have a moral obligation to the Kenosha workers and Wisconsin, or was it just responding to pressure?

b. Do arrangements like Chrysler had with the UAW loans and Wisconsin interfere with the ability to make business decisions? Review Iacocca's quote on business mistakes as you evaluate the issue.

c. Were the shareholders required to pay twice for the closing—once in severance pay and again in extended benefits?

d. Was Chrysler simply putting its duty to shareholders above its duty to Wisconsin, Kenosha, and its workers? Is this proper? Is it ethical?

e. Was Chrysler's action just a catalyst for needed economic development?

f. Iacocca, after having stepped down as chairman of Chrysler, made a takeover offer for Chrysler in 1995. What would Chrysler's ethical culture be like if Mr. Iacocca had succeeded in his takeover bid?

SUGGESTED ANSWERS:

a. There are differing schools of thought in ethics regarding the obligation of employers who close down plants to the workers from that plant and the communities in which they are located. One group imposes an obligation on the employer to leave the town whole. This obligation requires placement of the workers and economic redevelopment of the community all at the employer's cost with some contributions from governmental entities.

Another school of thought sees such additional obligations as a double tax to shareholders. Not only must they bear the cost of the cutbacks and economic downturn, they must now ensure that the workers and the community do not have to share in such losses. This view advances the notion that workers are always insulated from financial losses and economic downturns and may not have the appropriate incentives to retool.

b. Obligations to restore the workers and communities add costs to downsizing and prevent flexibility in making allocation and resource decisions. An additional cost is added to becoming more efficient and the incentives may make it easier to remain inefficient.

c. The rights of shareholders are often ignored in the interest of protecting the employees and communities. On the other hand, the communities give the employers the right to use the air and water sheds and the opportunity to benefit from the support of the government resources and often tax breaks.

d. Yes, Chrysler defined its duty as first and foremost to its shareholders. Businesses do have a primary obligation to their investors, but Chrysler did take on more investors here (community).

e. Chrysler's withdrawal may have ultimately benefitted the community.

f. Mr. Iacocca's focus would be on Chrysler's earnings. There are ethical risks with such a focus.

13. Leslie Fay Companies was a clothing conglomerate that produced lines of women's clothing and lingerie under the brand names Leslie Fay, Joan Leslie, Albert Nipon, Theo Miles, Kasper, Le Suit, Nolan Miller, Castleberry, and Castlebrook. In early 1993, it was discovered that senior Leslie Fay executives, in an effort to inflate profits and to mask an actual loss of $13.7 million, had perpetrated an accounting fraud. Paul

Polishan, Leslie Fay's chief operating officer, was placed on leave without pay in January 1993, along with Donald F. Kenia, the corporate controller. Mr. Kenia had first alerted the company to the accounting manipulations and worked with auditors to untangle the books.

By April 1993, Leslie Fay, under intense pressure from creditors, filed for Chapter 11 bankruptcy (reorganization) in Manhattan. Both Mr. Polishan and Mr. Kenia were fired. Mr. Kenia, charged with two counts of filing false statements with the SEC, has entered into a plea bargain with the U.S. Attorney in exchange for his cooperation in the continuing investigation of the Leslie Fay accounting improprieties.

Also in April 1993, two new outside directors were named to the Leslie Fay board. The audit committee of the board discovered, through continuing investigation, that accounting irregularities had inflated the company's profits for at least five quarters beginning in the fall of 1990.

As Leslie Fay continued its climb from bankruptcy, it was discovered that its law firm, Weil Gotshall & Manges, had failed to disclose its close ties to two board audit committee members. A federal bankruptcy judge ordered the law firm to pay fines totaling $800,000, which was the cost of having an independent review of the law firm's representation and conduct in the case.

In March 1995, Leslie Fay placed its flagship dress and retail business up for sale and offered its CEO a success fee of $1.5 million if those businesses were sold.

Also in March 1995, a report detailing accounting improprieties was released by the audit committee of the Leslie Fay board. The board found that when executives realized they would not meet pre-established goals, they would ship goods out to a Wilkes-Barre, Pennsylvania, facility to inflate sales. The executives also forged inventory tags, multiplied the value of inventory, developed phantom inventory and altered records to meet sales target. Some goods were invoiced to be shipped in the final day of a quarter even though they were not actually shipped until the next quarter. Numerous shareholders have filed suit against the Leslie Fay board and BDO Seidman, the company's auditor during this period.

John Pomerantz continued as CEO from 1993 onward. The company has tried to find a buyer but has remained unsuccessful in doing so.

a. What signals about the importance of earnings at Leslie Fay were sent to the officers who committed the accounting improprieties?

b. Wouldn't employees have been aware of the financial fraud? Why didn't they speak up? Why didn't they tell someone?

c. How might Leslie Fay have prevented what happened?

d. If you were the new chief financial officer, what message would you most want to impress upon all Leslie Fay employees?

e. Of what significance are the law firm's ties to the board's audit committee members? Did these ties set a poor tone at the top?

SUGGESTED ANSWERS:

a. The pressure to make quarterly earnings was so intense that the officers were willing to engage in deception, fabrication, shifting of sales, etc. to meet the earnings figures.

b. Employees may very well have been aware of the fraud, but with an ethical culture in which the officers were involved, it wouldn't have done any good to speak up. In a culture such as this one, employees would be afraid to bring such matters to anyone's attention.

c. Changing the signals to officers would have helped. The intense focus on earnings and pressure to meet goals set the stage for the deception.

d. The message would be:

Earnings the Right Way
Earnings Through Sales and Satisfaction
Integrity Without Compromise

e. There are conflicts of interest. Legal counsel for a business (which owes its business and account to the company) is not a good source for audit committee members. The ties suggest "good ol' pal network" and "you scratch my back...".

Note: At the time of the discovery of the earnings misrepresentation, Leslie Fay's stock was at $13 per share. In June, 1995, the price had dropped to 13/22. Leslie Fay continues to attempt to struggle out of bankruptcy.

14. Albertson's, the grocery retailer, has the highest profit margins in the industry at 6%. A union has filed suit against Albertson's for its "off-the-clock" without pay practices with respect to manager trainees. These trainees worked 4-5 hours extra each week without pay and did not complain because of promises of progression in the organization. When progression did not materialize, the trainees returned to checking positions and their union filed a class action suit on their behalf. The potential for back pay and penalties in the case is $200 million.

Albertson's notes that some managers may prod trainees to work longer without pay but that such is not company policy.

a. Who is responsible for the "off-the-clock" policy?

b. Is it each store manager or Albertson's?

c. Is "off-the-clock" an ethical policy?

SUGGESTED ANSWERS

    a. Students should discuss management's role in encouraging the practice even though individuals decide.

    b. Students should discuss pressure for breaches.

    c. The policy takes unfair advantage of employees who wish to advance and is a technical rules violation.

15. Fifty-nine auto dealers around the country were fined $200,000 by the Department of Labor for child labor violations. The car dealers hire 16- and 17-year olds to move cars from service bays to customer pick-up areas and from lots to show rooms. They are also employed to wash cars. The teenagers move the cars literally only hundreds of feet in the process, but they are driving the cars.

Under the Fair Labor Standards Act and the federal regulations, only those employees who are age 18 or above are permitted to drive as part of job requirements. The fine for a violation is $1,100.

The Department of Labor contacted dealerships and asked for the names of their employees under the age of 18. Once the Department had the names, it contacted the young employees to question them about their job duties. Upon discovery of the driving, the dealerships were fined.

About one-half of the dealerships have paid the fines and the remainder are protesting. The result has been that dealerships will now employ only those who are 18 and older because it is impossible to have an employee responsible for washing cars and not be able to move the car. The result has been that many special job programs for minority students and students in vocational schools have been eliminated.

    a. Do you think this type of driving was intended to be covered in the child labor statutes?

    b. Are auto dealers taking advantage of children or helping them?

SUGGESTED ANSWERS:

    a. Students should discuss purposes of law and protection of children.

    b. Discussion of impact of employing teenagers: pro and con. Issue of unfair advantage is important.

16. Steven Davis, a design engineer who formerly worked for Gillette, was indicted in Nashville, Tennessee on 10 counts of theft of trade secrets and wire fraud. Mr. Davis is accused of sending faxes and e-mail messages to Gillette competitors offering to reveal the characteristics of the new Gillette shaving system that has replaced the Sensor system and was unveiled in April 1998.

Mr. Davis used an alias in the messages, but one of Gillette's

169

competitors, upon receiving the fax offering the technology alerted Gillette to the problem. Gillette then worked with federal agents who posed undercover as persons interested in the technology. As a result of the competitor's notification, not much, if anything, about the new Gillette system was revealed through Mr. Davis's efforts.

a. Discuss the ethics of Mr. Davis's conduct.

b. What do you think of Gillette's competitor refusing to take up Mr. Davis on the offer and reporting the problem to Gillette?

c. What do you think was the downside of dealing with Mr. Davis?

d. When Mr. Davis was discovered, he recontacted the competitors and chastised them for being unethical by telling authorities. What do you think of his accusation?

SUGGESTED ANSWERS:

a. He was taking something that did not belong to him.

b. The competitor was honorable.

c. You couldn't trust Mr. Davis.

d. Mr. Davis remains confused about rights and ethics. He was wrong to take the secrets - those who reported him were not wrong.

17. Peggie Jean Gambarana was a real estate investor in the Las Vegas area whose substantial holdings enabled her to become one of the community's most generous philanthropists. Upon her death, her will provided that $1.5 million in cash and property be given to the University of Nevada at Las Vegas Foundation to benefit the James R. Dickinson Library.

The $1.5 million testate donation, the largest ever for the library, included $350,000 in cash, three properties, and a leasehold interest in a souvenir shop located at Fourth and Fremont Streets in downtown Las Vegas. However, by the time the funds and properties were converted to permanent library endowments, their value had been reduced by one-third. The reduction in value was the result of three real estate deals that involved members of the foundation.

The foundation sold all three donated properties below their appraised values. The Gambarana family home was sold to Arthur Nathan, who was moving from New Jersey to become the human resources director for the Mirage Hotel. The UNLV Foundation's chairwoman, Elaine Wynn, is an executive in Mirage Resorts, Inc., and her husband, Steve Wynn, is the corporation's chairman. Nathan purchased the home, which had an appraised value of $170,000, for $157,500. Golden Nugget, Inc., which later became Mirage Resorts, Inc., loaned Nathan the funds for the purchase. Wynn said she was not involved in the negotiations:

It's possible for me to represent both interests without . . . creating a conflict of interest in this, especially since I didn't benefit personally nor did Mr. Nathan benefit personally.

Ms. Wynn signed the sale documents for the property transaction.

The second property the foundation sold was appraised at $270,000 and sold for $206,628. The third property was appraised at $490,000 and sold for $320,000. After paying real estate commissions, the foundation received $296,200 from the sales. The commissions were paid to Madison Graves, a candidate for university regent in 1992 and a longtime friend of the foundation's director, Lyle Rivera. Rivera was also a broker for Graves' Flamingo Realty, the agency that handled the sales. Rivera saw no conflict of interest because Graves probably lost money on the sales, given the time it took to sell the property:

We always ask them to do it at a lesser commission than standard so most of these guys don't relish doing business with the foundation.

One of the purchasers of the third property was Shelli Lowe, who had also performed the appraisal on the property. Finally, with regard to the Las Vegas souvenir shop, the foundation lost $235,000 because it failed to exercise its option to renew the lease on the shop.

a. Was there a conflict of interest in the Nathan sale?

b. How would you have handled the Nathan sale differently?

c. Was there a conflict in having Madison Graves as the listing broker for the property appraised at $490,000?

d. Does a conflict exist when an appraiser purchases a property for which she has furnished the appraisal?

e. Did the foundation manage the funds as if they were its personal funds? Is this right or wrong?

f. What things would you have done differently if you had been a foundation member responsible for managing the gift?

g. Would disclosure forms and processes help the foundation's image?

SUGGESTED ANSWERS:

a. This is a classic case of a series of conflicts that arose as fiduciaries, given responsibility for the management of funds and properties, managed those funds and properties as if they were their own funds and were to be used for the benefit of themselves and others around them.

b. The Nathan sale should never have occurred unless at least the appraisal figure was paid and there was full disclosure to an independent panel of the foundation or an independent panel of the university.

c. Madison Graves had a conflict of interest. The award of the listings for the properties should have been done on a competitive basis. If Madison won the bid, as selected by an independent panel, then his commissions and results would have been more palatable.

d. The sales of the properties themselves were deservedly reported with questions. An appraiser should not also be the purchaser of the property unless there were other independent appraisals conducted when the appraiser indicated a desire to purchase the property.

e. The managers of this fund behaved as if the property was their own, in the wrong sense. They ignored propriety and the obligation to maximize the return on the contributed property. Managing funds as if they were your own in the trustee sense means managing them so that you take appropriate precautions and do all that you can to maximize profits.

f. A good foundation member would have set up a system of checks and balances and demanded more independence in the transactions. Also, the responsibility of effective management was required and the lapse of the lease option is evidence of a problem in adequate management.

g. Yes. Forms, processes, and approvals for members dealing with the foundation would be helpful. These processes anticipate public disclosure and provide above-board means for approval.

Legal Issues

There are duties imposed upon managers of trust properties and funds. This case shows self-dealing and breach of the duty to manage the funds and property prudently. The disclosure of interests in the various firms, employees and appraisers dealing with the foundation would be necessary. Documents would be required disclosing all of the assets and their disposition. The university, as a beneficiary, would have the right to claim losses for any mismanagement.

18. Frank Hoffman is the CEO of Triple Plus, Inc., a group of four successful restaurants in the Southwest. One member of the Triple Plus board of directors, Sam Wasson, has a daughter, Chelsea Wasson, who has just started Chelsea's Cloths, a business that supplies restaurant linens. Wasson has approached Hoffman to explain Chelsea's business. Chelsea's Cloths has adopted an environmental emphasis in its operations as a way of countering the industry trend toward the use of paper products in restaurants. Sam Wasson initially recruited Hoffman as CEO, was instrumental in having the board select Hoffman, and is one of Hoffman's strong backers. Wasson supported Hoffman when other board members were impatient with his new procedures, policies, and changes.

Ordinarily, when someone approaches Frank Hoffman with information on a new supplier, he takes the information and refers it to the purchasing/supply area or refers the person directly to the manager of purchasing. In this case, Frank personally presented the information to Triple's purchasing manager, Deidre Hall. Frank offered Deidre the Chelsea's Cloths brochure and card and explained, "She is Sam Wasson's daughter. She just graduated in marketing from State University last June and now has her own firm. See what you can do. Our contract with Lila's Linens is up for renewal. Maybe we can do something."

Deidre evaluated Chelsea's and Lila's proposals as well as that of an additional firm in making the purchasing decision. Although the pricing between Chelsea's and Lila's is equivalent, Chelsea's is too young a firm to have a track record, and Deidre is not convinced that Chelsea's can handle Triple's large account. Given Mr. Hoffman's interest, however, Deidre is confused about what recommendation to make.

a. Should Deidre recommend Chelsea's firm or offer her true recommendation?

b. Would it be ethical for Hoffman to change Deidre's decision?

c. What if Wasson had requested bid information so that his daughter could be competitive? Should Deidre supply it? Should Hoffman direct Deidre to supply it?

d. Can you solve the conflict without offending the director?

e. Does Hoffman need to be concerned about how his intervention would reflect the "tone at the top"? Could employees misinterpret his actions?

SUGGESTED ANSWERS:

a. Deidre is in a tense spot with which students can identify. They know the correct decision to be made but may be feeling some pressure from a superior to make a different decision.

   Deidre should make her recommendation as she has evaluated it and give her justifications. It is a business decision based on concerns about the viability and reliability of a new business. Deidre can also explain that Chelsea's is price-competitive and that she would be willing to consider Chelsea's once more references and a track record are available.

b. Hoffman should not reverse Deidre because it undermines her authority and confidence as the person responsible for purchasing. Also, Hoffman needs to consider the appearance of board presence and pressure being used to force the company to enter into contracts it would otherwise not choose. Troubles in the company at any time will bring a laundry list of these types of transactions that will prove damaging to Hoffman, Triple Plus and Chelsea's. Hoffman is in a position to explain to Wasson that his daughter's firm looks very good to them and that once she establishes a record with some smaller accounts, purchasing would be willing to have her work with them.

c. No bid information should be given to Chelsea's as a favor to Sam Wasson. See below.

d. Many corporations' ethics policies require directors to disclose

173

conflicts of interest; i.e., situations in which they or a family member benefit through a contractual relationship with the corporation. Wasson may have that obligation here.

e. Hoffman's intervention would send a signal to employees about the way the company does business and how contracts are awarded. It may seem like a one-time intervention, but Hoffman would actually be establishing the tone for the company. Employees would learn that who you know is the standard for behavior and not what's best for the company. Hoffman's intervention would do damage to the ethical atmosphere of the firm.

Legal Issues

Both Sam Wasson and Frank Hoffman are fiduciaries of Triple Plus. The transactions they enter into must be in the best interest of the corporation. Since the purchasing manager's decision has been made, neither should use their authority or influence to change that decision. Further, the disclosure of bid information in advance would be a violation of those fiduciary duties.

ADVANCED INSTRUCTIONAL MODULE
ETHICS

Prepared by Geoffrey P. Lantos
Stonehill College

Overview:
This lecture is concerned with constructing an ethical philosophy, i.e., with understanding the different moral principals, their strengths and weaknesses, and how they can be applied. We also look at difficulties that arise in business firms which hinder people from acting ethically as well as practical difficulties in using the moral philosophies. We conclude by focusing on analysis of ethical decision-making cases. We describe how ethics cases can be analyzed and provide some cases for classroom analysis.

The discussion on constructing an ethical philosophy deviates from most textbook discussions in that it begins at the most general level (often not discussed or only curtly treated):comparing two approaches to moral philosophy- relativism (the dominant approach) and absolutism. Four major sources of absolute standards are described, and the strengths and weaknesses of both relativism and absolutism are discussed.

Next, the six most frequently discussed perspectives for ethical decision making are reviewed. These break out into three major categories: intuitionism, teleological moral theories (utilitarianism, ethical egoism, Christian consequentialism) and deontological moral theories (rights, justice). A suggestion is then made on how to reconcile the different ethical philosophies.

Two areas of difficulty in being ethical in business are then discussed. The first is several pitfalls that hinder organizations from developing moral corporate cultures, and the second is a few practical difficulties that can prevent a decision maker from implementing her moral philosophy.

The lecture ends with Arthur Anderson & Co. SC's suggested approach for solving ethical dilemmas and cases. This approach is very similar in many respects to the methods used for solving traditional business school cases.

Then, several short, easily digested cases are presented along with suggested solutions patterned after the Arthur Anderson case study method. The module wraps up with an appendix which offers some helpful tips for the instructor in leading business ethics case discussions.

Learning Objectives: By the end of this module, the student will be able to:

1. Discuss the differences between a relativist and an absolutist philosophy towards resolving ethical dilemmas, the possible sources for absolute standards, and the advantages and disadvantages of using these two ethical perspectives.

2. Recognize and describe the use of six ethical theories: intuitionism, utilitarianism, ethical egoism, Christian consequentialism, theory of rights, and theory of justice.

3. Explain the advantages and disadvantages of each of the six ethical theories and how to reconcile these different perspectives.

4. Be alert to stumbling blocks which prevent many organizations from establishing moral corporate cultures.

5. Discuss the practical constraints which can hinder an individual from implementing an ethical course of action.

6. Solve a business ethics case using the Arthur Anderson Co, SC approach.

Outline:
I. Constructing an Ethical Philosophy
   A. Two Ethical Approaches/World views
      1. Moral relativism/situation ethics
      2. Moral absolutism/moral idealism
        a. Societal culture and norms
        b. Civil law
        c. Natural law
        d. Divine revelation
      3. Analysis of relativism
      4. Analysis of absolutism
   B Six Ethical Theories
      1. Intuitionism
      2. Teleological moral theories
        a. Utilitarianism
        b. Ethical egoism
        C. Christian consequentialism
      3. Deontological moral theories
        a. Theory of rights
        b. Theory of justice
      4. Conclusion on ethical theories

II. Areas of Difficulty
   A. Obstacles That Distract From Building Moral Corporate Cultures
   B. Practical Difficulties In Using Moral Philosophies

III. Solving Ethical Cases

IV. Appendix: Methods for Leading Discussions of Ethics

Lecture Notes:

Constructing An Ethical Philosophy
How one goes about constructing an ethical philosophy is the domain of

normative ethics, a prescriptive study that attempts to formulate and defend basic moral norms governing moral life. Normative ethics, studied by philosophers, aims at deciding what ought to be done, as opposed to what actually is done (descriptive approaches to ethics, studied by sociologists, anthropologists, and historians).

In order to render a moral judgement on the rightness or wrongness of the action taken in the ethical issue under consideration, one must apply moral standards. Also known as moral philosophy or ethical philosophy, these are rules or principles people use for deciding if something is right or wrong. People learn these principles through the process of socialization with family, friends, religious institutions, social groups (including the workplace), and formal education. Ultimately, ethical choices are based on the personal moral philosophy of the decision maker.

Moral standards include, first, moral values (absolute values, common morality, moral common sense), which embody a set of moral rules that most people agree on, at least in a given culture. In this section we will further explore the idea of absolute values, discuss their possible origins, and compare the absolutist approach to ethical decision making with the relativist perspective.

The second component of ethical standards is moral principles (moral perspectives, moral theories). These are particular approaches, some of which are relativistic and others of which can be used both absolutely and relatively to solve ethical dilemmas. Moral principles present guidelines for business people as they resolve specific ethical issues. However, there is no one universal moral philosophy applied by all persons in all situations; hence we refer to them as personal moral philosophies or perspectives. We will survey those moral perspectives which are most relevant to business decision making. We will discuss the advantages and disadvantages of each approach in order to aid the student in formulating his own personal moral philosophy, without recommending one approach or another. In fact, often it is helpful to analyze a given ethical scenario using several of these approaches.

All ethical philosophies deal with one of more of three characteristics of the behavior under question: the act itself (means), the consequences of the act (ends) and the actor's motives or intentions. Absolutism focuses on the act, teleological moral theories (utilitarianism, ethical egoism, Christian consequentialism) are concerned with the consequences, and the intuitionism looks to the actor's motives. Deontological moral theories (theory of rights and theory of justice) can focus either on the act (deontologists) or general moral principles combined with the situation (rule deontologists).

Two Ethical Approaches/World views.
There are two general approaches to ethics, i.e., two ethical philosophies or world views: moral relativism (a.k.a. ethical relativism, relative standards, situational ethics or speculative philosophy, based on a humanistic view) and moral absolutism (a.k.a. absolute standards or moral idealism, often based on religious and/or cultural values). Relativism tends to rely on moral theories whereas absolutism relies more on moral norms and values. Often these two

approaches will give different answers to the all-important question:"Is it right?" Most observers seem to agree that whereas once absolutism was predominant, in the twentieth century (especially during the second half) relativism has come into vogue. For instance, Alan Bloom, in The Closing of the American Mind, observes that most moral relativism dominates college campuses today. In the late twentieth century it seems that the notion of the timeless, universal principles of right and wrong has gone the way of buggy whips and pocket watches: rather quaint, but out of date.

Moral relativism/situation ethics. Using relative standards, one denies that there are absolute answers to ethical quandaries which hold true in all instances; rather, the correctness of a particular action depends on the situation. Morals are relative to the individual (e.g.,"You must do what's right for you"; "What's right for you might not be right for me"), the circumstances (e.g., premarital sex is fine if two people feel they are in love and the relationship will last; theft is justified if you cannot earn a living wage and meet you expenses; women go on "The Oprah Winfrey Show" and justify their acts of adultery with married men since the mens' wives aren't sexually satisfying them), and society (cultural relativism) (e.g., community standards used in obscenity trials; " the spirit of the age"). Relativists assume that right and wrong are just a matter of what a social group, or even an individual, approves or disapproves.

In other words, "There are absolutely no absolutes" and "The only thing that is absolute is that nothing is absolute." Ethics is autonomous (in Greek "self-law";you are a law unto yourself; we make up the rules as we go along). Moral values are derived from human experience ("Experience is the best teacher"), i.e., the basis of ethical values lies in the minds of men. The approval of one's peers or classmates can be used to validate one's decision; the "new morality" becomes acceptable.

This is humanism, the idea that humanity can determine what is best for society by its vast knowledge and technological capability; it exalts man and disregards or disbelieves God. Thus, we have heuristics such as "thou shalt not steal--ordinarily." There are all kinds of exceptions. This humanistic world view subscribes to Protagoras' assertion back around 400 B.C. that "man is the measure of all things." Unfortunately, humans are fallible (even fallen, according to biblical teaching).

Thus the relativist observes the actions of members of some relevant group and attempts to determine the group consensus on a given action. For instance, the Generally Accepted Accounting Principles gain their authoritative support from a political process in which interested bodies lobby the Financial Accounting Standards Board in support of their views on acceptable and unacceptable practices; the Principals change over time. Within many professions, such as accounting, law and medicine, it was until around 1980 considered unethical to advertise. As competition became more intense and as consumers increasingly demanded their right to know, these professions decided that advertising is an acceptable practice after all and concluded that restriction hindered free competition.

Relativistic rules are bound within a closed system; no appeal can be made to a principal or existence outside the system (e.g., God in an open system). Relativism is founded on the nation or Immanuel Kants' Critique of Pure Reason that we as human are responsible for the nature and structure of the world. An extreme fringe of relativists goes so far as to say that there is no such thing as objective truth; each of us has our own version of reality. Skepticism denies that truth in moral matters can be known.

Such worldly wisdom leads us to such maxims as: "Do unto others as you know they'd do unto you, given the chance," "Everyone does it, so that makes it okay" (vs. your mother's question, "If Billy jumped off the bridge, would you jump off the bridge?"), "As long as we all agree, then whatever we do is right," "Don't get mad, get even," "Go ahead and do it, just don't get caught" (or the variant ". . . just don't tell me about it"), "Might makes right," "It's a dog eat dog world," and "Whatever you do to me, I have a right to do to you" (vs. Two wrongs don't make a right").

Moral absolutism/moral idealism. Absolutism is concerned with the morality of the act itself or means, not with the consequences or other circumstantial factors. It judges the act on the basis of moral ideals or absolute universal standards ("traditional values") which hold true over time, place, and person. These permanent, immutable, rules are to be followed regardless of the circumstances, i.e., there are certain behaviors that are plain right and wrong, good and evil, whether prince or pauper, mighty or meek. Moral law is as unchangeable as the law of gravity. There are timeless truths which have worked well in the past and which will work well in the future. Plato insisted that we cannot be good without a timeless idea of goodness. Ethics is meaningless unless based on a solid value system.

For instance, Kantian absolutes are considered "higher truths" (e.g. compassion, honesty, kindness, protection of the weak). These are known as virtues, i.e., elements of moral excellence and righteousness. Aristotle advocated absolutes, whereas Plato admitted we can't always be certain what is right. Aristotle and Plato considered the four cardinal virtues to be prudence (practical wisdom), justice, courage, and temperance.

As a simple business example, the Director of Research for the Beech-Nut Corporation told the Food and Drug Administration that Beech-Nut was selling a blend of synthetic ingredients labeled as 100 per cent apple juice after his superiors ignored his internal memos. When asked why he did this, he replied,"I thought apple juice should be made from apples."

(Note: at this juncture you might want to ask your students, "How many of you think it is possible to know for sure if an ethical value is true or false?" Few hands will raise. Then ask, "How many of you think it's wrong to torture someone for the heck of it?" All hands will rise.)

There are degrees of absolutism. At one extreme, some absolutist claim that moral ideals are rigid, everywhere, and always the same. For instance, lying is always wrong, regardless of the situation. At the other extreme, some moral idealists believe that the most general principle of morality is absolute, but that as it is applied in various circumstances, certain lower-level norms may vary. For example, lying is generally wrong, but exceptions can be made to, for instance, protect a person's sensibilities ("little white lies"). A middle ground believes that moral principles and norms are everywhere and always the same, but that norms have exceptions. For instance, it is wrong to lie, except where a lie will protect human life.

Moral idealism sometimes considers certain rights or duties and standards of justice to be universal (e.g. JFK's Consumer Bill of Rights). These forms of moral idealism will be discussed as a subset of deontological moral theories (rights and justice) below.

In any event, the question naturally arises, "Where do moral ideals come from?" There is a difference between believing in universal moral principles and holding that one knows with certainty where they come from. Such a person might search in several places to answer the questions, "Whose values are valid? What or who is the ultimate authority to judge what is and what is not ethical?" We now look at the major sources of moral absolutes.

Societal culture and norms. Culture refers to the set of values, ideas, and attitudes of a society that are transmitted from one generation to the next, where a society usually refers to a group sharing common institutes and culture. Culture serves as a socializing force that dictates what is morally right and wrong.

Cultural relativism is the idea that cultures vary widely, and morality is relative to a particular culture, society, or community. This concept is very important in today's global marketplace. Anthropologists and sociologists have documented the fact that people in differing cultures, as well as people within a given culture, disagree on what is morally right and wrong (e.g. bribery, sexism, racism). Transcultural relativism means that there are differences in what is considered moral between cultures. For example, the ancient Greeks believed that infanticide was morally permissible, whereas we do not. According to the nineteenth century doctrine of Manifest Destiny the U.S. would convert the world to Christianity, capitalism, and democracy. It failed when anthropologists discovered diversity. Cartels are considered illegal and immoral in the U.S. but not in Europe. Intracultural relativism suggests that people within a given culture can disagree on what is morally acceptable. For instance, before the Civil Warm many Southerners insisted that slavery was morally acceptable while many Northerners did not. And, within the U.S. today, there is a heated debate on the morality of abortion. South Africa displays sharp cultural differences between the white majority and the black minority.

Differences in cultural moral values are due primarily to two factors. First, is differing conditions. Thus, a country with many men but few women might consider polygamy acceptable. A second factor accounting for cultural differences is factual beliefs. Hence, a society that believes the volcano gods demand human sacrifice will consider that practice to be moral.

Note that cultural relativism is descriptive, whereas ethical relativism is prescriptive. Thus, cultural relativism says that being ethical is doing whatever society accepts. An implication is that it is impossible to make moral judgements about other cultures. Everything is equally valid; nothing is better than anything else and nothing is worse. We can't judge the morality of a particular culture, we can only try to understand it. According to this approach, Sweden sees abortions as right, and for Sweden it is right, whereas Ireland sees abortion as wrong, and so for Ireland it is wrong.

However there are several problems with looking to a given society's morals for constructing a value system. First, cultural diversity might not be fact, especially since cultural and social laws are rooted in religious traditions which are founded on common moral values. For instance, in every country murder is considered wrong since if it becomes commonplace, society could not survive. Lying is always considered verboten because otherwise there would be no secure social interaction. Fortunately, there is sufficient agreement among societies to permit business to be carried on internationally, although a host of unresolved differences exist. For instance, does American business have a right to impose its ethical standards on foreign firms doing business here? (Most would say yes).

Second, if there is cultural diversity, diversity does not necessarily mean that both parties are right (despite the conventional wisdom). Some societies believe what is false. For instance, communist USSR (pre-1991) and the U.S. were often portrayed in the media as morally equivalent, even though communism is considered by many Americans as Godless and unnatural, hence, evil. Nazi Germany's murder of some six million Jews, although sanctioned by the government, was not moral. The same could be said for the policies of Saddam Hussein's Iraq. It a society becomes overly permissive, does that mean that adultery and fornication are okay? Which country's value system are we going to use? The dilemma is highlighted by the continuing by the continuing discussions of the Foreign Corrupt Policies Act. If bribing customers and government officials is an accepted business practice in a given country, why should a U.S. company doing business in that country be prohibited from the practice? Because it is wrong. The implication is that it's not always true that "When in Rome, do as the Romans do." This might be true concerning customs and folkways, but it's not always true regarding behaviors in the moral arena. We cannot always rely on society's decisions about right and wrong. Society makes its decisions in its own wisdom and for the welfare of its members. The idea that moral values vary over time and place contradicts the notion of fixed absolute standards.

Third, moral pluralism often exists. American society is diverse, a combination of various cultures and traditions. It is characterized by diversity, with many ethnic and racial groups. Not only is it culturally pluralistic, to some extent it is morally pluralistic.

Nonetheless, if a society is to properly function, it must have a large core of commonly held values and norms which form the common morality of a society. Respect for human beings, respect for truth, respect for other people's property, and other elements of moral common sense are all commonplaces in America, making business possible. In areas of serious disagreement (e.g. capital punishment, abortion), differences must be settled face by public debate and perhaps by legislation. But it is not true that when faced with moral claim against me or my business practices, I can dismiss them as simply being your opinions but not mine. Basic moral claims are universal.

<u>Civil Law</u>. Laws are society's values and standards that are enforceable in the courts. Laws and regulations are created by government to establish minimum standards for ethical behavior. Law regulating business conduct are passed because society does not always trust business to do what's right, especially in four areas. First, are laws regulating competition, i.e., practices that reduce or restrict competition among business. For instance, the Sherman Antitrust Act of 1890 prohibits monopolies, and the Robinson-Patman Act of 1936 restricts price discrimination against retailer and wholesalers. Second, are laws protecting consumers, i.e., that require businesses to provide accurate information about goods and services and that they follow safety standards. For example, the Consumer Product Safety Act of 1972 created the Consumer Product Safety Commission to establish safety standards and regulations for consumer products, and the Magnusson-Moss Warranty Act of 1975 created standards for consumer product warranties. Third, there exists laws protecting the government. Thus, the Clean Air Act of 1970 established air quality standards, and the Toxic Substances control Act of 1976 requires testing and restricts use of certain chemicals. Fourth, are laws promoting equity and safety in the workplace. An example of an equity law is title VII of the Civil Rights Act of 1964, as amended, which prohibits discrimination in employment on the basis of color, race, sex, national origin, or religion. An example of a safety law is the Occupational Safety Act, which is designed to assure healthful and safe working conditions

The term corporate compliance suggest that a firm will be law abiding. However, a common fallacy is that, "If it's legal, it's moral." An easy way to get off the hook is to let the lawyers decide what is ethical. The legalist believes that the law, and hence morality, is whatever the king says it is. However, moral standards aren't established or changed by the pronouncements of particular authoritative bodies. Sometimes the boundary between right and wrong is the same as that between legal and illegal. But sometimes it is not.

First, some laws simply are not relevant to morality, e.g., procedural issues such as how to evaluate a real estate contract.

A second problem with the law as an ethical signpost is that it is often of limited scope. Some moral situations are not covered by the law since legislators can't anticipate every problem area.

Third, some laws are immoral or unjust because they are the product of fallible humans. It is not excusable to dismiss an action by saying, "There isn't a law against it." St. Thomas Aquinas said, "An evil law is no law," Montesqieu believed that, "We should never create by law what we can accomplish by morality," and Oliver Twist's Mr. Bumble quipped, "The law is an ass, an idiot." Controversial laws include those related to abortion, capital punishment, legalized prostitution and gambling, and speed limits which slow us down to 55 mph on highways that were meant to be driven at 70 mph. George Washington committed an act of high treason against the British crown and yet was considered a morally great leader for what he did. As another possible example, you can ask your students if there should be laws to regulate the behavior of consenting adults (e.g., a prostitute and her client; two friends wagering a bet on a football game). It's legal to lay people off, but is it ethical? A final problem here is that an action might be illegal but morally compelling. Ethics should judge the law, not vice versa

Fourth, the law merely provides a floor or moral minimum for business conduct. The law is reactive, telling us what ought not to be done, rather than proactive, telling us what ought to be done (i.e., to exercise various virtues). It simply draws the line, telling us what the majority (or at least majority of the ruling body) feels is unacceptable conduct. The law can then degenerate into the question, "What can we get away with?" For instance, in the late 1980's the vague insider trading laws were pushed to their limits. In the savings and loan scandals, where one drew the line between constituent service and peddling influence wasn't clear. As the old saw goes, "It's difficult to legislate morality," at least regarding the gray areas (vs. Laws against rape, murder, theft, and other areas of common morality which we can all agree on). Laws don't make people moral. Too often people follow the letter of the law but not the spirit of the law. For instance, ask your students, "If a brilliant tax expert could legally cut you taxes by 90 per cent through some legal loophole while completely violating the spirit of the tax code, would you let her do it?" If enough people decide to break the law, of course, the law breaks down. Legislation is often viewed as coercive or restrictive. Business laws usually provide less stringent standards than trade or professional association rules; if they did not then the latter would merely be redundant or unnecessary. Industries and professional associations generally mandate less strict standards than do individual firms; after all, who would want to work for an organization which does not even adhere to standards in his own industry?

Fifth, laws can provide a confusing basis for morality since they are sometimes inconsistent, both over time (e.g., abortion laws) and place (e.g., certain state laws). For instance, product liability laws prior to the 1960's restricted a manufacturer's liability to persons injured using the manufacturer's product because of his negligence or fault. Today's liability laws are based on tort law as a means of social welfare to ensure that victims are compensated for their injuries regardless of whether the party forced to bear financial responsibility for the damage was at fault; the lawyers go after the "deep pockets," i.e., those parties even remotely involved in a transaction, which are best able to pay. Thus, laws can help people determine what is deemed right of wrong by society at a given point in time, but what is legally right today might vie as unethical tomorrow, and vice versa. Even at one particular time, different courts, or different state legislatures , may take different views. For example, the courts differ on what constitutes a "substantial" reduction of competition.

And, laws differ over places, especially in the interpersonal arena. For instance, many Koreans believe that the ideas of one person should benefit all. Thus, the Korean government rarely prosecutes infringements of intellectual property rights (copyrights, trademarks, patents), whereas in the U.S. unauthorized use of these is considered illegal and unethical. As another example, certain infant formula failed to meet U.S. safety standards, but local laws in third world countries permitted it. Should it be sold?

In general, sociological law has no fixed basis. It is arbitrarily determined by what group of people says it is good for society at the time. Thus, even Jesus broke the manmade rules about working on the Sabbath because he believed they contradicted a Higher Law. The major problem with using man-made rule as absolute yardsticks is that they are the product of fallible humans. The standards used are, as we have just seen, in fact relative, not absolute.

Natural law. The concept of nature refers to the proper ordering of the universe. Natural law is a body of laws that derives from nature (and God, if you believe that He is the creator of the nature), and the laws are believed to be binding upon human activity apart from or in conjunction with laws established by human authority. Based on the thinking of Aristotle, St. Thomas Aquinas, and john Locke, the idea is that an act is morally wrong if it is incompatible with universal human nature. Thus, human nature provided the key how people ought to live their lives. This rules out acts which cause potential physical harm, such as drunkenness (leads to sickness, vile behavior, etc.) and "casual sex" (STD's are not a casual thing).

The political philosophy of the Greeks (and later of Aquinas) said that natural law can be discovered be reason, i.e., by observing the operations of nature and society and drawing logical deductions. One relevant application to business ethics is the concept of natural rights, i.e., certain basic rights that are believed to be self evident; they stem from the nature of things. Such rights are based on the idea that there is an ideal standard of justice fixed by nature that is binding on all persons. This standard takes precedence over the particular laws and standards created by social convention, providing absolute standards against which laws and policies of a particular government and institutions are to be measured.

Thus, natural rights are considered to be fundamental rights irrespective of merit, due to be respected because they are rooted in a knowledge of certain universal regularities in nature. They are not to be usurped by the sovereign power of kings (i.e., government).

For instance, the right to life is based on our status as rational beings, worthy of respect, and ends-in-ourselves. The natural right to property was discussed by the British philosopher John Locke. In the Declaration of Independence the American Founding Fathers wrote about the natural rights of life, liberty and the pursuit of happiness in the context of the "laws of nature" and of "nature's God." Thus, their view of natural rights wasn't man centered, , it was God-centered. The idea was that all humans are endowed by God with certain rights and characteristics that no law or government can abridge, and that these natural rights exist apart from what laws or constitutions can give people.

Today it is more fashionable to speak of human rights than of natural rights. It is supposed that human beings have essential properties of human nature that determines their fundamental rights that are to be respected by other people and social institutions. We shall look at these later when we discuss rights theory.

Divine revelation.

Divine revelation (divine command theory) is the idea that God has revealed Himself, not only in nature, but also in other ways, e.g., through inspired writings in holy books (The Bible, Koran, etc.) prophets, etc. Theology, the study of the nature of God and religious truths, says that morality can be based on a "higher law," i.e., the revealed laws of our Creator. This higher law comes not from the minds of men, but from the word of God, i.e., divine revelation is God-centered, not man-centered. There is a standard above our ideas of right and wrong (i.e., a transcendent standard). This approach postulates the universe to be an open system (vs. a self-contained universe) where mortality is revealed from outside the human mind of the universe. Ethics is founded not on situational ethics, but on what God reveals on the situation. Out duty is to obey God and His revealed will.

Most religions claim to provide an absolute set of moral guidelines and advocate living an ethical life. In the U.S., most believers rely on the Judeo-Christian value system derived from the teachings of the bible (Orthodox Jews strictly adhere to the mandates of the Old Testament and Orthodox Christians adhere to the dictums of the New Testament, which claims God has added to His self-revelation in Jesus Christ, as well as the Old Testament teachings which haven't been superseded by the New Testament). In other words, the answer to how we know there are moral values is found in the line from the simple children's hymn, "Jesus Loves Me," "For the Bible tells me so."

Traditionally in American culture it was felt by the majority that the Bible's moral revelation provides fixed permanent guidelines which humans can choose to accept or reject; these values provided a moral consensus or common morality. The founding fathers believed in the Almighty and in the role of Divine guidance in human affairs. The Bible was considered to be a handbook of values, the best textbook ever penned on how to effectively and wisely live life. The basic truths of Western civilization were explicitly spelled out in the Old Testament (e.g.,the Ten Commandments) and the New Testament (e.g., the Sermon on the Mount) and implicitly in our great literature (e.g., A Christmas Carol teaches kindness and compassion, The Little Engine Who Could instructs on persistence in the face of adversity, and The Emperor's New Clothes warns of the danger of unreasoning conformity). There was a gradual turning away from this thinking in Western Civilization in the seventeenth century with the advent of rationalism and the consequent secularization of culture.

However, there is now some evidence that in the light of what many people see as a moral meltdown in society, they are either turning back to traditional religion or toward "New Age" spiritual beliefs, such as reincarnation. Most Americans still find strength and comfort in tradition and find that religion gives them "peace of mind" and "spiritual well-being." Bible-believing Christians believe that human nature is corrupt, and that when people lose something bigger than themselves to guide their behavior, society has no restraints to keep evil at bay. Some business executives are turning to prayer in seeking personal and a form of guidance.

Not to be denied is that disagreements will ensue if morality is solely determined by theology or faith. If faith and reason overlap this is not problematic. For instance, the Golden Rule is perfectly consistent with Kant's categorical imperative (discussed below). However, if ethics is based purely on personal faith and individual interpretations of revelation, not reason, arguments can ensue. One person says, "God says do X" and another says, "God says do Y." The dispute is not reconcilable. Also, not all people grow up with access to religious training, but non-religious people can nonetheless be ethical. And, within a given religious tradition people sometimes disagree on interpretations of the sacred writings. In any case, it cannot be denied that there is a body of moral values common to all religious traditions (common morality: don't lie, cheat, steal, etc.). Most conflicting truths among the various world's religions lie in the area of otherworldly concerns, such as the nature of God and the means of salvation (e.g., grace vs. works). Nevertheless, our common religious culture in the U.S. provides us a basis of moral consensus which can be applied to modern-day circumstances. For instance, Exodus 23:8 speaks of the evil of bribery. Following biblical commands, one would not permit misleading advertising ("Thou shalt not lie") nor corporate espionage ("Thou shalt not steal"). We learn from Scripture of Joseph's forgiveness of his brothers, David's cleverness and courage in facing Goliath, and the good Samaritan's kindness toward a stranger. In Dostoyovsky's novel, The Brother's Karamazov, three brothers debate the source of evil in the world. Finally, one brother cries out, "If there is no God, then everything is permitted." Sin becomes whatever makes us feel uncomfortable. Being good is replaced by feeling good. We become a law unto ourselves. Who is to say for sure that Hitler was wrong in murdering six million Jews?

Other possible sources of absolute values include parental standards (often the first thing students will mention when you ask them where absolute values come from), the educational system, and the workplace. However, these are all manmade sources and can be (and usually are) relativistic (changing) in nature.

Analysis of relativism. Relativism has some advantages to recommend it. It does presumably provide pragmatic, expedient solutions to moral problems, not idealistic, unworkable platitudes. Whatever works and gets the job done is acceptable. Convictions are not needed. Relativism leads to statements such as, "bribes are the only way to do business abroad." It works for politicians who wish to perpetuate their incumbency sticking a wet finger in the wind and making decisions on the basis of public opinions. "Safe sex" is safer than casual, unprotected sex, but is it moral?

Another plus for relativism is its flexibility and ability to adapt to changing circumstances. After all, if you live in the former USSR would you not lie if the KGB knocked on your door at midnight asking where your son was? And, in business the only constant is change. If it's best for our company or our situation, then all is well. This appeals to managers who wish to remain "state of the art" and move with the times. Morality becomes a moving target.

Also, this approach is considered "non-judgmental," or tolerant. In our society, scorn is heaped upon those who are judgmental or intolerant; it is considered best to be broad-minded or open-minded. However, where you draw the line on what you do or do not tolerate is not always clear. To say, "I'll tolerate what you believe if you tolerate what I believe" is not logical if we disagree.

Situational ethics has some serious shortcomings. It can lead to inconsistencies since analysis is done on a case by case basis. Thus, it can result in perceptions of decisions being unfair or arbitrary. For instance, if a professor grades on a curve, the grade that a student receives is a function of that great academic lottery known as registration. She will do better in a less smart section of the course than in a smarter one. Grading standards become inconsistent from section to section and semester to semester in a given course.

Additionally, relativism often means no consensus; seldom will there be agreement among all concerned parties that you have made a morally correct decision (except in obvious cases of common morality issues). Because the different ethical perspectives (which we'll look at next) sometimes support different alternatives, the result can be moral anarchy. The absence of agreement or consensus establishes the absence of truth. You think puffery in advertising is okay; I do not. Who is to say which one of us is correct? It is my opinion against yours. "You've got your morality, I've got mine. Where's the problem?" It's simply a matter of individual (or group or societal) preference. Being good has been replaced by feeling good. Wrongdoing is whatever makes you feel uncomfortable. The result could be a moral meltdown in society since almost anything goes.

Even if there is consensus, as determined by nose counting in which the Gallup Poll tells us what is moral, polls can be used to create public opinion rather than measure it; they become self-fulfilling prophecies. At best, morality is reduced to a show-of hands in which the majority, plurality, or those in positions of power determine what is right and wrong. However, just because something is average does not mean that it is normal. Average is the way most people are; normal is the way people should be. (Lions ought to have manes. If a plague hits, maneless lions will be average, but they are not normal.)

The result when morals are in perpetual motion is uncertainty ("What's right? Got Me.") standards built on the shifting sands of personal subjectivity are no standards at all; relativistic principles are as fixed as water. We end up drifting in the shifting tides; without firm anchors our values are merely blowing in the wind without a moral rudder, and it is hard to steer clear of troubled waters. This makes us feel insecure in the correctness of out decisions since we have no anchors for those decisions. Teaching in a vacuum of values teaches that no values are right. Psychologically, the notions that there are many kinds of ultimate reality, that truth is relative, and that no one possesses the whole truth are confusing. They are cause a sense that life is meaningless, since meaning can only be built on certainties and convictions. In the business world, often the rules of the game change with the changing of the guard, as management turns over and a "new broom sweeps clean." Employees end up in a state of confusion and anxiety (codes of ethics and other techniques for institutionalizing ethics can help overcome this problem).

Finally relativism is criticized as being morally impotent and corrupt. Clever formulas take the place of good old-fashioned morality. Due to our inherently corrupt nature, immorality will prevail by default. Relativism is considered by some to be the "yeah, but," "it depends" school of thought. "Doesn't that seem improper?" "Yeah, but, hey, this is 1993. Get with it, man," or "yeah, but my situation is different." These are often just rationalizations.

Analysis of absolutism. Absolutism offers much more certainty than relativism. It gives the most definitive answers to moral questions. There are truths with a capital "T" which can be implemented with consistency over time and place (Yet relativists like Pontius Pilate, rhetorically ask, "What is truth?" They don't think it can be answered). Things can be more black and white than murky gray. At least among absolutists there can be consensus.

Another advantage of absolutes lies in their simplicity. We don't need fancy jargon, esoteric theories , complex formulae, and the like. Any five-year-old can grasp the basic notions of honesty, kindness, individual responsibility, and other ethical norms. Also it is easier to judge someone's actions than their motives, net gain to society, and other relativistic yardsticks we will be examining.

Furthermore, moral absolutes have been tested and proven to consistently work. History teaches that societies crumble when they jettison traditional values (e.g., ancient Greece and Rome, ancient Israel time and again, and perhaps the USA today).

Additionally, absolutes tend to be impartial and thus just. Everyone's behavior, whether prince or pauper, is judged bu the same standards; in fact, discrimination is a violation of absolute norms.

Finally, moral idealism is not idealistic--it is rational (the name is "moral idealism," not "moral idealistic"). By it's nature truth is absolute. When we arrive at truth we assume a conformity between mind and reality.

However, there are some perceived and real problems with an absolute approach to ethics. Perhaps the greatest difficulty is the fact that gray areas still abound; reasonable people can differ on how to interpret a given principle and at what point a person trips over the ethical line.

Thus, some would argue that what absolutes command is blind, unthinking adherence ("Just following orders"). However, believing in moral absolutes isn't as simplistic as some believe; one still needs to make moral judgements. The trick is properly putting the principles into practice. For instance, if you believe in being "fair and just" in treating your suppliers and dealers, you must still interpret whether certain behaviors in given situations are "fair and just." Or, what, exactly is "bad taste?" Even fundamentalist Christians disagree on the morality of such issues as dancing, playing cards, drinking alcoholic beverages, listening to rock music, attending R (or even PG)- rated movies, and the like, because while the Bible provides general guiding principles, it does not, for the most part, provide detailed standards of conduct. Should beer and wine be advertised to adults, so long as the pitch is moderation and drinking is not glamorized? Should we go shopping on Sunday, given that we are to "observe the Sabbath day, to keep it holy"? When we are faced with such less than clear-cut issues, the wise aphorism probably is "When in doubt, don't."

Another objection to absolutes is that they are perceived as being too rigid and inflexible. They do not adapt to nor bend for extenuating circumstances. Isn't it okay for the destitute widow to steal in order to provided food for her children? Admittedly implementation must still be done on a case by case basis.

Closely related is the charge that holding only to traditional values is "narrow-minded"; we need to "loosen up." The question is: how broad should broad-minded people be? Where do you draw the ethical line?

Others do not like the fact that absolutes are intolerant. However, says the absolutist, what they do not put up with is wrongdoing, i.e., what they aren't tolerating are not just opinions but violations of true standards. A proper level of tolerance is a virtue, but one must draw the ethical line somewhere. For instance, the great faiths of the world pretty much expect the same virtues in their followers. Far from being narrow or intolerant, their moral values reflect the consensus of humanity about what makes for a good life and society.

People say that to rely on absolutes is to be judgmental. However, the judgment is based on a person's actions, not on what is thought to be in the heart. Every honorable individual has a responsibility to speak out against evil, to render moral judgments to say that this is right and that is wrong and that those who transgress are wrongdoers. The critics would subscribe to the ethics of noninvolvement: "I don't want to force my views on others; therefore I won't get involved." This is the person who would have said, "I do not believe it is right to murder innocent Jews, but I do not wish to impose my views on others; therefore I will remain silent." This is the politician who subscribes to the "personally opposed" view of morality: I'm personally opposed to (such and such an action or policy), but who am I to impose my opinion on others?" Yet you steal their wallet and they will find it absolutely wrong.

Then, there is some argument that traditional values are obsolete or "Neanderthal." They belong back in the stone age; they are out of tune with the times; traditionalists are trying to "turn the clock back" on what relativists call "progress." As an extreme example, Nietze declared that God is dead and therefore religion cannot be used to determine values. Yet, some things in life are not to be manipulated or adjusted. This is understood in mathematics, science, and other intellectual disciplines, yet it is often denied regarding standards for behavior. Common values live because they are invaluable.

Another perceived problem is that to teach absolutes is to indoctrinate. But, the dictionary defines a doctrine as something which is taught; hence we cannot teach without imparting doctrines.

Admittedly, to abide by moral ideals demands integrity--having the courage of one's convictions. It takes intestinal fortitude for a person to stand up for what they believe in the face of hostility and opposition. Biblical prophets such as Jeremiah, Ezekiel, et.al. were prosecuted for speaking out against immorality. The unbelievers killed the messengers instead of dealing with the bad news. Usually, of course, it is not that bad; while there are people who ridicule a person with ideals and standard, most people admire persons who do what is right and do not fear to speak out, rather than merely going along to get along. Integrity is sorely needed today when looking good, showing up well, and receiving favorable press coverage dominate. Integrity involves sacrifice, struggle, and perhaps non advantageous (in the short-run) decision making. For instance, when a conflict develops between an employee's ethics and his company's, he basically has three choices. He can choose loyalty, ignoring his own values and staying with the company. He can vote with his feet, exiting with his values intact. Or, he cam raise his voice, either to complain or dissent against what he believes is wrongdoing--and that requires integrity. Economic security is not worth the psychological torment that normally follows a wrong choice.

To believe in absolutes is said to be arrogant: "How can you know for sure?" asks the relativist. Admittedly, answers will vary, depending upon which sources we examined you turn to for your value system.

Thus, a final and probably the most important sticking point with absolutes is disagreement on the source of the standards. Who is to judge what is ethical and what is not? Which religion? Which law? Which society's norms? Who is the ultimate authority? (Students should be challenged to think through what their world is and the source of ultimate authority for the moral principles they hold.)

Five Ethical Theories
Work in the field of normative ethics in this century has evolved from three basic kinds of moral theories. Each approach uses different kinds of criteria to evaluate the ethics of human behavior, and hence the different perspectives

often provide entirely different conclusions on what ought to be done. They are utilitarian theory, the theory of rights, and the theory of justice or fairness. We will also discuss the more simplistic approaches of intutionism, ethical egoism, and Christian consequentialism.

By and large these approaches are all relativistic in nature (except when rights and justice approaches adhere to absolute standards of rights and justice). They are more abstract and don't yield as indisputable as absolutism. Utilitarianism, egoism, and Christian consequentialism all use teleological frameworks, i.e., they focus on duties to respect rights and promote justice.

Intuitionism. The intuitionist judges the actor's motives or intentions. The answer to whether the behavior is ethical is relative to the individual. Thus, this approach is also known as naive relativism, which is the idea that all human beings are themselves the standard by which their actions should be judged. The decision is correct if the individual's conscience tells him that it is right. As Jiminy Cricket told Pinnocio, "Let your conscience be your guide." If the person can "fell in her bones" and knows in her "heart of hearts" that it is proper, then for her it is. As long as she feels that her motives are good (i.e., she is "sincere"), she does not intend to harm anyone, and she feels comfortable doing it ("If it feels good, do it") then all is well. It is the "what's right for me" value system. The only authoritative is the self, i.e., your common sense. What happens right to you is, indeed, right. "I'm okay, you're okay."

The method has several things going for it. First, it is easy to justify (I made a good faith effort"). Second it is simple to implement; no hard thinking or heavy lifting required. Hence, be default it is probably the most widely-used approach to ethics. Third, it is often experience-based, and as the old saw says, "Experience is the best teacher." The well-seasoned manager knows best.

Fourth, for independent types, there is no authority to answer to but yourself. Fifth presumably an intuitive approach allows one to sleep at night. It is guilt free; one feels good about themselves if they can say "I wrestled with my conscience, and my conscience won." No cognitive dissonance creeps in.

But, there are some things going against intuitionism, too. A person can be well meaning but misguided, sincere but sincerely wrong. There is a lot of truth to the old adage, " The road to hell is paved with good intentions." "There is a way the seems right to man, but its end is the way of death," says a biblical proverb. Frequently, feelings deviate from what is ethical. There is no objective guideline.

This approach is the least likely to yield consensus. Whose intuition can we trust? Ours? Certainly. Our co-workers'? Maybe. Our boss's? Possibly. At the extreme, each person become a law unto themselves. And yet, humans are imperfect (an understatement). The great Russian author Aleksandar Solzhenitsyn said that if people believe all that matters is what feels right, they have no means to disarm the evil within them and do good.

Also, a person's feelings can be changing and contradictory. Think of a youngster faced with the temptations of adolescence, a frustrated couple considering divorce, or a businessperson struggling with a difficult decision. How do they know which impulse is right? Feelings can go astray. Did you ever get the impulse to bump a lousy driver who cut you off?

Finally, there is the delicate issue of judging another person's motives. Since we can't read minds, this is difficult to do. And actually, we are not permitted to, for each person knows best (a logical contradiction if we disagree).

<u>Teleological moral theories.</u> Theology (from the Greek word "telos" which means "end" or "result") refers to moral theories which consider an act morally right if it produces desirable end results or consequences, be it pleasure, fame, fortune, career growth, or whatever. The following moral theories are also referred to consequentialism.

<u>Utilitarianism.</u> The utilitarian model is a direct descendant of Adam Smith's work and was more precisely formulated by Jeremy Bentham and John Stuart Mill in the eighteenth century. It has an economic basis and is therefore widely accepted in business (research shows that it is the most widely used ethical perspective in business). Adam Smith believed that when each individual pursues their own self-interest, the invisible hand will assure that the good of the whole society is met. The focus was on aggregate economic welfare: the market works by itself to ascertain that individual needs are satisfied, according to classical economic theory. Corporations are accountable to the marketplace where consumers are deemed sovereign and government policy should be laissez faire. Perfect competition leads to use of resources and prices which enable consumers to maximize the utility (satisfaction) per dollar spent.

In its modern formulation, utilitarianism looks at the societal (not just economic) consequences or end results of an act to determine its moral worth; "the proof is in the pudding." The underlying idea is to act so as to produce good for the greatest number (rather than just good of the individual or of the firm). If the consequences of an action result in a net increase in society's well being or welfare (or at least not a decrease), then the act is considered to be morally right. Thus, two types of acts are considered unethical: (1) those that do not produce the greatest good for the greatest number and (2) those that represent inefficient means to accomplish such ends (i.e. one should consume as few outputs as possible and minimize external or social costs (externalities) of organizational activities on stakeholders.)

Restated, the goal is to increase benefits and decrease harms for all stakeholders. Thus, an action is morally appropriate if it maximizes benefits and minimizes overall harms for all stakeholders, i.e., if it maximizes the societal good. For instance, at the systemic level, squandering of societal resources would be considered bad, since it is an inefficient means. Capitalism is often considered ethical since it tends to produce the greatest

good for the greatest number. Monopolies or large conglomerates might be most
efficient, resulting in an optimal allocation of society's resources. If a
company is polluting the air or water, it should invest in pollution control
devices to the point where it costs equal the benefits society derives from
pollution control (it internalizes the externalities, i.e., social costs).
Job discrimination against minorities and women is wrong because society's
productivity is optimal only if jobs, promotions, and pay raises are awarded
on the basis of competency and merit, rather than on the basis of race or
gender. At the corporate level, it would be unethical to sell product A to a
customer if product B gives greater utility per dollar spent (bang per buck).

Measurement of the "greatest good" is done using a formal ethical calculus
variously in terms of pleasure and pain, satisfaction of individual revealed
preferences, and overall economic well being (welfare economics) using
societal cost/benefit analysis to arrive at a utilitarian coefficient.
Alternately, the calculations can be done intuitively, considering the
advantages and disadvantages of a given course of action.

The procedure utilitarian decision makers are required to use is:
    (1) Identify relevant stakeholders.
    (2) Identify alternative strategies.
    (3) Estimate costs and benefits of each alternative for each stakeholder.
    (4) Select the best option, i.e., the one that produces the greatest good
for the greatest number.
For instance, a firm could establish cost-benefit tradeoffs for decisions
involving potential employee risk of occupational accidents, illnesses, and/or
deaths. Or, a firm could justify a minor deception in conducting marketing
research (such as concerning the sponsor of or purpose of the research) if the
resulting lack of bias on the part of respondents leads to more valid
research, which, in turn, results in better products and services.

Utilitarian moral philosophers are conventionally divided into two groups, act
utilitarians and rule utilitarianism. Act utilitarians hold that each act
should be subjected to the utilitarian test. Although we can have general
rules of thumb which work in most cases to maximize utility, such as, "Don't
break contracts," these are just generalizations about past instances, and
some particular future instance might just prove to be an exception to the
rule. Rather than being categorically wrong, an act might be contingently
wrong. In a particular case, breaking the contract could be morally
permissible if it leads to the greatest good for the greatest number. The
justification for this approach is that it considers the merits and demerits
of each individual action. The criticism of the approach is that we can't
always know all of the consequences and it leads to a bias toward breaking
moral rules.

Rule utilitarians, on the other hand, hold that there are general moral (e.g.,
"Bribery is wrong.") as to what we should do to maximize utility which cannot
be compromised by the demands of particular situations. Such compromise would
threaten the general effectiveness of the rules. Rules are not subject to
change by demands of individual circumstances. The correct moral rules are
those that would produce the greatest good for the greatest number if everyone

were to follow them all the time. Thus, by looking at general consequences of breaking contracts in the past, we conclude that it is never right to break contracts, no matter what. Likewise, we should never lie, steal, murder, etc. The justification for this approach is that it considers general norms and values. The criticism is that it neglects each case might be unique; exceptions to the rule might sometimes maximize utility.

There are several advantages to the utilitarian approach. First, it results in "optimal" solutions (Pareto optimally in the language of the welfare economist). Most people end up satisfied and better off.

Second, presumably it uses rational, objective analysis (vs. intuition) and yields quantifiable results. And, the most fundamental lesson in business is that in making decisions you should compare benefits to costs.

Third, it is goal oriented (teleological); therefore managers feel comfortable using it and it is easy to justify to others. For instance, it is often argued that if business decisions increase profits, market mechanisms ensure that most customers are better off; otherwise they would buy from someone else (this ignores stakeholders other than customers).

Fourth, it considers stakeholders, including animals (e.g., in animal research by cosmetics and pharmaceutical companies). Fifth, pleasure and pain are important considerations. Sixth, it encourages efficiency and productivity. Finally utilitarianism impartiality takes everyone and all interests into account.

On the downside, there are some serious shortcomings to the utilitarian model. First, due to convenience and the fact that hindsight is 20-20, there is a tendency to neglect long-run outcomes and only measure short-term consequences. Thus, unintended, unanticipated long-run consequences are not accounted for. For instance, "free sex" might be pleasurable, but in the end the result could be a communicable disease or an unwanted child. Marketing flavored cigarettes or junk food can make customers happy but yield ultimate negative results.

Second, minorities often suffer the "tyranny of the majority," i.e., someone or some group gets burned when the majority rules, resulting in an unjust allocation of resources and/or individuals being deprived of their rights. That is, utilitarianism ignores the important concepts of rights and justice. For example, in the "bad old days" many marketing efforts were targeted toward WASPs while largely ignoring ethnic minorities. As another example, state lotteries are generally favored by taxpayers (the majority) since their tax money can be slightly reduced. But those who suffer are the heavy users, i.e., the poor who cannot afford to throw away their hard-earned dollars and gambling addicts whose addictions are further fed. In the difficult issues of abortion for poor single mothers, welfare costs and inconvenience to the mother are minimized, but what about the rights of the unborn child? Or, an automobile manufacturer could build a lower level of safety into each car, saving each customer, say, $150, but the results would be the death or serious injury to one of each 115,000 consumers. Can we balance lives against cost savings? Utilitarian analysis forces us to make such cold calculations, placing a value on human life. (The Ford Pinto's cost/benefit analysis showed that it was more profitable to settle out of court claims from life-threatening fuel system systems rather that recall the product.)

Thus, a third difficulty is that using utilitarianism can be a calculative nightmare. It can take much time and effort to make calculations and forecasts for many different stakeholders. Although it is usually straightforward to measure costs since these are tangible items, intangible benefits are more problematic to quantify and measure. How do you measure the worth of a human life? In fact, interpersonal comparisons of utility are impossible; there is no scientific way to measure the increase in welfare to the majority against the decrease in well-being to the minority. For instance, no smoking on continental airlines is now federal policy. Does the satisfaction to the 80% of nonsmokers outweigh the frustrating pain visited upon the 20% smokers? Many benefits, and sometimes even costs, are difficult to forecast in advance. To partially alleviate calculative problems, boundaries can be placed on the utilitarian measurements. For instance, often calculations are confined to the economic realm or else only the interests of those directly affected are considered. Anyway, the objectivity of the measurements is open to serious question.

A fourth problem is that utilitarianism encourages individualistic, selfish behavior since it ignores and can result in an abridgement of others' rights. It could be used to rationalize almost any behavior, including emotional acts. For example, the parties to an adulterous act might be happy, but what about the spouse and the underlying moral issue which can remain unaddressed?

Fifth, a desirable end might be caused be an unjust means or a bad motive. For instance, Robin Hood, with a "soak-the-rich" mentality, stole from the rich to assist the poor. The American Heart Association could justify running false and misleading advertising if the result is to discourage many young people from smoking. In effect, utilitarianism is analogous to the Marxian notion that "the ends justify the means." If the student's end is to get good grades so as to land a good job and the means is to cheat, fine. Using this line of reasoning some have advocated fetal harvesting as long as the fetal tissue is used for "humane" purposes such as transplants or medical research. We can presumably even justify having prostitutes work out of church basements if we use the money for feeding poor and missionary work. In fact, some studies suggest that most unethical acts in business are committed by basically honest people under pressure to achieve bottom-line results, which are believed to be all that really matters. In effect, sometimes we are saying , "Let us do evil, that good may come."

Sixth, despite supposedly hard and fast calculation, there is still some uncertainty since the definition of "the greatest good" is left open to dispute. For instance, which stakeholders should get more happiness? (Different groups can be weighed, but this involves subjective judgments and biases.) There is also uncertainty in the sense that, at least with act utilitarianism, no actions are always right or wrong. For instance, dishonesty or theft might be justifiable if it increases net benefits.

<u>Ethical Egoism.</u> This approach defines acceptable behavior in terms of consequences for the individual decision maker. Ethical egoism says that one should promote their own self interest, seeking the most good (consequences) for themselves above that of all others ("You've got to look out for number one"). Maximization of self interest is defined differently by each person. Depending on the egoist, an act could be considered right if it gives one more pleasure than pain, gives one the most power, results in fame, promotes a satisfying career, etc. In short, "do the act that promotes the greatest good for the self."

An enlightened form of egoism, postulated indirectly by the philosopher Thomas Hobbes, takes a long-term perspective and allows for consideration to one's personal well-being. In other words, one should consider the interests of others when it suits their own interests. One should accept moral rules and assume certain obligations only when doing so promotes one's welfare. One should back down on an obligation (e.g., to tell the truth, fulfill an obligation) whenever it is not in one's best interest. Thus, an enlightened egoist might call management's attention to a colleague who is cheating customers, but only to safeguard the firm's image and hence the egoist's own job security. A lot of philanthropic and "socially responsible" actions appear to be motivated by enlightened ethical egoism rather than true altruism. By being a good "corporate citizen," the firm receives good public relations.

The major advantage to egoism is that it benefits the individual. This is seen by some thinkers as being reasonable; in fact, acting against one's own interest is viewed as contrary to reason--conventional moral standards are fraught with irrational sentiment and unreasonable constraints on the individual. If enlightened egoism is practiced, some feel that this leads to utilitarian outcomes (e.g., Adam Smith's invisible hand, discussed shortly).

Problems are that it is hedonistic and selfish (and therefore morally unacceptable); ethical egoism ignores other stakeholders (possibly even stepping on toes), and therefore invites regulation; and this perspective can lead to conflicting directives in situations of moral conflict (e.g., a consumer activist fights to halt production of an unsafe car while the manufacturer fights against the activist's initiatives). However, Adam Smith argued that the public good evolves out of a suitably restrained clash of competing interests (the guiding "invisible hand" ensures that public good is served when each person pursues their own agenda). Thomas Hobbes, on the other hand, proposed the need for the all-powerful sovereign state (in modern terms, government regulation) to ensure the public good (although Hobbes believed government's powers should be fairly limited). Many modern business people recognize that when their interests do clash with those of others within the established rules of the competitive game, they should pursue their own interests. However, business practices are thus restrained because self-interest is subservient to the rules of business practice.

<u>Christian consequentialism.</u> Although Judeo-Christian morality is founded on absolute moral rules, some Christians have tried using a relativistic approach, in the form of Christian consequentialism. This says that an act is

right if it causes one to love his neighbor or to further the Kingdom of God. Aquinas labeled this "perfect good" and Augustine called it "happiness."

Cited advantages are that it focuses on positive and negative results, is flexible, follows the spirit rather than the letter of the law, and avoids legalism and rules. However, on the negative side of the ledger, it tends to be vague, Jesus did not come "to abolish the law but to fulfill it," (Matthew 5:17) and we presently "see through a glass darkly," i.e., we don't know for sure if our actions further the Kingdom of Heaven. Scriptural support for this approach seems to be lacking. The Bible denounces the days when "everyone did what was right in his own eyes." (Judges 21:25).

Deontological moral theories. Deontology refers to moral philosophies that focus on duties (deontology is derived from the Greek "duty"), on the rights of individuals, and on the intentions or motives of the moral agent. Being duty based, deontological moral theories deny what teleological moral theories assert--that only the consequences of actions and rules count. Deontological theories consider the means of actions, whereas teleological theories consider the ends. Thus, there are some things we should not do, even to maximize utility. For instance, the fact that one has made a promise obligates one to keep the promise, even if it becomes clear that keeping the promise will not lead to the greatest good.

Thus we have duties such as being fair, keeping promises, fulfilling debts to others, or abiding by a contractual relationship, regardless of consequences, Corporations have special moral obligations to their customers employees, independent of the general good.

As was true of utilitarians, deontologists can be divided into two groups: those who focus on moral rules and those who focus on the nature of the acts themselves. Rule deontologists believe that conformity to general moral principles determine ethicalness. For example, the traditional Judeo-Christian approach to morality is rule deontological (e.g., the Golden Rule). These rule deontologists also hold that individuals have certain absolute rights which should not be violated, such as freedom of conscience, freedom of consent, privacy rights, and free speech rights, among others. Rule deontologists regard the nature of moral principles as permanent and stable, and they believe that ethical people act in accordance with these principles.

Act deontologists hold that actions are the proper basis on which to judge morality. Act deontology requires that one use equity, fairness, and impartiality in decision making, and that rules serve only as general guidelines.

One perspective on deontology, prima facie duties, says that there are certain duties that are to always be acted upon, except if in a particular situation a given duty conflicts with a given or stronger duty. Thus, prima facie duties are not absolute; they can be overridden under some conditions. Prima facie duties "tend to be our duty." For instance, if the prima facie duty to keep promises were to conflict with the duty to protect innocent persons from harm, then the actual duty would be to protect innocent persons, overriding the prima facie duty to keep promises.

Deontologists also insist on the importance of motives. The same action could be different intentions. For instance, the person who keeps a promise simply because she knows she'd look bad by breaking that promise is less ethical than the person who keeps the promise because she really cares about the other party's welfare.

There are two major deontological theories: the theory of rights and the theory of justice. The theory of rights, a type of rule deontology, focuses on individuals' rights and the corresponding duties of moral agents to respect those rights. The theory of justice, a type of act deontology, focuses on equity, fairness, and impartiality in decision making. These theories can be relative or absolute in nature, depending on how they are interpreted.

Theory of rights. The theory of rights (or moral entitlements or duty), with its roots in the seventeenth century work of Thomas Hobbes, John Locke, and Immanuel Kant, recognizes moral entitlements of individuals. Moral rights are fundamental personal rights based on moral norms and principles, like the right to life, freedom, health, safety, and property. They are universal and therefore exist prior to and independent of social conventions and laws; they cannot be abolished by political powers. These rights exist irrespective of merit, just because we are human. Thus, these fundamental human/personal rights are given as birthrights (rather than as a privilege for being a Ph.D., member of a certain institution, etc.). Our humanity is said to confer rights to impartial treatment in matters of justice, freedom, equality of opportunity, and the like. The theory of rights mandates that any individual has the right to be treated in ways that ensure the dignity, respect, and autonomy of that individual.

Such rights as free/informed consent, privacy, freedom of conscience, free speech, and due process have been codified in the U.S. Bill of Rights, in the Declaration of Independence, and in the U.N. Universal Declaration of Human Rights. The Declaration of Independence asserted that these rights come from God (". . .We are endowed by our Creator with certain inalienable rights. . .life, liberty, and the pursuit of happiness.").

It is respect for these rights which should guide decision making. Most rights theorists believe that the rights of individuals take precedence over the rights of organizations and institutions. Rights theory is duty based; we judge the actor's fulfillment of her duties/obligations to other individuals in the exchange process. Focus is on the means rather than on the consequences of the actor's behavior. The arguments for rights are twofold: (1) It is necessary for individuals to have self-respect and (2) rights support freedom and well-being. Thus, rights boil down to: (1) the need for self-respect and (2) the need for freedom and well-being. Rights, in effect, show respect for humanity. Our obligation is to respect others' moral rights.

Business, then, should be viewed not simply as an economic institution but as a moral institution. Consequently, various stakeholders should not be treated with respect for their rights.

In the workplace, some commonly accepted rights include employees' right to equal pay for equal work and consumers' right to know (and JFK's other three consumer rights). Managers sometimes complain that unions violate their right to manage, and investors grouse that taxation violates their property rights.

One variation on rights theory is the Golden Rule model, with its foundation in the Bible. This states that one should choose the action which treats others with the same dignity and respect that he would expect (costs or consequences are only of secondary importance). Thus, an action is morally appropriate if it treats all the stakeholders with the same respect and dignity one would expect from others.

Another variation on rights theory is the Kantian model, which holds that each person has a basic right to respect and to be treated as a free person equal to everyone else, and everyone has a duty to treat people this way. An action is morally correct if it minimizes the violation of the rights of all stakeholders. Kant emphasizes performing one's duty for the sake of duty and not for any other reason (such as utility or self-interest). The person's motive for acting must be fulfillment of one's moral duty. Moral law states an imperative--something must be done. We must do out duty categorically, i.e., unconditionally, no matter what, no exceptions.

Kant's categorical imperative is something that must be done and is applicable to all and binding on all unconditionally. Everyone has a right to be treated as a free person equal to everyone else, and everyone has a duty to treat people this way.
Kant gave three formulations of the categorical imperative. A moral action must: (1) be universally applicable, (2) respect human beings as ends in themselves, and (3) stem from and respect the autonomy of rational beings. These three formal conditions all derive from reason and what it means to be a rational being. They suggest that self centered (non cooperative, self seeking) behavior is not always in each person's best interests.

Kant's first principle is universalization (or universalizability): what is morally right for you must be morally right for everyone else. Kant said that reasonable, thinking people would arrive at that judgement that, if universally applied, would be best for everyone. As Kant said it, "I ought never to act except in such a way that I can also will that my maxim should become universal law." In other words, ask the following question regarding the action in principle: "what if everyone did that?" That is, if everyone were to behave as you do (to act on principle) and the result were chaos, then your principle is immoral. For instance, cheating on an examination only succeeds if others do not cheat; everyone cannot receive an "A." Cheaters must free ride of honest people. Or, consider that if everyone lied, there would be no social order; language would lose its meaning. Liars must free ride off of truth tellers. Lies increase what in economics-speak are known as transaction costs, making exchange (the essence of marketing) less efficient. Or, think about queuing and the character that drives in the right-hand lane while others merge left, and then cuts into the left-hand lane at the last possible moment. If there were universalized cutting in line the result would be social chaos. If the majority of business people became dishonest or unethical, the result would be destruction of the economic system as it operates today.

Another criterion for Kant's first formulation of the categorical imperative is reversibility: your reasons for acting must be reason you'd be willing to have all others use, even as a basis for how they treat you. In other words, "How would you like it if he did it to you?" or "How would you like it if you were in her place.

The second formulation of Kant's categorical imperative says to respect people as ends (a rational person) in themselves, not as means. Always act with recognition of every person's right, including self, to be treated with respect and dignity. Each person has intrinsic value; therefore one should not use other people as means for her own ends (advancing her own self-interest). Thus, in the immortal words of Immanuel Kant, "Act so that you treat humanity, whether in your own person or in that of another, always as an end and never as a means." For instance, to subject employees to health risks without their knowledge would be to violate this principle. Deception and coercion are immoral because they fail to respect peoples' freedom to choose for themselves. Job discrimination and sexual harassment are immoral because they treat certain people as less than fully human, i.e., as less than free persons equal to all others. Likewise, lying, theft, and murder fail to show respect, treating people as means. The kind of treatment that people deserve as rational beings, as ends in themselves, is sometimes put in terms of the rights we are discussing here.

The third formulation of the categorical imperative is that moral law must stem from and respect the autonomy of human beings. We have the freedom to choose to accept the moral law and to act morally or immorally (vs. animals, who act on instincts), and we should live as members of the moral community in accordance with the moral law.

Many different human rights have been proposed. Some are controversial, i.e., some people consider them wrongs (e.g., childrens' rights, animal rights, gay rights, rights of various special interest groups), while the limit on the scope of many rights is not clear; most rights are not absolute. For instance, in 2000 years of Western Civilization, there has never been a recognized right to absolute control over one's body, such as taking heroin or committing suicide. Even though we have free speech rights, you don't have the right to yell "fire" in a crowded theater, nor do you have the right to perjury, libel, incite violence, or fraudulently advertise. My right to swing my fist ends where your face begins. And, rights are certainly not the same concept as virtues. For instance, is there a right to sexual gratification outside of marriage?

Two basic categories of rights can be identified: rights to liberty and rights to welfare. Liberty rights, (A.K.A. negative rights), recognized by all philosophers who are rights theorists, suggest that people should be free from restriction or control. An individual should have the right to act, believe, or express himself as she wishes. Basic liberty rights include privacy, free speech, freedom of conscience, and free consent. These traditional rights mean that people have the right to be left alone and suggest limits on state power. Free markets protect two natural rights: the right to be freedom (voluntary exchange) and the right to private property. An example of a controversial liberty is the freedom of association (many men's clubs have been forced to admit women in recent years; some country clubs exclude blacks).

Second, are welfare rights (A.K.A. positive rights or entitlements), which are not recognized by libertarians. Generally these boil down to health, happiness, and general well-being, and they assert a right to a minimum standard of living where a person can't provide for themselves but these are available. Specifically, welfare rights include employment, food, housing, and education.

Traditionally, such rights were felt to be a government responsibility (and they enhance the state's power), not a business responsibility. Today, more businesses, acting as "good corporate citizens," are paying more attention to these and are helping to meet some community needs (e.g., McDonald's Ronald McDonald houses). Another example of a welfare right would be an employee's right to an enhanced quality of life, which could be infringed by an organization that promotes or grants raises only to those who spend large amounts of in the working environment at the expense of family, church, and community.

The concept of duties or obligations means that for every right that someone has, there is a duty of someone else to expect that right, either by refraining from taking certain actions (liberty rights) or by taking certain actions (welfare rights).

Regarding liberty rights, the duty is simply not to interfere with another person's intended course in life, i.e., one need not really do anything to fulfill his duty. For instance, my right to life negates your "right" to kill me. One could argue that one should not prevent another from going to the grocery store, going to a porno theater, or even from having an abortion (the latter perhaps ignores the baby's right to life). The Bill of Rights in the U.S. Constitution says that the duty of government is to not interfere in certain areas of citizen's lives (civil liberties). For instance, people have the right to worship as they choose (although the line is drawn in places like animal sacrifice and drug use). An advertiser has the right to honest free commercial speech. A businessperson has the right to use, sell, or destroy personal business assets.

With respect to welfare rights, the duty is to provide people with what is needed (an education, food, shelter, employment, adequate health care, etc.). These are called positive rights because others have a positive duty to provide a person with whatever she needs to pursue her interests. Thus, homelessness could be viewed as a failure to provide one's right to shelter. Inner-city dwellers could be viewed as having a right to be served efficiently by retailers. Roles or positions within social institutions and organizations create positive rights. For instance, a married couple has the duty to care for their children, doctors have a duty to care for their patients' health, and business managers have a right to care for the organization they manage (the law of agency).

Welfare rights can clash with liberty rights; tradeoffs are sometimes necessary. Some people could feel that their liberty rights (e.g.,right to use their property as they see fit) are infringed by those telling them they have a duty to provide. For example, lawyers sometimes are expected to do pro bono work to aid the poor. The lawyers challenge the fairness of being asked to work for no pay, while proponents of this policy say that it is only fair that poor defendants have legal counsel. This gets back to the debate--do business organizations exist solely to make money for their stock holders, or do they have responsibilities to other constituencies as well?

Some people view contractual rights and duties as a third set of rights. These arise when someone enters into an agreement with someone else in a specific transaction. Each party has the right to receive what they were promised in the contract and the right to be left free and fully informed when contracts are made.

Here are some examples of generally agreed upon rights (although interpretations vary in certain situations, e.g., does a woman's right to privacy permit her to get an abortion?), along with marketing applications.

1. The right to free/informed consent. Individuals have the right to be treated only as they knowingly and freely consent to be treated. This suggests that marketing research data collected secretly against an individual's agreement (some kinds of observational studies) might be immoral.

2. The right to privacy. People have the right to do whatever they choose to do outside of working hours and to control information about their private life, including information not intended to be made public. This suggests that retailers who enter customer's names and addresses into computer files and later sell the data bases to other marketers are violating customer's privacy rights.

3. The right freedom to freedom of conscience. Individuals have the right to refrain from carrying out any order that violates moral or religious norms to which they adhere, as long as these are commonly accepted norms. Thus it would probably be immoral for an ad agency to force an ad executive to work on a cigarette or beer account if they object to the morality of those products.

4. The right to free speech. This includes individuals' right to criticize conscientiously and truthfully the ethics or legality of others or of an organization, so long as the criticism doesn't violate others' right. This argues in favor of whistle blowing; some say that an employee has a duty to whistle blow to honor the employer's right to know about unethical business conduct. It argues against false criticism of another company's salespeople.

5. The right to life and safety. This suggests that products that pose needless safety hazards shouldn't be marketed.

The procedure rights theorists are required to us is:
1. Identify all relevant stakeholders.
2. Determine all of each stakeholder's rights.
3. Figure out management's duties to the various stakeholders.
4. Prioritize the duties.

Rights theory has certain advantages to recommend it. One is its relative simplicity. One should (at least regarding negative rights) just avoid interfering with others' rights. Acts are rejected when they victimize just one person, even if societal welfare could be increased. Rights theory takes an individual perspective (vs. making utilitarian calculations involving many people and society). Second, rights theory assures minimal levels of satisfaction for all individuals (vs. some suffering the tyranny of the majority). Third, it can lead to certainty if absolute rules/principles are followed in determining rights. For instance, natural rights are absolutes, although legal, positive rights can be relativistic since they are manmade.

On the negative side of the ledger, there is often disagreement on which rights are right and which rights are wrongs. Do children have certain rights which can be asserted against their parents? Do employees have the right to advance notification of termination of employment for just cause? Do teenagers have the right to have sex and to have it with whomever they want? The Declaration of Independence suggests that rights come from the Creator, and so some major religions proscribe the latter "right." If rights are relativistically derived, of which human rights can we be certain and how? Where do rights come from?

Second, as already noted, the limits of rights aren't always clear. Does the right to free speech allow flag burning or nude dancing? Should we suppress speech which is distasteful, offensive, or disturbing to a few? To many? How much advance notification should be given employees prior to a plant closing?

A third, and very difficult problem, arises when there are conflicts among rights of competing individuals or groups (there almost always are). Positive rights often conflict with negative rights (e.g., welfare rights vs. liberty rights). For instance, affirmative action quotas embody the liberal view that group rights should take precedence over individual rights. One person's exercise of their rights might infringe on another's rights. In the abortion issue, we have the woman's right to control her body vs. the rights of the father and of the unborn child. Consider the issue of drug testing in the workplace. On the one hand, the employee has the right to privacy, but on the other hand employers and other employees have the right to know whether certain employees are likely to pose a threat to a safe work environment. Or, how do we balance the rights of smokers to enjoy a drag against the rights of nonsmokers to breathe clean air? How about privacy rights of AIDS victims vs. the right of the general public to health and safety? Environmentalists argue that the people have a right to a clean environment, that business people have a duty not to foul our natural resources no matter what the cost, while some people hold that this could interfere with their private property rights. Employees claim the freedom to unionize while employers claim the right to hire nonunion labor. Property rights sometimes conflict with zoning restrictions on use of private property. Consequently, there is sometimes the difficult task of prioritizing duties. This necessitates examining the relative importance of the interests that each right protects, an admittedly subjective process.

Another problem is that rights theory can encourage individualistic, selfish behavior when people scream about "my rights." If taken to an extreme, this could lead to anarchy.

Finally, rights theory, as opposed to utilitarianism, can lead to sub optimal consequences since consequences are inconsequential. Personal prerogatives might set an obstacle to productivity and efficiency, as in the case of drug-impaired employees.

<u>Theory of Justice.</u> The final theory of justice or fairness, with its origin in the fifth century B.C. writings of Aristotle and Plato, holds that equity, fairness, and impartiality should guide decision making. This means that a person receives "what they deserve." A person has been treated justly when she has been given what is due or owed, what she deserves or can legally claim. What might be deserved can be either a benefit or a burden. Any denial of something to which someone has a right or claim is an injustice. Thus, in the abortion issue, some would say that taking the life of an unborn child is unjust while others would argue that denying the woman the right to control her body is unjust. There are three types of justice, each defining differently the concept "that they deserve": distributive justice, retributive justice, and compensatory justice.

The concept of distributive justice focuses on distribution effects of actions or policies. Distributive justice refers to the proper distribution of social benefits and burdens, including economic goods and political rights. Justice arises from fairness in the distribution of benefits and burdens in society. For instance, should the special needs of certain geographic, ethnic, age, or religious segments receive special or unequal treatment? Canons of justice include distributive rules and principles for administering rules.

Distributive rules put an emphasis on equal treatment, i.e., fair treatment: equal ought to be treated equally and unequals unequally. Programs or services designed to assist people of a certain class must be made available to all members of that class.

First, differentiated treatment of individuals should not be based on arbitrary characteristics: individuals who are similar in the relevant respects should be treated similarly, and persons who differ in relevant respects should be treated differently in proportion to the differences between them. Thus, financial rewards, promotions, and opportunities to have additional authority and responsibility should be commensurate with the quality and quantity of work performed (rather than being based on political considerations). For instance, job discrimination in terms of distributing benefits such as salaries and promotions is wrong. If Jack and Jill each hold the same job, have the same skills, equal experience , etc., and Jack is paid twice as much as Jill, this is an unjust situation if gender is an irrelevant characteristic. Bribery can be considered unjust in that it unfairly favors the bribe payer. Executive compensation has become a disputed issue; some believe many CEO's are receiving a greater share of corporate profits than they deserve. Some people see affirmative action programs as unjust in that they give preference to women and minorities, resulting in "reverse discrimination." However, some people would justify differential treatment based on differing degrees of need.

A second distributive rule says that relevant attributes and characteristics on which differential treatment is based must have a clear relationship between goals an tasks. Price discrimination is illegal except where price differences to different buyers are cost justified. Large industrial accounts receive quantity discounts which small firms do not get. In some circumstances the job, age, discrimination might be justifiable if older people tend to perform more poorly due to physical restrictions.

Thus, an action is morally correct if it treats all stakeholders the same except where there are sound reasons for giving different treatment to different individuals. An unfair/unjust/discriminatory action awards benefits or imposes burdens on a basis not related to relevant statistics or needs.

However, there is disagreement on what are valid rules for distributive justice. The following is a sample list of major candidates of valid principles of economic distributive justice:
1. To each person an equal share.
2. To each person according to a person's need.
3. To each person according to that person's rights (e.g., economic and social liberty).
4. To each person according to individual effort.
5. To each person according to societal or group contribution.
6. To each person according to merit.

Different rules are considered o be appropriate in different situations.

The different views on relevant characteristics for equal/unequal treatment have led to rival theories of social justice at the systemic level (a full discussion of each of these is beyond the scope).

1. Egalitarianism. To each person an equal share of society's benefits and burden's (e.g.,free public education). There are no relevant differences among people that can justify unequal treatment.

2. Capitalism (capital justice). To each person according to societal or group (e.g., the firm) contribution. This could be measured in terms of work effort (input) or productivity (output, the usual measure in business).

3. Socialism/Marxism. "From each according to ability, to each according to need." Work burdens should be distributed according to peoples' abilities and benefits should be distributed according to peoples' needs.

4. Libertarianism. To each person according to her rights to social and economic liberty. Any distribution of benefits and burdens is just if it is the result of individuals freely choose to exchange with each other the goods the person already owns. "From each as they choose, to each as they are chosen." Libertarians see excessive taxation as robbing Peter to pay Paul, i.e., as coercive and confiscatory.

There are two major principles for administering rules and policies. First, rules are clearly expressed, administered fairly, enforced consistently and impartially. If someone feels that they have been unfairly treated, they should have a right to an impartial hearing. Fair administration of rules and policies should occur both within the organization (e.g., a bonus plan for the sales force should be available to all salespeople) and outside of the organization (e.g., performance-based discounts should be equally available to all distributors). Second, those who act in ignorance, under duress, or involuntarily, are excused.

One particular theory of distributive justice concerns itself with justice of process vs. justice of results. The term "distribution" may refer to the procedure of distributing, or it may refer to the results of the distribution process.

The first concern is for a just procedure ("fair play" or "due process"); focus is on the means. If the process is fair in that the system operates fairly and procedures are in place to safeguard individual rights, the outcome is irrelevant. For instance, if a fair trial was held but the wrong party was judged guilty, this would be okay if the concern were only just procedure. Sexual harassment certainly does not involve fair play. A superior who takes credit for subordinates' successes but lets them take all the blame for their mistakes is operating unfairly. Economic and social conservatives tend to favor just procedure.

A second concern is for just results; focus is on the ends. The act is just only if the outcome is fair, regardless of procedures used to arrive at the outcome. For instance advocates of comparable worth wish to rectify the 60% wage gap between males and females, not by relying on the free forces of supply and demand which determines labor market rates, but by trying to determine the relative value of various jobs to an organization. Underlying the welfare state is the concept of "social justice" in which material equality is the goal. Liberals tend to prefer just results.

Business people like to point out that the competitive free enterprise system leads to fair distribution of wealth because it offers (at least in theory) equal opportunity to all. Unfortunately, it does not guarantee and does not result in quality results for all. Ideally it is desirable to have both just procedure and just results, but in practice there is often a tradeoff between the two.

The advantages of relying on just procedure are that it focuses on equal opportunity and rewards merit. On the downside, it ignores needs and is harsh on the less fortunate or less naturally endowed (as a result capitalistic economics usually have some sort of welfare built in).

The positives for using just results are that they focus on consequences, consider need, and result in an egalitarian distribution of wealth. The negatives are that incentives might be stifled and needs are rewarded over merit (for instance the socialist catch phrase "From each according to his ability, to each according to his need").

A second type of justice is known as retributive justice. This is concerned with the justice deserved by the person who did wrong. It focuses on distribution or imposition of penalties and punishments on those who do wrong. For example, a firm polluting the air could internalize the external costs by either paying those harmed or paying the cost of pollution control equipment. However, if a person was either ignorant or unable to freely choose to do right or wrong, then they can't be justly punished or blamed. Thus, if the owner of a cotton factory whose conditions created brown lung disease didn't know about the hazardous condition, he would be blameless. The insanity plea is used to excuse murderers since they were supposedly unable to choose to do right. Also, a due process system should be used to ascertain whether the person really did wrong (e.g., circumstantial or flimsy evidence isn't good enough). And, punishments must be consistent over time and place and proportional to the wrong; the penalty should be no greater than the harm done (this argues against treble damages and punitive damage awards). This is because the punishment's purpose is to deter others from committing the same wrong or to prevent the wrongdoer from becoming a repeat offender.

The third type of justice is known as compensatory justice. The idea here is to provide a just way of compensating people for what they lost when wronged by others. A just compensation is one that is proportional to the loss. Norms of compensation/restitution exist for injuries or harm, both economic and psychological. First, individuals are not held responsible for matters over which they have no control. Second, individuals should not be compensated for their losses by the party responsible for those losses. Examples include monetary compensation for damage done and media make goods for advertisements which do not run as scheduled.

A controversial concept of compensatory justice in the business world is that of "preferential treatment" or affirmative action. This involves programs that attempt to remedy past injustices against groups (especially minorities). Does justice mandate that members of a group formerly discriminated against be compensated by being given preferential treatment in hiring, training, and promotion procedures? Or is such treatment itself a violation of justice by violating the principle of equal treatment? Does justice require quotas of minority members even if this necessitates turning down more highly qualified non minorities?

In general, the advantages of justice approaches to ethics include that it ensures a "fair" allocation of resources (however one defines "fair"), is democratic in that it does not allow a society to become status- or class-conscious, it protects the interests of minorities, and can result in certainty when absolute standards of justice are applied.

However, it is difficult to apply justice criteria (e.g., determining the criteria upon which differential is based), justice can encourage a sense of entitlement that reduces risk/innovation/productivity as well as diminished incentives to produce goods and services (especially true for just results), it can result in curtailing some people's rights to achieve canons of justice (affirmative action, for instance, has been labeled by some as "reverse discrimination"), and there often arise conflicts among different claims of justice, especially where fixed standards aren't in place.

Regarding clashing claims of justice, there is a conflict between just procedure vs. just results; different economic systems for ensuring economic justice (capitalism vs. socialism, etc.); seniority vs. merit, and market values vs. other criteria in determining compensation. Affirmative action opponents say that quotas violate out country's principle of equal treatment for equal skills; supporters say that justice demands compensation for the horrors of past discrimination. Some view attempts to redistribute wealth as unfair since policy makers take money away from one section of the community to give it to another. Looters in the 1992 Los Angeles riots following the Rodney King verdict claimed they were just getting "justice." Is "vigilante justice" really justice?

<u>Conclusion on ethical theories.</u> Work in the field of normative ethics in the twentieth century has evolved from two basic approaches: teleological theory (focus on consequences) and deontological theory (focus on duties). The major teleological theory is utilitarianism, and the major deontological theories are rights theory and justice theory.

One might ask: why do we need moral theories? Why not just rely on generally accepted moral rules (conventional morality) such as "Do no harm," "Do not kill," and "Tell the truth"? First, although these rules are generally sufficient in black and white cases they are not always so in gray areas. The theories are especially useful for resolving difficult moral issues, i.e., ethical dilemmas. Second, using these ethical theories for moral reasoning makes it possible for an individual who makes a moral decision to explain and justify it to others. For instance, the manager who hires and fires employees must be able to explain the fairness of her decisions to others.

Each of the different moral theories uses different kinds of criteria to evaluate ethical behavior, and each looks at ethical dilemmas from a different moral point of view. None of the theories captures all of the factors that must be considered when rendering moral judgements (e.g., utilitarianism considers social welfare, rights theory considers individual moral rights, and justice theory considers the distribution of benefits and burdens among individuals). Therefore all three theories should be given consideration, although only one might be most relevant in a particular situation. These are not moral decision rules per se but, rather, constitute moral perspectives to be used in analyzing cases and scenarios. They enable use of critical reasoning skills in reaching a post conventional level of analysis.

Different ethical theories sometimes promote rival answers to moral dilemmas, which present obvious problems for corporate executives, employees, or others who are called to make ethical decisions. When there is a conflict among the results yielded by the different approaches judgement should be used in weighing the different theories. Some ethicists feel that rights take precedence over justice, which take precedence over utilitarian consequences. Where there is conflict among criteria within a given approach (e.g., between utilitarian consequences, between the rights of competing individuals, or between different canons of justice), again a weighting procedure is recommended. Also, the ethical theories can be combined with application of moral rules. In any case, ethical theories force critical and constructive reflection on moral problems.

Areas of Difficulty--Obstacles that Detract from Building Moral Corporate Cultures

The state of perceived and perhaps actual ethical business conduct is at a low level. Business has been weighed in the moral balance and found wanting. Why is this so? Perceptual reasons could include the fact that society is increasingly pluralistic regarding beliefs and values (e.g., environmentalism vs. unbridled free enterprise and growth), business decisions are increasingly being judged publicly by groups with diverse values and interests (e.g., R.J. Reynolds' decision to market Uptown cigarettes to blacks was applauded by some marketers and booed by black community leaders and anti smoking groups), and the public's expectations for ethical business conduct have increased. There are also some real reasons why business ethics might actually be in freefall.

First, there is the pressure for performance. An overemphasis on economic values (vs. moral values), on beating competition, and on a constant eye on the bottom line can create an atmosphere where it is easy to give in to the short-term pressures. The bad barrel argument says that corporate cultures become unethical, not because individuals are rotten (the bad apple argument) but because pressures create such a state. Most ethical lapses are probably unpremeditated acts committed by basically hard-working people with moral fiber who are thrust into situations where they are pressured to wrestle with their conscience and win (vs. white collar criminals who engage in outright crooked goings on as selling bogus securities or embezzle funds from the corporate coffers). Thus people give in to temptation and end up doing questionable things like accepting gifts shipped to their home by suppliers and approving advertising which stretches the truth a bit to make the cash registers ring. Many people become involved in white collar crime not out of greed or malevolence, but out of weakness or due to blunders which lead them to step over the ethical line rather than cross it purposively. The pressure on corporate executives for favorable quarterly earnings increases creates a dog-eat-dog environment whereby everyone looks out for themselves.

Second, decisions in the workplace are sometimes invisible. Many decisions are made in groups or pass through multiple approval points. Thus, it becomes easy to hide behind the corporate shield.

Third, ties are less personal at work, especially in large corporations. In such environments, it becomes easier to, for instance, be loyal to the boss, no matter what it takes.

Fourth, too many top corporate managers are hypocrites who only pay lip service to ethics or talk out of both sides of their mouth. They are competent administrators but leaders in terms of moral guidance when they informally set different standards for different levels in the corporate hierarchy. In effect, they say, "Do as I say, not as I do." And yet, as the saying goes, "The fish rots from the head down."

Fifth, is the dehumanization of employees and customers. Too many organizations are only concerned with efficiency and productivity, not with employees' quality of life. Instead of treating employees with respect and dignity (as Kant would suggest), managers treat them as cogs in a machine, depriving them of meaningful work lives. And, if employees see that top management views customers as gullible, unenlightened, and as easy prey for deception, they might fear that management will treat them similarly.

Sixth, is the overemphasis on image. Too many activities done in the name of social responsibility and alleged concern for ethics are merely public relations ploys (ethical egoism in practice).

Seventh, is nonparticipative management, top down dictation of rules and procedures. A more ethical climate evolves where, instead, employees are encouraged to freely express ideas, concerns, and personal values. Corporate power, responsibility, and wealth are shared, which helps build the trust which allows employees to work more collaboratively and selflessly.

Finally, some would say that a major barrier is the omnipresence of immorality in society overall, due to decline in the family structure and in religion institutions in preaching good old-fashioned morality. The highest values in a society lie in the integrity and quality of relationships among people. These values in a society lie in the integrity and quality of relationships among people. These values are cultivated primarily in family institutions (via direct teaching using rewards and punishments) and religious institutions (via instilling the importance of knowledge of and obedience to God's will).

With the decline of the family and formal religion, the burden of instilling ethics is increasingly being left to educational and workplace institutions. Yet it is curious that, despite all the efforts of the last 15 to 20 years, standards of business conduct have not been raised and might still be falling. Some have speculated that this demonstrates the pitiful failure of the predominant relativistic approach in ethics education. Ethics should, they day, be moved from being merely an intellectual exercise to one in which sound values are internalized.

<u>Practical Difficulties in Using Moral Philosophies</u>
Two problems arise in trying to apply the theoretical moral philosophies in order to do the right thing. If either or both of these conditions are present, the individual isn't morally responsible or culpable and can be excused for her immoral decision. One is a lack of information by the decision maker on either the moral standards or factual information needed to render a moral judgement (e.g., intangible consequences for utilitarian decision making). For example, asbestos manufacturers claimed they didn't

know that conditions in their plants would cause lung cancer. However, the person isn't excused if she deliberately kept herself ignorant or if she negligently failed to take adequate steps to keep herself informed.

The second problem is the decision maker's lack of ability to employ the criteria in the moral theories (e.g., is she is not permitted to or she is pressured by her supervisors). This is usually due to lack of power, skill, opportunity, or resources to act. If a person is under great pressure or duress, their responsibility for immoral actions is correspondingly reduced.

These two problems can occur at all three levels of analysis.

At the systematic level, for example, there is the impact of the law, which, although usually an ally of ethics, can also be an enemy. For instance, an employer can be sued for telling an ex-employee's prospective employer negative things about the fired employee. Thus, he withholds potentially valuable information, which seems to be morally problematic since it violates the prospective employer's right to know. Or, as liability laws get stricter, we will see more drug testing, which violates the employee's right to privacy. Another systemic level difficulty can be the impact of unfair competition, which makes operating above board and earning a profit difficult. Cultural differences, i.e., the fact that different societies play by different rules (such as bribery) poses another problem, as we have seen. Industry practices can also be constraining factors.

At the corporate level, corporate cultures or corporate policies which encourage immorality can make moral behavior challenging. Incentive systems encourage short-run opportunistic behavior such as pressure selling. A dishonest superior can make moral turpitude tempting. Constrained corporate resources might make unethical behavior the easy way out.

Finally, at the individual level, the clash of values between an individual and his peers, an inability to act, pressure from superiors, personal hardships and risks, personal financial constraints, and conflict between family/church/community organizations and the business organization can lead to difficulties. For instance, although a professor could spend all of her spare time doing scholarly research, this would be fair neither to her family nor to her students.

Solving Ethical Cases
A seven-step model has been developed by Manuel Velasquez and has been used by ethicists working in conjunction with Arthur Anderson & Co., SC.(this author is developing it a bit more fully here). The model can be used by a person confronted with an ethical dilemma and in using the case method. The approach is similar to the traditional case analysis approach used in most business courses, and it is an attempt to apply general rules to the full complexity of specific circumstances. It consists of seven questions to be asked in a class discussion where various viewpoints can be brought out and assertions can be probed and challenged.

   1. What are the relevant facts? Recall that the second element in the

moral reasoning model was factual information concerning the policy, institution, or behavior in question. The decision maker should separate out facts that are not needed to identify the ethical issues. The decision maker must also be able to clarify/distinguish facts from her assumptions and interpretations in the situation. And, decision makers should be critical of information sources (watch for possible biases).

2. What are the ethical issues? An ethical issue is a problem, situation, or opportunity requiring an individual or organization to choose among several actions that must be evaluated as right or wrong, ethical or unethical (e.g., conflicts of interest, unfairness, discrimination, bribery). Critical ethical issues, i.e., possible violations of moral standards or common morality, need to be defined at all three levels of analysis. Ethical values can be classified as either bad (e.g., violence, threats, property damage, violation of rights, deception, unequal distribution of wealth) or good (e.g.,freedom, equality, respect for individuals, justice, integrity, honesty, courage). One must identify the moral agent(s)(individuals, organizations, government policy makers, etc.) and whether they know the ethical value of the act or policy question.

3. Who are the primary stakeholders? Rather than coming up with an exhaustive list of individuals or groups which might be affected by a decision (which is usually impossible), key persons and groups should be identified.

4. What are the possible alternatives? The possible courses of action should be creatively identified without regard to their ethical impact.

5. What are the ethics of the alternatives? Moral standards (the first component of the moral reasoning model) are applied to the situation. The three ethical theories (utilitarianism, rights, justice) should be used to determine how each alternative affects all stakeholders and which alternatives offer an acceptable moral solution. Moral rules/norms/values can also be applied, especially where the ethical theories give conflicting answers.

6. What are the practical constraints? Factors which might limit the decision maker's ability to implement an alternative, such as ignorance (e.g.,where one couldn't foresee consequences of an action) or lack of ability (e.g., an involuntary choice) should be identified.

7. What actions should be taken? A moral judgment (the third component in the moral reasoning model) is made on the rightness or wrongness of the behavior in question. This includes selection and implementation of an alternative, along with justification why this was chosen over alternative courses of action. Key considerations are the ethical evaluation and the practical constraints.

Appendix: Methods for Leading Discussions of Ethics

The following is non-lecture but, it is hoped, provides useful background information on teaching ethics and integrating ethics into the marketing curriculum. Most of the ideas here come from materials supplied by Arthur

Anderson & Co., SC, although other sources and the author's own experiences are also drawn upon.

The Place of Ethics in the Curriculum

There are three possible ways to integrate ethics into the business curriculum. First, it can be as a stand-alone course, taught by either a philosophy, theologian, business professor well-versed in ethics, or by a combination of these. The advantages are that this course offers a concentrated, systematic look at the subject, and it is usually taught by professors formally trained in ethics. The downside is that the professor is often not very familiar with business issues.

A second possibility is to use the integrative approach whereby ethics is treated as an intrinsic part of various functional area business courses. The ethical dimensions or marketing subject matter can be discussed throughout the course. This does not mean that you merely have an "ethics day " or "ethics week," which leaves the perception that ethics is merely an add-on, afterthought, or separate area of business. Rather ethics is taught and ethical issues are discussed at several points during the course. The advantages are: if students keep hearing about ethics, they begin to realize what an important component of business decision making ethics is; the professor has expertise in business and her functional area; and there is no burning need to add an additional business ethics course into an already overly crowded business curriculum (such additions are, of course, always thorny political issues). The downside is that the professor might feel uncomfortable in teaching this material and might lack effectiveness since she isn't formally trained in ethics (more on this next).

A third possibility, which is ideal if there is room in the curriculum, is to use a combination approach: include both a stand-alone course and integrate ethics into the various business and marketing courses, thereby obtaining the advantages of both of the above approaches. The business ethics course need not be a full-semester course; it could be a workshop during freshman orientation, a half semester course or minicourse, a significant component of an Introduction to Business course, etc. You need not be an expert.

You don't need a Ph.D. in ethics or to be an accomplished ethicist to teach the basics of ethics and to lead ethical discussions. The material in this lecture should be more than ample to equip you with the basic ethics concepts and models. If you plan to devote one 75-minute lecture to this material, you will find what you need to be selective in what you present. However, the additional material you don't have time to present will give you additional background information to help you feel more confident and be able to answer student questions. You will need to communicate the foundation ethical reasoning models and guide your students your students through the ethical decision making process.

Your Task

This is the controversial issue. The prevailing opinion is that your task is not to change the moral character of your students but rather to sensitize them to the moral dimensions of the business. Your job is to provide them with the intellectual foundation for moral reasoning.

The problem here is that being ethical involves more than just going through an intellectual exercise. We need to touch the conscience. This can only come through a strong emphasis on the idea that there is a right and wrong, good and evil. An emphasis on moral values is sadly lacking in most ethics curricula.

The related advice given by the "experts" is to avoid introducing value judgments. This would be to "indoctrinate" students.

However, the question is: "What's wrong with indoctrination?" The word simply means to impart doctrines. Isn't that what teaching is about? It is amazing how we are able to teach basic rules and truths in math, science, and other disciplines, including business, but not in ethics. Thus, while the ethicists solemnly warn us not to tell our students what is right and wrong, the author suggests that this is nihilistic; it teaches that right and wrong are just matters or personal preference. What we suggest is to defer revealing moral standards until near the end of a discussion. This allows for freer and more airing of student opinions. If the students are encouraged to voice and analyze their positions in an organized fashion and if the instructor carefully respects these various opinions, then disagreement can be tolerated and the discussion can move forward. If there is disagreement in the classroom following an ethics discussion, try to achieve closure by reconciling the results of the ethical theories with the moral values. Students must be challenged to think through what their world view is (e.g., absolutism vs. relativism) and the source of authority for the moral principles they hold (culture, religion, etc.). They must then search out what moral principles are relevant in a particular ethical scenario.

Use Lecture
The most critical thing to emphasize in the lecture is the foundation concepts about world views, moral theories, and how to systematically conduct an ethical analysis. Present other material as it suits your student's needs and interests.

Use an Ethical Reasoning Model to Facilitate an Analytical Perspective of Business Ethics
The Arthur Anderson & Co., SC seven-step model is not the only reasoning model available for analyzing and resolving ethical dilemmas. However, it ties in nicely with the Moral Reasoning Model it is becoming widely used by the many business and marketing professors who have been through Arthur Anderson & Co.'s business ethics conferences, and it is well-suited to case discussions since it is similar to the case analysis process.

This case method teaches by discussion instead of by lecture, and it focuses on a concrete event instead of theoretical concepts. Students are expected to take a stand on the ethical issues in the case and to provide reasoned arguments for their position. They are to put themselves in the shoes of the moral agent (ethical decision maker) and not merely be a passive observer. The instructor leads the discussion through Socratic questioning, keeping it moving and on track. The case method trains students in analytical thinking and sharpens their decision making skills. The seven-step model helps here by leading students through a logical decision-making process. However, the model shouldn't be viewed as a rigid set of steps which must be followed in lock-step fashion. Rather, it provides a general logical procedure to use in ethical reasoning; generally, the later steps build on the earlier steps. However, sometimes steps can be skipped and returned to later if this makes more sense. Thus, the model is both flexible as well as systematic.

The following are a few additional pointers, most from Manuel Velasquez, for each step in the seven-step model:

1. Identify the relevant fact. Students must determine which facts are critical to understand the ethical issues. Often they will say that they need additional information in order to render a moral judgment. Is so, one possibility is for you to remind them that in the "real world" decisions are often made without adequate information. Or, in some cases it might be more fruitful to have them (or you) make reasonable assumptions. Alternatively you can direct them to the library to gather additional background information.

2. Identify the ethical issues. This is where moral standards can be emphasized, since an ethical issue is generally a question about whether a behavior, policy, or institution is consistent with personal or societal moral standards.

3. Identify stakeholders. Your goal here is to get students to see things from different perspectives to learn to empathize and identify with others.

4. Develop alternatives for resolving the ethical issue. This is where students can put on their creative thinking caps. The instructor's job will be to help students winnow down a potentially long list of viable alternatives to the best few for further analysis.

5. Evaluate the ethics of each alternative. This is the heart of the ethical analysis, and it will require a good portion of the discussion time to apply the three major ethical theories. Here are some suggestions for guiding the discussion using each ethical theory:

a. The utilitarian perspective. For each alternative, ask students to spell out the costs and benefits each stakeholder incurs. Then students must estimate which alternative is ethically best from the perspective of utilitarianism. Since students will differ in their estimates of benefits and harms, these differences should be discussed and resolved where possible.

b. The rights and duties perspective. Students should be asked what moral rights they believe each stakeholder has and what moral duty each owes other stakeholders. Then, students must weigh or prioritize the various rights and duties. Finally students must identify the alternative which promises to respect the most important rights and duties of the stakeholders. This alternative is "ethically best" from the perspective of rights theory. Since students will differ in their views of what constitutes rights and theories, they should be asked to defend their ideas.

c. The perspective of fairness or justice. For each alternative, students should be asked which of these distributions is the fairest (the "ethically best" alternative) and why. Since students will differ in their answers, they should be asked to support their reasoning by describing the criteria they used for defining fairness.

While these three perspectives will tend to rule out those alternatives that are unequivocally unethical, often more than one alternative will be recommended by the analysis. In this case, ask students which one of the three ethical theories makes the most sense to use in the particular situation. Also, analyze the alternatives in terms of the moral norms.

6. Consider the practical constraints. This encourages students to think pragmatically as well as theoretically.

7. Choose and implement an alternative. A decision is made, based on the ethical evaluation and possible constraints. Use Minicases.

Use Minicases from textbooks, casebooks, and the Arthur Anderson collection as a basis for group discussion (either the entire group or breakout groups). The advantage of short cases is that they are quicker for students to grasp and hence a more efficient way to apply ethical principles.

Another option is for you or even your students to create your own minicases. Here are a few guidelines for doing so:
- Be sure that the situation is suitably ambiguous.
- Select realistic business situations.
- Center the vignette around situations that entry-level business would face
- Make sure that only one person faces a dilemma, so that students can put themselves in that person's shoes. When students develop their own vignettes, they draw upon personal ethical dilemmas they have faced in their academic or professional careers.

Use Role Plays
You can set up a role playing session where students volunteer to assume the roles of various characters in an ethics case or minicase, and have them act out the situation.

Use Videos
More and more textbook publishers are offering videos free to adopters of their texts. Some of these either focus on or (more often) have integrated into them ethical issues. The Arthur Anderson videos are also very useful (see the resources section for a description). One of the strengths of vignette videotapes is that your students can start thinking about what it will be like to encounter ethical dilemmas in their first full time job outside of college.

Use Articles

Articles in national newspapers (Wall Street Journal, USA Today, Marketing News, etc.) and in local papers and magazines report current ethical issues and ethical lapses. These can be described and discussed in class.

Use Guest Speakers
Local business leaders, faculty experts, or former students/alumni can be invited to speak on the importance of ethics and issues they have grappled with.

Key References

Arthur Anderson & Co., SC. Business Ethics Program Reference Guide. St. Charles, Illinois, 1990.

Robert A. Cooke. "Ethics in Business: A Perspective." Arthur Anderson & Co., SC, 1991.

Geoffrey P. Lantos. "Arthur Anderson Business Ethics Overview," in Christianity and Business: A Collection of Essays on Pedagogy and Practice, ed. Edward S. Trunfio. Christian Business Faculty Association, 1991, pp.3-28.

Manuel G. Velasquez. Business Ethics: Concepts and Cases. Englewood Cliffs, N.J., 1982.

Table of Transparencies

Types of Ethical Dilemmas

I. Individual Values and the Business Organization
    A. Employee Conflicts of Interest
    B. Inappropriate Gifts
    C. Security of Company Records
    D. Personal Honesty
    E. Government Contract Issues

II. Individual Rights and the Business Organization
    A. Corporate Due Process
    B. Employee Screening
    C. Employee Privacy
    D. Sexual Harassment
    E. Affirmative Action/Equal Employment Opportunity
    F. Employment at Will
    G. Whistle-Blowing
    H. Employee Rights
    I. Comparable Worth

III. Business Operations
    A. Financial and Cash Management Procedures
    B. Conflicts Between the Corporation's Ethical Code and Accepted Business Practices in Foreign Countries
    C. Unauthorized Payments to Foreign Officials
    D. Workplace Safety
    E. Plant Closures and Downsizing

F. Environmental Issues
G. Purchasing: Conflicts and Bribery

IV. Business and Its Competition
    A. Advertising Content
    B. Appropriation of Others' Ideas
    C. Product Pricing

V. Business and Its Product
    A. Contract Relations
    B. Product Safety
    C. Product Quality
    D. Customer Privacy

VI. Business and Its Stakeholders
    A. Shareholders' Interests
    B. Executive Salaries
    C. Corporate Contributions
    D. Social Issues

Language to Watch For:
Rationalizations for Ethical Breaches

1. "Everybody else does it"

2. "If we don't do it, someone else will"

3. "That's the way it's always been done"

4. "We'll wait until the lawyers tell us it's wrong"

5. "It doesn't really hurt anyone"

6. "The system is unfair"

Categories of Unethical Behavior

1. Taking things that don't belong to you

2. Saying things you know are not true

3. Giving or allowing false impressions

4. Buying influence or engaging in a conflict of interest

5. Hiding or divulging information

6. Taking unfair advantage

7. Committing personal decadence

8. Perpetrating interpersonal abuse

9. Permitting organizational abuse

10. Violating rules

11. Condoning unethical actions

12. Balancing ethical dilemmas

Resolving Ethical Dilemmas:

Blanchard/Peale

1. Is it legal?

2. Is it balanced?

3. How does it make me feel?

Front Page of the Newspaper Test

"Contemplating any business act, an employee should ask himself whether he would be willing to see it immediately described by an informed and critical reporter on the front page of his local paper, there to be read by his spouse, children and friends. At Salomon we simply want no part of any activities that pass legal tests but that we, as citizens, would find offensive."

Warren E. Buffet
Chairman, Salomon, Inc.

"If we were making that decision now in light of the press scrutiny we have been receiving, we probably would not have taken that risk."

Robert C. Winters
Chairman, Prudential Insurance

Resolving Ethical Dilemmas:

Laura Nash Model

1. Have you defined the problem accurately?
2. How would you define the problem if you stood on the other side of the fence?
3. How did this situation occur in the first place?
4. To whom and to what do you give your loyalty as a person and as a member of the corporation?
5. What is your intention in making this decision?
6. How does the intention compare with the likely results?
7. Whom could your decision or action injure?
8. Can you discuss your decision with the affected parties?
9. Are you confident that your position will be as valid over a long period of time as it seems now?
10. Could you discuss your decision with your CEO, board, friends, boss, family?
11. What is the symbolic potential of your action if understood? If misunderstood?
12. Under what circumstances would you make exceptions to your position?

Case 1.1: Commodities, Conflicts, and Clintons

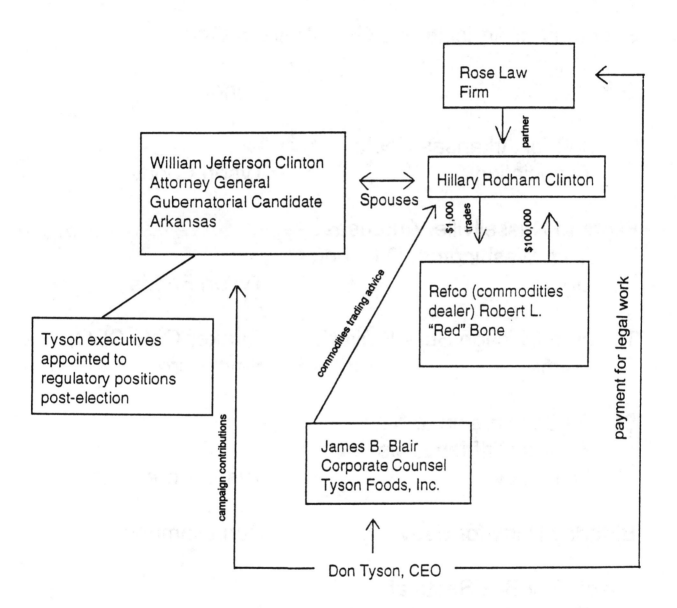

Case 1.6: The Secretary of Agriculture, Chicken Processors, and Football Sky-Box Seats

Secretary of Agriculture's Gifts While in Office:

Gift	Donor
Lodging for Arkansas Poultry Association	Tyson Foods
Flight to Russellville, Arkansas from Washington, D.C. and Back	Tyson Foods
Ticket to Chicago Bulls Playoff Game	Quaker Oats CEO, Smithburg
$1,200 Scholarship to Mr. Espy's Girlfriend, Ms. Dempsey	Tyson Foundation
Birthday Party for Espy	Sun Diamond
Tyson Sky-Box Seats at Dallas Cowboys/New York Giants Playoff Game	Tyson Foods

Case 2.1: Ann Hopkins, Price Waterhouse and the Partnership

The Differing Descriptions

"Deft touch"

"Outstanding professional"

"strong character, independence, integrity"

"extremely competent, intelligent"

"strong and forthright"

"very productive, energetic, creative"

"intellectual clarity"

"stimulating conversationalist"

"highly competent"

"overly aggressive"

"unduly harsh"

"difficult to work with"

"impatient with staff"

"macho"

"overcompensated for being a woman"

"needs to take a course at charm school"

"lady using foul language"

"appealing lady partner candidate"

"walk more femininely, talk more femininely, dress more femininely, wear make-up, have her hair styled, and wear jewelry"

Case 2.2: Handwriting Analysis and Employment

HANDWRITING ANALYSIS

More than 100 personality traits are scored in handwriting analysis, and the results may be used to determine whether an applicant is right for a job. The samples below illustrate how a handwriting trait may be isolated to define a personality trait in an individual.

The sales job
Two applicants trying to land a job in sales.

A *[handwriting sample]*

B *[handwriting sample]*

Trait highlight
A more rhythmic pattern of writing and dotting the i's to the right is believed to indicate a persuasive personality.

Trait highlight
Extra humps on n's and m's, and an erratic writing pattern, are said to show less persuasiveness.

Overall analysis
Applicant A scored higher than Applicant B in several traits pertinent to a sales job, including "persuasive," "energetic," "shrewd" and "self-motivated."

The management position
Two applicants for a management job.

C *[handwriting sample]*

D *[handwriting sample]*

Trait highlight
Simplified letters and angular shapes in writing are believed to show ability to handle pressure.

Trait highlight
Elaborate letters and a tendency to overlap descenders are said to show less ability to handle pressure.

Overall analysis
Applicant C appears to have a personality that better fits the job than does Applicant D. Applicant C scored higher in the "analytical," "organized," "decisive" and "handles pressure well" categories.

Source: Handwriting Research Corp.

The Arizona Republic

Case 2.16: Beech-Nut and the No-Apple-Juice Apple Juice

1977	Beech-Nut and Interjuice contract for apple concentrate
1978	LiCari sends Beech-Nut employees to Interjuice plant; access to tanks denied
1979	Nestlé buys Beech-Nut
Early 1981	LiCari goes to plant manager Lavery with suspicions and circumstantial evidence; "Chicken Little" meeting
August 1981	LiCari takes chemical tests to Lavery; "Team Player" meeting
August 1981	LiCari takes evidence and tests to Hoyvald; "Naivete and Impractical Ideals"
November 1981	LiCari leaves Beech-Nut
1982	Processed Apples Institute lawsuit against Interjuice; Beech-Nut cancels Interjuice contracts
March 1983	Bogus juice sales stopped
1986	Lavery and Hoyvald trials (conspiracy, fraud, food and drug law violations)

Case 2.18: Dow Corning and the Silicone Implants: Questions of Safety and Disclosure

History and Ownership of Silicone Implant Manufacturers

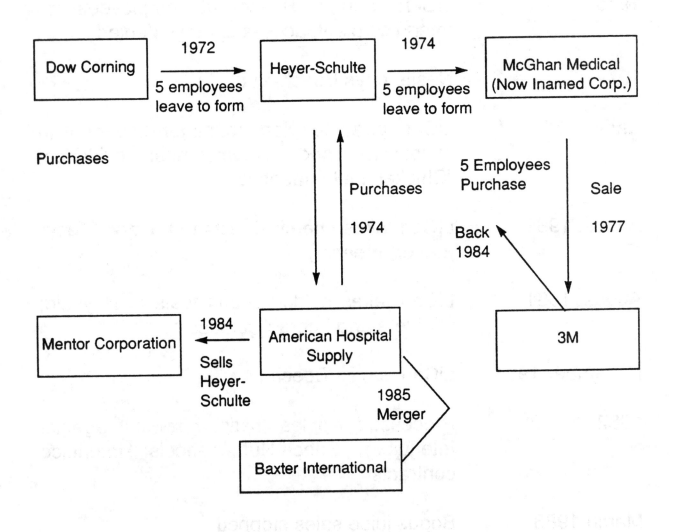

Case 2.18: Dow Corning and the Silicone Implants: Questions of Safety and Disclosure

Dow Corning Chronology

1960s	Implants first developed
1976	Thomas Talcott, Dow engineer raises safety questions
1976	Heyer-Schulte "Dear Doctor" safety letter
1980	Salesman questions sale of implants
1984	Bill Boley, Dow Corning scientist, says no safety data established
1984.	Stern case in Nevada; $1.5 million in punitive damages against Dow Corning
1987	Dow Corning does not dispute leaks; only connection with harms
1987-1991	Increasing litigation; medical documentation of immune system problems
1991	New York $4.5 million verdict
Oct. 1991	FDA Hearings
Dec. 1991	Hopkins' $7.3 million verdict against Dow
January 1992	FDA requests ban on sales of implants
Mid-Jan. 1992	Dow Corning's stock falls $10
March 1992	Dow Corning withdraws from implant market

Case 3.1: BCCI and the Role of Internal Auditors

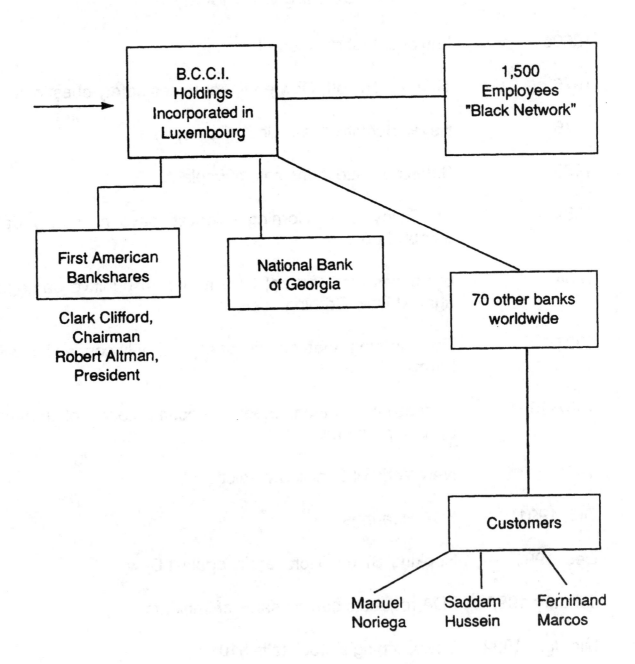

Case 3.2: Medical Billing Errors and Practices Terminology

Upcoding	code as different procedure to bring more compensation from insurers
Unbundling	breaking surgeries into parts to bring more compensation from insurers
Exploding	breaking tests into various parts to bring more compensation from insurers
Code creeps	unbundling, exploding, and upcoding
Miscoding	Routine uncovered tests coded as something else to ensure coverage
Bundling	Insurer's practice of package price for procedures

Case 3.4: MiniScribe and the Auditors

Employee Cooperation in Fraud

1. Shipments to customers are two times the amount that they actually ordered; sales fully booked

2. Manipulation of reserves

3. Pretend inventory (construction bricks wrapped as disk drives)

4. Alteration of auditors' work papers

5. Shipping practices and passage of title and booking of sales

Case 3.6: The Ethics of Derivatives

Entity	Loss
Charles County	$8.3 million (98 percent of its assets in collateralized mortgage
Cuyahoga County	$137 million (leveraged its $1.8 billion fund)
West Virginia	$279 million
Florida	$175 million
Metallgesellschift	$1 billion
Askin Capital Management	$2 billion (firm is liquidated)
Procter & Gamble	$102 million
Gibson Greetings	$23 million
Bankers Truss	$130 million

Lawsuits

Paine Webber	(settled for $33 million)
Piper Jaffray	(settled for $70 million)
Bankers Trust	(pending)
Gibson Greetings	(settled for $23 million)

Case 3.15: Electromagnetic Fields (EMF): Exposure for Workers and Customers

Chronology of Events

1950	First studies; U.S. Public Health Service
1968	Navy ELF project in Wisconsin
1972	Becker recommends further study
1973	Power line siting issue erupts in New York
1979	Werthemeier Denver cluster studies on wire configurations and childhood leukemia
1979	PAVE PAWS impact examined
1980-83	Adey studies appear; press coverage of PAVE PAWS on Cape Cod
1985	Houston case on refusal of power lines
1986	Women near PAVE PAWS have higher cancer rate
1988	New studies
1992	EPRI involvement
1994	EPRI study on utility workers

Case 3.17: Generics of Downsizing

Year	Company	# of Employees
1998	AT&T	15,000
1998	Seagate Technology	10,000
1998	Intel	1,100
1998	J.C. Crew	100
1997	Kodak	2,000 (middle managers); 10,000
1997	General Motors	42,000
1997	Fruit of the Loom	2,900
1997	Waste Management	1,200
1997	Polaroid	5,000
1997	Kemet Corp.	1,000
1997	RJR Nabisco	2,800
1997	Apple Computer	4,100
1997	H.J. Heinz	2,500
1997	Hasbro	2,500
1997	Boeing	12,000
1997	Levi Strauss	6,395
1996	Best Products	10,000
1996	Aetna	8,200
1996	Sunbeam	6,000
1996	Wells Fargo	3,800

Case 3.23: Exxon and Alaska

Damage to Prince William Sound:

> Spill covered 1,000 square miles
> 1,000 dead otters
> 34,400 dead sea birds
> 151 Bald Eagles
> Fishing industry

Damages Assessed and Costs to Exxon:

> $2 billion clean-up
> $50,000 fine - Hazelwood
> 800 civil suits still pending
> $180,000 to fishermen (settlement)
> $1.15 billion fine (criminal case by U.S. and Alaska)
> $900,000,000 (civil case by U.S. and Alaska)
> $287 million to fishermen
> $9.7 million for damages to Native American land
> $1.5 billion for wildlife damage
> $20 million to native Alaskans for damages to their villages

Case 3.24: The Death of the Great Disposable Diaper Dilemma

PRO

Only 2% of solid waste

Greater environmental
    impact of cloth if
    energy and water
    in laundry included

4 of 5 Americans prefer
    disposable

CON

7,800 diapers/child

2-5 years for plastic to
    break down

20 states regulate
    municipal regulations

Case 4.4: The Obligation to Screen? The Obligation to Reject, *Soldier of Fortune* Classifieds

Ads at Issue

The Hearn Ad

Ex-Marines -- 67-69 'Nam Vets, Ex-Di, weapons specialist -- jungle warfare, pilot, M.E., high risk assignments, U.S. or overseas. (404)991-2684

Note: "Ex-Di" means ex-drill instructor; "M.E." means multi-engine planes; and "high risk assignments" means work as a bodyguard or security specialist.

Previous Ads

Gun For Hire: 37-year-old -- professional mercenary desires jobs. Vietnam Veteran. Discreet and very private. Bodyguard, courier, and other special skills. All jobs considered. [phone number]

Gun For Hire: Nam sniper instructor. SWAT. Pistol, rifle, security specialist, bodyguard, courier plus. All jobs considered. Privacy guaranteed. Mike [phone number].

Case 4.12: Salomon Brothers and Bond Pricing

The Mechanics of the Salomon Squeeze

1. Salomon bids its 35% share in government bond auction (price is high)

2. Salomon bids same high price for customers

3. Government accepts bids

4. Salomon buys bonds back from customers
    Market is cornered

5. Salomon can name its price as other buyers struggle to buy

Case 5.9: Ford and Its Pinto: Cost Analysis Tables for Pinto Redesign

Table 1

Costs of the 1970 Potential Design Modification
Strategy: Low Estimate[1]

Calendar Year	Sales (1,000)	Estimated Unit Cost ($)	Estimated Total Cost ($ million)	Present Value of Estimated Costs in 1970 ($ million)
1970	76	8.00	.608	.608
1971	328	8.00	2.624	2.385
1972	287	8.00	2.296	1.897
1973	268	8.00	2.144	1.611
1974	192	8.00	1.536	1.049
1975	170	8.00	1.360	.844
1976	106	8.00	.848	.479
		Total		8.873

[1]*Automotive News*, Almanac Issues for 1971-1979, Slocum Publishing Company, Detroit, 1971, and Marketing Services, Inc., Detroit, 1972-1979.

Case 5.9: Ford and Its Pinto:
Cost Analysis Tables for Pinto Redesign

Table 2

Costs of the 1970 Potential Design Modification
Strategy: High Estimate[1]

Calendar Year	Sales (1,000)	Estimated Unit Cost ($)	Estimated Total Cost ($ million)	Present Value of Estimated Costs in 1970 ($ million)
1970	76	18.66	1.418	1.418
1971	328	18.66	6.120	5.564
1972	287	18.66	5.355	4.425
1973	268	18.66	5.001	3.757
1974	192	18.66	3.583	2.447
1975	170	18.66	3.172	1.969
1976	106	18.66	1.978	1.116
			Total	20.696

[1]*Automotive News*, Almanac Issues for 1971-1979, Slocum Publishing Company, Detroit, 1971, and Marketing Services, Inc., Detroit, 1972-1979.

Case 5.9: Ford and Its Pinto:
Internal Memo on Value of Life

The total benefit is shown to be just under $50 million, while the associated cost if $137 million. Thus, the cost is almost three times the benefits, even using a number of highly favorable benefit assumptions.

Benefits:

Savings:	180 burn deaths, 180 serious burn injuries, 2,100 burned vehicles
Unit cost:	$200,000 per death, $67,000 per injury, $700 per vehicle
Total Benefits:	180 x ($200,000) plus 180 x ($67,000) plus 2100 x ($700) = $49.15 million

Costs:

Sales:	11 million cars, 1.5 million light trucks
Unit cost:	$11 per car, $11 per truck
Total costs:	11,000 x ($11) plus 1,500,000 x ($11) = $137 million

Case 6.3: Levels of Executive Compensation: How Much Should The Boss Make?

Company	CEO	Pay (For 1997)
Travelers Group	Sanford Weill	$230,725,000
Coco-Cola Co.	Roberto Goizueta	$111,832,000
Healthsouth	Richard Scrushy	$106,790,000
Occidental Petroleum	Ray Irani	$101,505,000
Nabors Industries	Eugene Isenberg	$ 84,547,000
Cadence Design Systems	Joseph Costello	$ 66,842,000
Intel	Andrew Grove	$ 52,214,000
HBO & Co.	Charles McCall	$ 51,409,000
Morgan Stanley Dean Witter	Philip Purcell	$50,807,000
Monsanto	Robert Shapiro	$49,326,000
General Electric	Jack Welch	$39,894,000
American Express	Harvey Golub	$33,457,000
Health Management Assoc.	William Schoen	$30,945,000
Bristol-Myers Squibb	Charles Heimbold	$29,211,000
Providian Financial	Shailesh Mehta	$28,365,000
Allied Signal	Lawrence Bossidy	$28,237,000
Pfizer	William Steere	$28,120,000
America Online	Stephen Case	$26,913,000
Travelers Property Casualty	Robert Lipp	$26,301,000
Colgate-Palmolive	Reuben Mark	$25,390,000

Case 7.6: The Degrees-for-Grants Program Comparison of Thesis/Dissertation Language and Contract Reports

1. The most prevailing wind directions at Tower 301 are from the north, northeast, southwest, and northwest especially in the spring and summer. Over 60 percent of the wind is from north. Significant diurnal variation of wind speeds occurs in the summer and fall months.

FWG Associates report to NASA by H.P. Chang and Walter Frost, February 26, 1987.

In addition to the spatial velocity and reflectivity fields of the JAWS microbursts, which were analyzed and reported by Frost, et al. (1985), JAWS data sets also provided turbulence information in the form of radar-measured pulse, wind, and total standard deviations (defined below).

'Development of a Microburst Turbulence Model' by H.P. Chang and Walter Frost, March 1987

1. The most prevailing wind directions at Tower 301 are from north, northeast, southwest, and northwest especially in the spring and summer over 60 percent of the wind from north. Significant diurnal variation of wind speeds appeared in the summer and fall months.

Peggy S. Potter master's thesis, December 1989.

In addition to the spatial velocity and reflectivity fields of the JAWS microbursts, which were analyzed and reported by Frost, et al. (1985), JAWS data sets also provided turbulence information in the form of radar-measured pulse, wind, and total standards deviations (defined below).

Dennis A. Faulkner doctoral dissertation, May 1990

Advanced Instructional Module -- Ethics
Teleological Theory

1. Utilitarianism

2. Ethical Egoism

3. Christian Consequentialism

Advanced Instructional Module -- Ethics
Deontology

1.   Rights (Kant)

2.   Justice